Investigation for Determination of Fact

A Primer on Proof

Investigation for Determination of Fact

A Primer on Proof

Richard A. Myren
American University (Emeritus)

Carol Henderson Garcia
Nova University

Brooks/Cole Publishing Company
Pacific Grove, California

Brooks/Cole Publishing Company
A Division of Wadsworth, Inc.
© 1989 by Wadsworth, Inc., Belmont, California 94002. All rights reserved. No part of this book may be reproduced, stored in a retrieval system, or transcribed, in any form or by any means — electronic, mechanical, photocopying, recording, or otherwise — without the prior written permission of the publisher, Brooks/Cole Publishing Company, Pacific Grove, California 93950, a division of Wadsworth, Inc.

Printed in the United States of America
10 9 8 7 6 5 4 3 2 1

Library of Congress Cataloging-in-Publication Data
Myren, Richard A., [date]-
   Investigation for determination of fact : a primer on proof /
Richard A. Myren, Carol Henderson Garcia.
      p.   cm.
   Includes bibliographies and index.
   ISBN 0-534-09348-5 :
   1. Criminal investigation. 2. Burden of proof. 3. Research.
I. Garcia, Carol Henderson, [date]-   . II. Title.
HV8073.M97 1988
363.2′5—dc19   88-3770
                                                                  CIP

Sponsoring Editor: *Claire Verduin*
Editorial Assistant: *Gay C. Bond*
Production Editor: *Phyllis Larimore*
Production Assistant: *Marie DuBois*
Manuscript Editor: *Janet M. Hunter*
Interior Design: *Stephanie Workman and Katherine Minerva*
Cover Design: *Stephanie Workman*
Art Coordinator: *Sue C. Howard*
Interior Illustration: *Graphic Arts*
Typesetting: *Harrison Typesetting, Inc.*
Cover Printing: *The Lehigh Press, Inc., Pennsauken, New Jersey*
Printing and Binding: *Arcata Graphics, Fairfield, Pennsylvania*

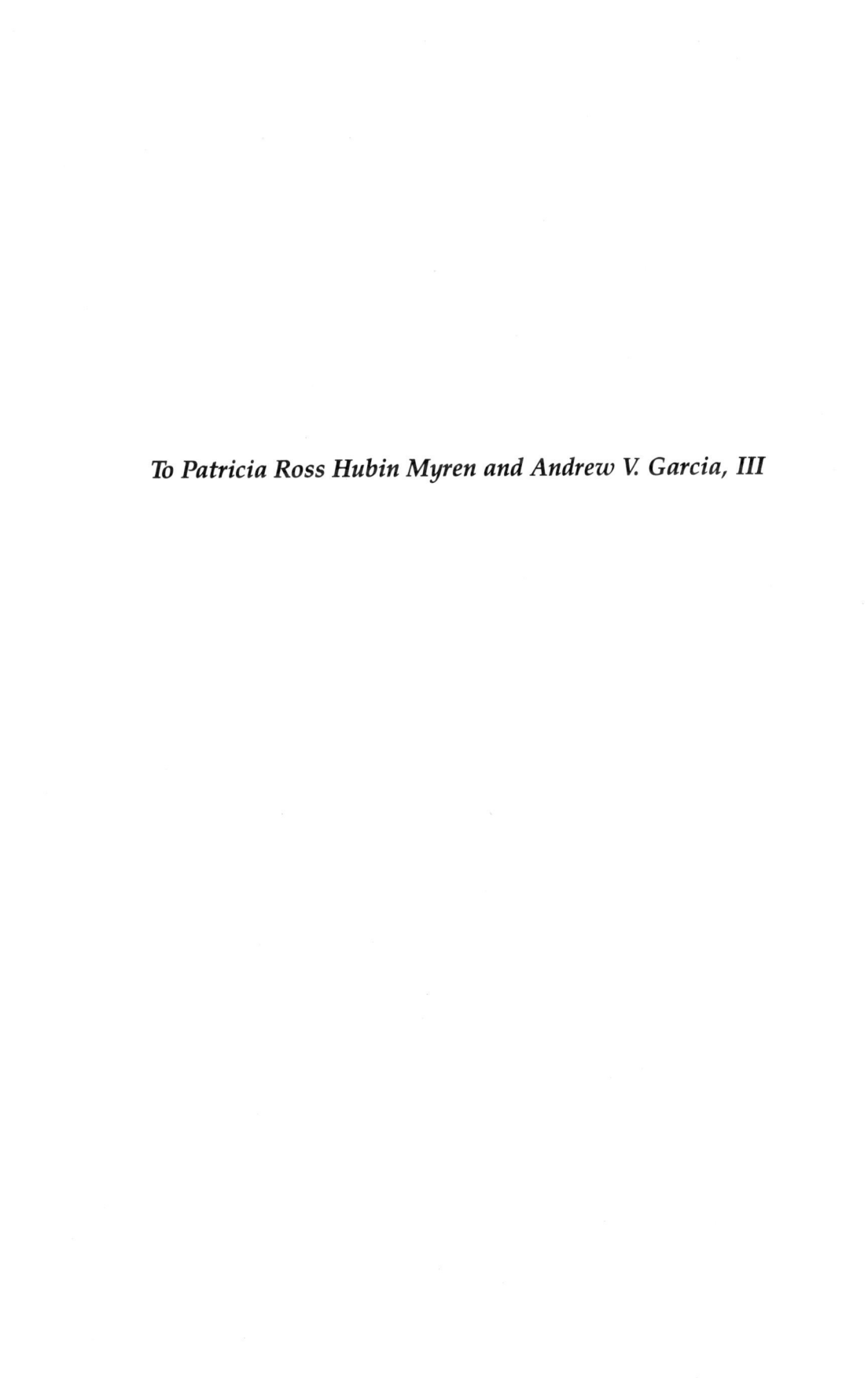

To Patricia Ross Hubin Myren and Andrew V. Garcia, III

This book deals with the investigation process, the process that is necessary to establish the basis for a determination of fact. It is a primer on proof. The concepts it covers have previously been addressed in fragments through various kinds of books. Here, they are brought together in a comprehensive discussion of the field. Our focus is on the social science of investigation and the ideas, concerns, and values behind it, rather than step-by-step details of particular investigative techniques. The book is designed for use in criminal investigation courses taken by criminal justice majors, pre-law students, and those studying to be paralegals; we expect that it can have still broader use.

Determinations of fact must have a basis. They are most frequently reconstructions of the past, decisions about how certain events occurred. That is why investigators, who build cases for those who make the actual determinations of fact, have much in common with investigative reporters and historians. But more recent events, or facts, are also the object of another type of investigator, namely, physical and life scientists. And still others gather current facts as a basis for predicting what future facts will be, a valuable political as well as scientific activity. Although these different kinds of determinations of fact are similar processes, this book focuses on reconstruction of past events and on the formal decision making in governmental organizations that revolves around disputes that must be settled—which person, which crime, when, how, and so on.

Determinations of fact occur in many settings, from the purely personal and informal to the most public and formal. The archetype of the public and formal is, perhaps, the court trial of a person for a capital offense, an alleged violation of the criminal law for which the punishment may be death. At the personal and informal end of the spectrum are such mundane decisions as what one will wear on a particular day and what one should eat for breakfast. To make any of these decisions wisely, regardless of their importance, facts must be marshaled and considered. This book explains, in a fundamental way, the investigations in which that marshaling of facts occurs and the results of that consideration.

There are four parts to any process resulting in a determination of fact. They are

Definition of the problem and of the issues that it raises
Collection of the information relevant to resolution of the issues
Organization and analysis of the information
Presentation of the information to the decision makers in such a way as to persuade them to make a particular decision

This chronological list corresponds with the four parts of the book. Chapter 1 of Part One sets forth the important concepts of *fact* and *determination,* as well as a definition of the circumstances—the problem—in which facts must be determined. It also discusses the vast number and variety of settings in which determinations of fact occur. In Chapter 2 we spell out the similarities and differences between investigation and research. Chapter 3 covers legal and ethical considerations in the gathering of information, extremely important facets of the process.

In Part Two, the discussion moves on to collecting relevant information, the heart of the book. In Chapter 4 we consider, in a general way, potential sources of information: people, documents, and other kinds of physical evidence. Chapter 5 takes up testimony by scientists and the investigator's use of modern technology. In Chapter 6 we discuss in detail the two primary processes for obtaining information from people, interviewing and interrogation, and then we move on to an overview of police investigations in Chapter 7; Chapters 8 and 9 elaborate on that overview for two principal types of criminal investigations: traditional and economic crime. We end Part Two with a discussion of administrative agency and legislative investigations in Chapter 10.

Part Three of the book covers organization and analysis of the investigative work product. Chapter 11 focuses on organization of the data and Chapter 12, its analysis.

Part Four brings the reader to the culmination of an investigation: presenting a decision maker with the information that has been collected. In Chapter 13 we cover organization of the analyzed information in a way that will enhance the effectiveness of its presentation. And, we bring the book to an end in Chapter 14 by considering the procedures, strategies, and techniques of effective presentation.

The text covers a wide range of material, thoroughly and logically organized, and the structure of the chapters is designed to aid the student. For instance, the salient points of each chapter are reviewed in a summary section and reinforced by a series of study questions. A list of readings particularly relevant to the topics of the chapter follows. Then, each chapter concludes with notes documenting sources and pointing the interested reader to further discussion.

Three appendixes and a glossary supplement the text. Many of the terms that are new or used in a special way in the book are gathered in the glossary as well as being explained in the text. Appendix A sets forth a detailed list of readings that investigators may find useful in their education, training, and work. Appendix B provides names and addresses of agencies and organizations that are of special interest to investigators. In addition, the name of a contact at the agency is often included.

As authors, we believe this book represents a fresh and innovative way of approaching the popular criminal investigation course taught in the justice studies programs of colleges and universities. We have seen little change in the narrow and technical way the course has been taught over the last thirty years, despite a change in the academic programs from a *police*, to a *criminal justice*, and finally to a *justice studies* orientation. Criminal investigation courses, still ubiquitous, are also still narrow and technical. They cry out for replacement by a broader course designed to prepare students for all kinds of investigations leading to determinations of fact. This book is intended to be the text for such an expanded approach.

As authors we also believe firmly that this book has an even broader utility. It provides a much needed base for courses in research methods and can serve as a basic text for those who seek careers in government, where fact determination is of paramount importance, and for future paralegals and lawyers who regularly participate in fact determination proceedings.

Thus, we posit a broad audience for this work, and we think you'll find it of considerable interest. "Try it; you'll like it."

ACKNOWLEDGMENTS

We decided to write this book when we were colleagues at the American University a few years ago. The ideas for the book were actually conceived during Richard Myren's discussions with Professor James W. Osterburg at Indiana University, Bloomington, some twenty-five years ago. Once the writing process began, we sharpened and supplemented the earlier concepts and developed the manuscript by using early drafts in our classes at American University. This book is the result.

The long writing process was made possible by the continued support of our families and friends. Others who facilitated our work include Jenny McGough, then Associate Dean for Administration of the American University School of Justice, who helped in many ways. Chairman Tom

Johnson of the Department of Criminal Justice at California State University, Sacramento, provided computer facilities during compilation of the index, and Donna Gillott and Kathy Dunnam provided advice on the use of those facilities.

The text was substantively improved as a result of suggestions from the following reviewers, to whom the authors are indebted: Professor Emeritus James W. Osterburg, University of Illinois, Chicago; Richard Bennett, American University; Edwin Donovan, Pennsylvania State University; Joachim Goldsmith, California State University, Sacramento; Edward Latessa, University of Cincinnati; Donal MacNamara, San Jose State University; Frank Morn, Illinois State University; Paul Sutton, San Diego State University; and Richard Ward, University of Illinois, Chicago.

Richard A. Myren
Carol Henderson Garcia

PART ONE
FACT DETERMINATION PROCESSES 1

1 INVESTIGATION FOR FACT DETERMINATION 3

Problem Definition 4
Fact Collection 9
Fact Presentation 10
Fact Determination Settings 12
Summarizing Commentary 15
Study Questions 16
Recommended Additional Reading 17
Notes 17

2 RESEARCH VERSUS INVESTIGATION 18

Research and Investigation Defined 19
Research and Investigation Methods 20
Who Does Research? Who Investigates? And Why? 22
Preparation of Investigators and Research Personnel 25
Impact of the Setting 27
Summarizing Commentary 28
Study Questions 29
Recommended Additional Reading 29
Notes 30

3 LEGAL AND ETHICAL PRECEPTS 31

Legal Precepts Governing Investigation 32
Ethical Considerations 40

xii　CONTENTS

Summarizing Commentary　43
Study Questions　45
Recommended Additional Reading　45
Notes　45

PART TWO
INFORMATION COLLECTION　47

4　SOURCES OF INFORMATION　49

Information from People　50
Documents as Sources　56
Other Physical Evidence　60
Reference Sources　61
Summarizing Commentary　64
Study Questions　65
Recommended Additional Reading　66
Notes　66

5　INFORMATION FROM SCIENCE　68

General Considerations　68
Utilizing Scientific Experts　71
Using Lie Detection Tests and Hypnosis　79
Utilizing Technology　81
Summarizing Commentary　83
Study Questions　84
Recommended Additional Reading　84
Notes　84

6　TALKING TO PEOPLE　86

Talking to Whom?　88
Finding Persons to Interview　89
Interview versus Interrogation　90
Conducting the Interview　93
Problems in Special Cases　97
Summarizing Commentary　99
Study Questions　101
Recommended Additional Reading　101
Notes　101

7 A POLICE INVESTIGATION OVERVIEW 103

Traditional Criminal Investigation 104
Managing Criminal Investigations 105
Fine-Tuning the MCI Concept 110
Portability of the MCI Concept 112
Summarizing Commentary 113
Study Questions 114
Recommended Additional Reading 114
Notes 114

8 TRADITIONAL CRIME INVESTIGATIONS 116

Commonalities among Street Crime Investigations 118
Special Considerations of Specific Offenses 120
Summarizing Commentary 126
Study Questions 127
Recommended Additional Reading 127
Notes 127

9 ECONOMIC CRIME INVESTIGATIONS 130

Special Legal Problems 130
Special Accounting Problems 133
Investigative Approaches to Economic Crime 134
Continuing Criminal Enterprise Statutes 140
Summarizing Commentary 144
Study Questions 145
Recommended Additional Reading 146
Notes 146

10 LEGISLATIVE AND ADMINISTRATIVE INVESTIGATIONS 148

Investigation for Legislative Action 149
Investigation for Administrative Action 150
Relevant Federal Regulations and Statutes 154
Summarizing Commentary 155
Study Questions 156
Recommended Additional Reading 156
Notes 156

PART THREE
ORGANIZATION AND ANALYSIS OF THE INVESTIGATIVE WORK PRODUCT 159

11 ORGANIZATION OF INVESTIGATIVE INFORMATION 161

Organizational Components 161
Pertinent Rules of Evidence 162
Uses of Investigative Reports 170
Summarizing Commentary 171
Study Questions 172
Recommended Additional Reading 172
Notes 172

12 ANALYSIS OF INVESTIGATIVE INFORMATION 174

Case Components 175
Investigations for Planning Purposes 181
Analysis of Reports for Investigator Evaluation 182
Summarizing Commentary 183
Study Questions 185
Recommended Additional Reading 186
Notes 186

PART FOUR
PRESENTATION OF THE FACTS 187

13 PREPARATION FOR PRESENTATION 189

Case Preparation 189
Submission of the Case to the Prosecutor 190
Uses of the Case Submission Report 191
Anticipating the Opposition 194
Master Case Presentation File 196
Summarizing Commentary 197
Study Questions 198
Recommended Additional Reading 198
Notes 199

14 CASE PRESENTATION   200

Impact of the Setting   201
Specific Preliminary Concerns   204
Presentation Concerns   207
Summarizing Commentary   212
Study Questions   213
Recommended Additional Reading   213
Notes   213

Glossary   215

Appendix A: Readings for Investigators   219

Appendix B: Agencies and Organizations of Interest to Investigators   225

Index   230

FACT DETERMINATION PROCESSES

The only proper answer to the question of why we should accept both the conclusion of a logical argument and the evidence of our senses is that we just do so as a matter of course. We are simply made that way. We are rational and perceptive creatures, so we believe what our reason and our senses tell us.

Iredell Jenkins
Social Order and the Limits of Law

INVESTIGATION FOR FACT DETERMINATION

Investigation is a process that fits into a context of determination of fact for decision-making purposes. It is the activity that produces the facts on which our decisions are based. It is an all pervasive function, central in both our personal and professional affairs.

This book explains the process of investigation. The information presented is useful to every person; we all investigate to determine the facts upon which we base our decisions. In addition, some of us earn our living as investigators, by gathering facts through investigation to present to others for their decision making. Investigation occurs in many settings, but the principles governing the process remain constant, whether the factual work product is used personally or professionally. Those principles are discussed in detail in later chapters. In this first chapter, our attention focuses on the context in which investigations take place, the process of decision making.

An investigation always has a goal. It is an end-oriented function, not engaged in for its own sake. The end is determination of fact. Once established, the facts are usually used in some decision-making process, but may, as in the case of pure science, be sought for their own intrinsic worth. Because investigations are goal oriented, that goal must be specified, the problem to be investigated must be defined, before the investigation can be planned. As the investigation progresses, its work product—the information gathered—must be organized and analyzed. Only through such organization and analysis can one know when an investigation is complete. Once the facts have been determined, they are then presented to some consumer, usually to someone who will make a decision based on those facts, but occasionally to someone interested in the facts themselves because they contribute to a body of knowledge. In this book we are concerned with investigation of a defined problem and presentation of the facts as they have been discovered. We do not discuss, except incidentally, the use made of facts once determined: the art and science of decision making or the role of newly determined facts in scientific expansion of knowledge.

This discussion focuses on investigations leading to formal decision making in governmental organizations, but the insights and knowledge revealed are useful in any decision-making process. Attention is directed to determinations of fact in two of our principal formal, legal, justice systems: the civil and the criminal. Perhaps the most demanding of these determinations is the trial of an adult alleged to have committed a serious violation of the criminal law. Because the stakes are so high—loss of freedom or even of life itself—the trial requires a very high level of care in determination of fact. For that reason, special attention is given to investigation in that setting.

PROBLEM DEFINITION

There are many different kinds of problem situations involving a need for investigation to determine fact. Some of these situations are trivial, others quite serious. Some are personal and others involve organized groups. We all make personal decisions about such matters as whether to go for the daily paper, whether to pursue a certain career, whether to make a specific financial investment, whether to marry a particular person—all based on varying determinations of fact. It is not unusual to hear someone say, "I talked myself into it." Small informal groups go through the same processes, as do formal organizations.

An individual making a personal decision that does not directly and materially affect others may be quite casual about the decision-making process; or, if the decision looms large in that person's life, may set up a formal process of investigation and may establish criteria for judgment once the investigation is completed. The same is true of informal and formal groups, including states. Formal organizations, however, are usually more systematic in making even minor decisions because the officers responsible are accountable to others for their actions. To meet that responsibility, formal procedures are followed and a record kept of the actions at every step.

Situations in which there is a need for determination of fact may arise differently: the problems may be immediately apparent or those affected may live with the situation for some time before they realize that there is a problem. Examples of the former come from our everyday lives.

- You rise in the morning hungry. What should breakfast be?
- The car breaks down, and the mechanic consulted says that it is not worth repairing. What kind of replacement should be purchased?
- The morning mail brings a registered letter informing me that my

neighbors, who allege that the fence I built last month is on their land, have brought a civil suit against me. What is necessary for defense of the suit?
- In a more serious police setting, some person has been killed. Was it an accident or an intentional homicide? If the latter, was it a criminal act? If so, who did it?

In all of these cases, the problem is readily apparent.

But there are also common situations in which the problem is more difficult to recognize and define.

- Very gradually, you realize that your car sounds and acts differently than it has in the past. What is wrong with it?
- While sitting reading in my study, I become aware of some discomfort. What is it? Only when the cause of the discomfort can be pinned down can it be faced.
- One day my boss calls me in and suggests that our agency just isn't functioning as well as it should. She can't pinpoint the problem, but she is certain that something is wrong, and my assignment is to set it right. How do I start? What is the source of her impression? Is it low productivity? Excessive costs? Failure to work well with other agencies? Complaints about lack of courtesy to members of the public? Improper accounting procedures?

In these cases, problem recognition and definition is required before further action can be taken. The skills required to carry out that process are quite valuable and are highly compensated in the real world.

Basic to such skills is an expert knowledge of the context in which the problem arises. But that kind of knowledge is not enough. Coupled with it must be an ability to sort out the relevant from the irrelevant. Some individuals develop a reputation for having that ability. About those persons, we frequently say such things as she gets right to the point, he can put his finger right on the trouble spot every time, she will get to the bottom of it very quickly, he will tell you what's wrong if anybody can.

Imagination and intuition—a disciplined curiosity—are indispensable assets in *problem definition*. An imaginative approach uses rational associations, "fancy," and perhaps chance circumstances, as W. I. B. Beveridge puts it. The result is frequently an intuitive diagnosis. Beveridge posits seven conditions "most conducive to intuitions."[1] They are

1. A mind steeped in the detail of the problem situation
2. Freedom from competing interests and worries
3. Freedom from distractions and interruptions
4. Periods of rest away from conscious concentration on the problem
5. Intellectual stimulation from colleagues
6. Freedom from mental and physical fatigue

7. Facilities for recording the usually fleeting intuitive thoughts as they occur

Focusing an educated and experienced intellect on a problem situation under these conditions will lead to recognition and sharp definition of the problem and, frequently, to an intuitive knowledge of where to look for the solution.

Thus far two prerequisites for good problem definition have been mentioned: a thorough knowledge of the context in which the problem is set, and the intellectual capacity to form intuitive insights about the nature of the problem. A third prerequisite is careful consideration of problem symptoms. In many cases, the gross symptoms are readily apparent but their cause is not; a methodical backward search may be necessary to detect where the malfunction causing the symptoms is occurring. The malfunction may be in either a physical component of some system or in some person performing a specific role in the system. The indicators of possible component malfunction are too varied to specify in any general way; instead, detailed knowledge of the normal functioning of the problem context is frequently necessary for successful diagnosis.

Definition of a problem for investigation is similar to the task of scientists who must assess current knowledge in order to design new research projects.[2] Their knowledge of the facts known at the moment leads them to a tentative *theory*. Theories are based on facts, suppositions, and conclusions that are continually subjected to reexamination to determine whether they can continue to be relied on.

Scientists order the facts that investigators have observed as a first step in building a theory to explain them. In so doing, gaps in the fact picture are noted that require new, planned observations in the future. A scientist will then make an educated guess, a supposition, a *hypothesis*, as to what will be found when those observations are made. With the fact picture thus tentatively completed, the scientist begins explaining it, begins the building of a theory. However, the situation is complicated by the fact that more than one theory may explain or imply known and supposed facts. When faced with such a problem, the scientist does not reject any possible theory, but, for the time being, picks as most promising the simplest, the one requiring the least elaborate assumptions to explain the known facts. Scientists have given this preference for simplicity a number of different names: the Canon of Parsimony, Occam's razor, Lloyd Morgan's Canon.

Other factors that may guide the tentative choice among alternative theories are that one may explain a wider range of facts than the others, one may fit the facts with greater precision, or one may imply a set of as yet unobserved facts that seem more probable than those implied by the other theories. It is important to note that not every theory that may explain the known facts must be accepted. To the contrary, two or more conflicting theories are sometimes tentatively accepted and explored with a view to eliminating all but one.

Once a theory or set of possible theories has been tentatively decided upon, scientists begin the testing process. New observations will be made in an attempt to verify or disprove actual existence of the previously reported facts on which it is based, and to determine whether the facts implied by the theory can actually be found. *Formal implication* as a component of scientific reasoning has been explained this way:

> One *assertion* [emphasis added] or set of assertions implies another when it can be shown that if one accepts the former one necessarily commits oneself to the latter. The former may be referred to as the *implicans* and the latter the *implicate*.[3]

It is useful to note in passing some of the other terms used in formal scientific reasoning. A statement of two or more *simple* assertions or propositions jointly creates a *compound* proposition of which there are a number of types. A and B when referred to together are a *conjunctive* proposition. If one proposition depends upon another (if A, then B; if A and B, then C), the statement is an *implicative, conditional,* or *hypothetical* proposition. The second or result part of the proposition is the *consequent* component which may be special, may be frequent or common, or may be universal.

Scientific reasoning distinguishes between *validity* and *truth*. Validity is formal. A stated implication is valid if it is logically correct, if the implied conclusion must follow from the previous assertion. Truth, on the other hand, is factual. False assertions can be used to make a logically valid argument.

Science disproves its tentative hypotheses and theories through *falsification*. If it can be shown by observation that facts implied by the theory do not exist, the theory has been demonstrated to be false and must be discarded. If, however, the implied facts are observed, the theory is not proven true, only tenable. Competing theories may imply the same facts.

Explanation is a core concept of scientific reasoning, although there are competing beliefs as to what it is.

> There are two views of what constitutes an explanation, with no doubt some views involving an admixture of the two. The first stresses insight, intuition and even mystical revelation.... The second view of explanation is...that we have explained some phenomenon when we can show that it follows logically from premises which include some general rule, principle or law and which have not been shown to be untenable.[4]

The second of these views involves deduction, reasoning from the general to the specific, as opposed to induction, which is reasoning from the specific to the general. In actual investigation of any kind, both proceed together.

In its reasoning, science also recognizes the necessary and the contingent. The necessary is that which could not have been other than it is, that which would make the theory self-contradictory if denied. The contingent is that which is possible and perhaps even probable but that could have been different. Although contingent facts may be quite regular and stable, they need not be as they are. For that reason, they are sometimes called accidental, fortuitous, or random.

Scientists differ in the positions they take as to the basis on which beliefs about nature should be justified. The two main views are called *rationalism* and *empiricism*. Rationalists stress the explanatory theories of science; empiricists stress the observed facts themselves. Rationalists stress deduction while empiricists stress induction as the "best" method for attaining knowledge.

In their less charitable moments, rationalists sometimes accuse empiricists of being superficial and without concern for the essential. Empiricists tend to search for irreducible elements. The pure method of the rationalist, sometimes described as *hypothetico-deductive*, is a three-part process: formulating the hypothesis, exploring its ramifications, and testing whether its implied facts or events exist or occur. It is generally recognized that hypotheses do not materialize out of nothing. With a possible exception in the realm of pure mathematics, where theorems are deduced from postulated axioms, hypotheses are based on a general knowledge of the subject matter out of which they arise.

But it is frequently alleged that the deductive model is the closer to reality, that inductive inference of theory from facts alone simply does not occur. The assumption is that suggestions and clues come from the facts, but that theory is imagined or invented, perhaps working through analogy to other better known and understood situations. Rationalists continually stress that observations may be false and, at the same time, that theory must continually be tested. Even the most accepted of theories may be disproved tomorrow, at least in part. In evaluating their ongoing tests, scientists speak of evidence that will confirm or verify, infirm or falsify their theories. Complete confirmation is said to constitute verification and complete infirmation to constitute falsification. But only falsification is ever final. Verification is always qualified as being on the basis of what is now known.

These concepts from scientific investigation, although they cannot be applied in full measure to more mundane investigations, nevertheless provide sound guidelines for all fact-finding processes. They make organization and analysis of the collected information for presentation to the decision maker an easier task.

It isn't possible to set out a checklist for investigators to use in defining the problem to be investigated. Whether a given investigator is good at problem definition can only be judged by hindsight. The test is whether the investigator "gets on the track" quickly and stays on it until solution of the problem, or whether there are many false starts leading to blind alleys not only initially but during the progress of the investigation.

FACT COLLECTION

Once the problem has been recognized and defined, the next step in fact determination is collection of all of the available relevant information. This is done through investigation. The bulk of this book, the seven chapters (out of a total of fourteen) that constitute Part Two, discusses fact collection through investigation. But at this point, it is necessary to consider the preliminary question of the nature of the "fact" that the investigator seeks.

Depending on the context in which it is used, the word *fact* may take on any one of several meanings. In most situations, it is obvious that simple concrete things and actions are both included. Things may be important in and of themselves but their usual significance in determination of fact is their relationship to something that was done, their role as evidence concerning the nature and circumstances of a deed. Thus frequently "fact" may mean a unit of action—an event or segment of an event. In this book, emphasis is on proof of facts that will convince a decision maker that specific consequences should follow from acceptance of the proof. For example, the decision maker may be convinced that further proceedings should take the course sought, that persons should be required to act in a certain way in the future, or that the state should pursue a certain course of action through its government.

Generally speaking, a fact is an element of reality that can be directly and personally experienced. It can be a physical or mental event that one becomes aware of through direct observation or that can be inferred with certainty from direct observations. Because of this grounding of facts in reality, we tend to think of them not as truth but as components from which truth can be discerned.

Facts, then, are not truth. It is the task of the advocate to convince the decision maker that a specific set of facts exists which leads to a truth that should be accepted as having been established. Facts standing by themselves, without reference to their relationship to other facts and without interpretation as evidence of the truthfulness or falsity of some assertion, are sometimes called *brute* or *indifferent* facts, items subject to observation and needing no interpretation.[5]

But facts can take on a different significance when used in argument. They then become assertions about aspects of what is alleged to have happened. In a legal proceeding, the facts are distinguished from the law to be applied to the facts as found. When the law is applied to the facts, certain consequences follow. That application is made by an authorized decision maker who may be a judge, a jury, an administrator, a board, a commission, or some other legal entity. The decision-making responsibility may be split, with one entity (for example, a jury) deciding questions of fact and another (for example, a judge) deciding questions of law.

It is thus clear that in many determinations, facts must be proved at two levels: first, as brute or indifferent facts that simply exist; and second, as evidence that meets the required standard of proof so that the matters at issue can be determined with one outcome rather than with another. These two levels are sometimes differentiated by referring to the first as *findings of fact* and the latter as *determination of the issues*. For example, decision makers in many settings are required to make reports that comprise findings of fact, the rules applied, the decisions on the issues, and the reasons for those decisions based upon the application of the law to the facts as found.

Once facts have been collected, they must be organized and analyzed to determine their significance. These processes are discussed in detail in Chapters 11 and 12 of Part Three. They proceed simultaneously with fact collection. They are used to assess the progress of an investigation, to keep it on track, to decide whether it needs redirection, and to determine when the investigation is complete.

FACT PRESENTATION

Culmination of any investigation comes with the actual presentation of the assembled material to the designated decision maker. Part Four of this book covers this final stage in detail, but some preliminary comment here will set the scene.

It is at this point in determination of fact that commentators frequently say that the determination is actually made. What does the word *determination* signify in this context? There are at least three meanings that are relevant to this discussion.

1. The act of drawing a conclusion or making a decision that settles or ends a controversy. Judicial decisions are frequently referred to as "coming to a determination."
2. The discussion itself, the process of argument and reasoning by which a decision is reached.
3. The actual conclusion or decision reached, the end product of the fact determination process, the final conclusion as to which among several asserted versions of an event or deed is the one that actually occurred.

The task of the decision maker is to determine what actually happened on the basis of the information presented. Decision makers in formal proceedings must convert brute or indifferent first-level facts into interpretations, generalizations, and finally conclusions that, after application of the proper rules, will lead to fixed and binding results for the future. This is true whether the proceedings are public and required by law or private and merely authorized and facilitated by law. And it is interesting to note that the determination, once made, becomes itself a fact.

Although brute facts exist that can be verified by simple observation and require no interpretation, formal determinations of fact in human affairs usually involve consideration of the significance of such facts in the context of others. This complication in consideration of the fact situation usually involves influence of what might be called the *value set* of the decision maker. For example, consider the following fact situation:

> John Smith, married and the father of three children born to his wife, Jane Smith, acknowledges that he is the father of an infant born to Mary Jones, who lives just down the block. Blood tests, although they cannot verify the relationship, do establish its possibility. Jones also asserts that Smith is the father of the infant.
>
> Shortly after the facts just given emerge, Smith dies suddenly without leaving a will. His estate is valued at about one million dollars. The state statute on inheritance provides that children of persons dying without a will share 50 percent of the estate of the deceased parent if there is a surviving spouse, who then also takes 50 percent of the estate.
>
> Suit is brought by Mary Jones on behalf of her infant alleging that the infant, as Smith's child, should receive 12.5 percent of Smith's estate. No court in the state has yet decided whether the word *child* in the statute means any natural child or only a child born in wedlock. Should the Jones infant receive a share of the estate?

In this situation, the basic fact is Smith's parenthood of the Jones infant. That fact takes its significance from other data in the context: Smith's wealth, his marriage to Jane and parenthood of three children born in wedlock, his death without a will, the state statute on inheritance, and the suit brought on behalf of infant Jones. Within this context, the right of the infant to recover is dependent on the other relevant facts, but the issue raised has significance beyond this particular fact situation. It demands a decision as to whether infants born out of wedlock are "children" under the state inheritance statute. Whether a court will decide that "child" means any natural child or only a child born in wedlock will depend on the value systems of the judges on the court. It is interesting to speculate on which traditional values will push the decision one way or the other.

In commenting on his belief that eyewitnesses do not mechanically reproduce the facts but only their error-prone judgment of the facts, Judge Jerome Frank makes the interesting observation that judges and others who make determinations of fact are themselves witnesses—to the process of proof.[6] They determine what the facts are from what they see and hear during the proceedings, a determination that is not a simple mechanical act.

Although observers can be trained to be objective, the result is never perfect. The formal decision maker, usually a person of advanced education and experience, brings to the process a value set growing out of that education and experience that determines the way in which the facts of the situation will be weighed. This value set is sometimes recognized by the decision maker and sometimes not.

In governmental settings such as the legal justice system, a particular value set is sometimes specified, frequently by the political process. The interest group with the greatest political power succeeds in having its value set accepted. Not infrequently, however, no single interest group has the power to prevail, in which case the one chosen is a compromise. Exercise of discretion influenced by an unarticulated value set is sometimes involved. It is important to recognize this role of values in determination of fact. As one scholar has put it:

> Citizens left to believe that burdens flowing from a judgment inevitably flowed from pre-existing law, when in fact decision on the law (or on the facts) might have been the other way, are in a sense being deceived. The right to know the architect of our obligations may be as much a part of liberty as the right to know our accuser and our judge.[7]

In any given determination, the value component of the decision may overshadow any mandate from the facts.

Once the decision maker has been persuaded that a given version of the facts should be accepted, the appropriate rules are applied to yield the decision. Where do those rules come from? That depends on the nature and the context of the decision being made. In informal personal and organizational settings, the participants will usually apply rules that they learned as they grew up and were educated—as they matured. A sociologist might call such rules internalized social norms. Some of them will be rules that persons accept quite uncritically. Others will have been accepted only after much study and thought. Some are accepted only tentatively; they continue to be questioned, restudied, and sometimes eventually modified or rejected. But in more formal situations, such as those concentrated on in this book, the rules are usually given to the participants by law. In those cases, the decision maker need only choose which law to apply. This may in itself be either a simple or a complex process.

FACT DETERMINATION SETTINGS

This book is concerned with the process of investigation that results in determinations of fact. It covers many settings, but focuses more on the formal than the informal, more on the governmental than the private, although it does discuss mediation and arbitration as alternatives to traditional governmental action. This section sketches some of the more important governmental settings in which presentations of investigative work product are made that lead to determinations of fact.

The first such setting is the legislative, of which Congress is typical. Legislators sit as determiners of fact in a number of situations. For example, in committee hearings they attempt to define needs for legislation. They seek to define problems and then to obtain as much information about them as possible. In another kind of hearing they seek the facts necessary to monitor the performance of executive agencies charged with implementing previously passed legislation. They also on occasion sit in judgment on the conduct of their own members.

In these situations they are aided by their personal and committee staffs. The Legislative Reference Service of the Library of Congress does much of the necessary research. Officials from executive and administrative agencies are called to testify, as are interested and knowledgeable outsiders such as university professors, trade association representatives, and members of the staffs of a wide variety of other special interest groups. Where criminal activity might be involved, testimony will be taken from law enforcement agencies at all levels: federal, state, and local.

A second common type of governmental setting for determinations of fact requiring investigative effort comprises the executive branch and administrative agencies. Both use formal proceedings for making routine decisions in administering and monitoring programs established under previous legislation. Both conduct investigations and research to build support for proposed new legislation. They also search for and document violations of existing law. In addition, administrative agencies frequently have adjudicative functions in which administrative judges perform very much like their counterparts in the courts.

But the prototypical settings for determinations of fact are the judicial: judges hearing pretrial motions, deciding cases, presiding over trials in which juries are the decision makers, and hearing appeals. Pretrial motions are frequently decided on the basis of affidavits and briefs, seldom on the basis of oral testimony. A single judge may hear many such motions in one day. In all of these proceedings, the work of investigators regarding the issues at stake will be presented, usually with the aid of lawyers.

Mediation and arbitration hearings, as settings in which determinations of fact are made based on investigative work product, may involve government employed or independent third party mediators and arbitrators. The purpose of mediators is to make sure that each of the parties understands the positions of the other, that they are not talking past one another without communicating. Mediators make sure that everyone understands just what the issues and alternatives are, what the practical matters involved may be (such as economic position), and what matters of principle are raised. Arbitrators, in contrast, are decision makers performing much the same functions as judges but in more informal settings. There are usually fewer restrictions on fact assertion in the rules of evidence used in arbitration hearings, the standard of proof is usually the same as it would be in a court in a similar case, and arbitrators generally possess and use specialized subject-matter knowledge in their decision making.

In addition to the governmental and private settings discussed, investigations are undertaken and determinations of fact are made as a matter of routine in scientific settings. Most scientists find and use facts in a somewhat different way than they are found and used in administration of justice. Physical, or "hard," scientists are concerned with discovery of what is and explanation of why it is. They come closer to working with absolutes than do government decision makers. Social, or "soft," scientists use the language and, to the extent possible, the same scientific method as do their hard science colleagues, but most recognize that dealing with individuals, groups, and organizations makes their work qualitatively different.

Perhaps the social scientist whose task is closest to that of the government investigator is the historian. Both focus primarily on the past. As one historian put it:

> History, then, is a science, but a science of a special kind. It is a science whose business is to study events not accessible to our observation, and to study these events inferentially, arguing to them from something else which is accessible to our observation, and which the historian calls "evidence" for the events in which he is interested.[8]

But, because their purposes are different, the tasks of the investigator preparing for a determination of fact and of the historian are not identical. Time is frequently an important factor in court trials. Defendants in criminal cases have a right to a speedy trial. There is also strong social and political pressure to resolve expeditiously the disputes brought to the civil courts. To meet these time deadlines, courts must frequently be satisfied with less certain "proof" than they desire. Scientists, on the other hand, at least in the ideal, are not under the same time pressures. They can withhold judgment until they believe that they have irrefutable evidence to support one inevitable conclusion.

However, despite this difference, the analogy between governmental and scientific determination of fact is useful. One government decision maker who is more free than the trial judge to ignore time pressures is the legislator. Trial courts must decide promptly issues properly presented to them; legislatures are free to postpone decision in most cases. The pressures to which they must respond are political, not legal, although those pressures may be very strong indeed.

Another difference in the way in which facts obtained by investigation are used in government and scientific settings is that, in the former, facts or matters in controversy are evidential facts that furnish a basis for decision on the matters at issue. In contrast, in scientific settings, facts are used primarily to build belief systems, to explain the world that has been observed and to predict what will be found when new observations are made in the future. The belief systems of scientists are their theories.

SUMMARIZING COMMENTARY

Investigation, which establishes the base for fact determination, is a very common function. It varies in its formality from the most casual to the most ceremonious of processes. It is involved in the solution of many kinds of problems, some of which immediately present themselves in unmistakable detail and some of which must be teased out of their context before they can be faced. The process of problem recognition and definition may itself be a formidable problem. Imagination and intuition are invaluable aids to one so involved.

But mental agility cannot help until a great deal of information from a great number of facts has been collected about the problem and its context. In discussion of what facts are, it is quickly apparent that facts must be proved at two levels, first as to their brute, or indifferent, existence and second as to their significance in a resolution of the issue at hand.

An investigation resulting in a determination of fact culminates with the actual presentation of the assembled information to the designated decision maker. A determination of fact is defined as a conclusion as to which among several asserted versions of an event or deed is the one that actually occurred. Such determinations are likened to those of historians who must consider not only brute facts but relationships among those facts. In considering the significance of facts, the simplest theory that will do the job is preferred.

Values are involved both directly and indirectly in fact finding. Although some brute facts are significant standing alone, others are important only in relationships within a setting. Consideration of those relationships leaves room for discretion on the part of the decision maker. At that point, both personal and societal values enter into the process. These must be recognized and made apparent so that they can be judged. If they operate invisibly, accountability in the decision-making process is impossible.

When the findings of fact are complete, the appropriate rules are applied to them to reach a decision. The rules are sometimes internalized social norms, sometimes prescribed by law. Their choice and application are not mechanical, but guided by value sets.

Determinations of fact occur in many different settings. The knowledge, skills, strategies, and tactics of effective presentation vary with the setting, although the basic principles of investigation do not. In this text, the discussion focuses on investigations that lead to formal governmental decisions, but attention is also paid to mediation and arbitration, more informal processes alternative to adjudication.

Decision makers in formal legal proceedings find and use facts differently than do physical scientists who, in turn, find and use them differently than do social and behavioral scientists. Perhaps the closest analogy to governmental investigation is the task of historians. Both historians and governmental investigators are engaged in reconstruction of the past. The main difference in their work is in their time frames. Governmental fact determination must be made in defined, relatively short periods of time. Historians, on the other hand, can wait until they believe that all the evidence is in. In that respect, historians are more like legislators who can also wait (absent overbearing political pressure for immediate action) until they believe they have all the information required for a just and wise decision. In science, fact and theory, although usually differentiable, are sometimes mixed. Similarly, although lawyers usually can separate issues of fact from those of law, they do on occasion discuss mixed questions of fact and law.

Analysis of the collected facts also proceeds differently in governmental than in scientific settings. Scientists have developed formal processes to guide their investigations. Simple facts are stated as propositions. These, which are of a number of different types, are used by scientists in description, prediction, and explanation. There are different views of explanation, the most accepted being a modified deductive process. It is believed that scientific theories may be *suggested* by the facts, but not *induced* from them. Theory formulation is regarded as a more creative process than a pure induction method would imply. It is widely asserted that pure induction just doesn't occur in real life. Paralleling this distinction between deductive and inductive methods are the rationalist and empiricist schools among scientists. Although the pure scientific methods are not completely applicable to governmental determinations of fact, they do offer sound guidelines for all determinations of fact.

From this preliminary discussion of the context in which the investigative function is employed, Chapter 2 moves on to a comparison of two familiar fact-finding procedures: investigation and research.

STUDY QUESTIONS

1. Why does the world value the ability to define issues in a problem situation?

2. In what sense is it accurate to describe most investigations resulting in determinations of fact in government settings as reconstruction of the recent past?
3. What is the primary difference in goals between fact finding in governmental settings as opposed to scientific settings?
4. How do the value sets of decision makers affect their deliberations?

RECOMMENDED ADDITIONAL READING

- Beveridge, W. I. B. *The Art of Scientific Investigation*. New York: Norton, 1950.
- O'Neill, William Matthew. *Fact and Theory: An Aspect of the Philosophy of Science*. Sydney, Australia: Sydney University Press, 1969.
- Stone, Julius. *Social Dimensions of Law and Justice*. Stanford, Calif.: Stanford University Press, 1966.

NOTES

1. This discussion draws on W. I. B. Beveridge, *The Art of Scientific Investigation* (New York: Norton, 1950), Chapters 5 and 6.
2. This discussion of how physical or "hard" scientists use facts is based on and generally follows William Matthew O'Neill, *Fact and Theory: An Aspect of the Philosophy of Science* (Sydney, Australia: Sydney University Press, 1969), passim.
3. Ibid., p. 74.
4. Ibid., p. 106.
5. O'Neill discusses brute facts at page 26 of *Fact and Theory*, op. cit.; indifferent facts are discussed by Wolfgang Kohler, *The Place of Value in a World of Facts* (1938; reprint, New York: Liveright, 1966), p. 320.
6. Jerome Frank, *Law and the Modern Mind* (New York: Brentanos Publishers, 1930), p. 109.
7. Julius Stone, *Social Dimensions of Law and Justice* (Stanford, Calif.: Stanford University Press, 1966), p. 678.
8. R. G. Collingwood, *The Idea of History* (New York: Oxford University Press, 1956), pp. 251 and 252.

RESEARCH VERSUS INVESTIGATION

Determinations of fact occur in many settings. Both research and investigation may be involved, but the meaning of those words has come to have a practical difference in everyday life. In this chapter we explore that difference as it is demonstrated primarily in the work of three different groups: historians, investigative reporters, and government investigators.

These three groups are quite different, yet each is involved principally with reconstruction of the past. In talking about their work, historians are apt to call it research; reporters and detectives are more apt to call it investigation. Despite that difference, all would probably agree that their result is rarely absolute proof, absolute certainty. The best that they can hope for in most circumstances is a very high degree of probability. The police detective, whose work may result in loss of liberty or even of life for the person accused, ultimately must meet the standard of *proof beyond a reasonable doubt*. Note that not all doubt must be eliminated in criminal prosecutions, only reasonable doubt. Although investigative reporters also strive for certainty, their bottom line standard is most likely to be enough proof to defeat a charge of libel in a court. There they must meet a lesser standard of proof, which may be proof by a simple *preponderance of evidence,* the common standard that must be met by most plaintiffs in civil law suits. Depending on the jurisdiction, however, it might be the more stringent civil action standard of proof by *clear and convincing evidence.* For historians, the issue has been well put by Robert Jones Shafer, who said:

> No facts speak for themselves to lighten the historian's task, not even facts as objects – a chariot wheel or a baby's crib – to say nothing of facts as events or ideas. So, facts must be made to speak, in the light of the historian's varying purposes, erudition, sense of the fitness of things, and abilities to deal with problems of proof and probability. And there is the rub: the proof is rare and probability comes in many sizes, only to be judged with art and a sense of responsibility.[1]

In other words, historians must support their assertions with proof that will convince their peers that they have exercised a professional "sense of responsibility." All three groups—reporters, detectives, and historians—are said to meet the standards of proof imposed upon them through research and investigation. Is there a difference between these two endeavors?

RESEARCH AND INVESTIGATION DEFINED

Literally, the word *research* means, of course, to search again, to repeat the process of looking in order to verify or expand the first result. That literal meaning emphasizes that research is a very carefully planned, painstaking, and exhaustive process of searching for information. That search includes controlled experimentation with observation and recording of the results. Its purpose is the development of new knowledge, either in the absolute sense or as reconstruction of the past: recovery of knowledge that once existed in some person but is now hidden by that person or has been lost with the passage of time. Quite obviously, research involves investigation, albeit a special kind—a critical and exhaustive investigation. This means that research and investigation are, if not identical, at least closely related concepts.

One of the definitions of the transitive verb "to investigate" is "to follow the trace of" or "to track," meanings that come directly from the Latin word *vestigium*, meaning "footprint," "trace," or "sign." As a noun, investigation means the act of investigating or of inquiring into some matter.

It seems clear, then, that there is no absolute distinction between research and investigation. Popular usage, however, has, in the past, differentiated between the two. Research has generally meant an investigation designed to generate new knowledge for its own sake. Sometimes that meaning has been more clearly indicated by calling the activity basic research. When the new knowledge was sought for immediate practical application, it was called, in contrast, applied research. On the other hand, *investigation* has been used primarily to mean reconstruction of the past for some immediate action purpose, such as in investigative reporting or police detective work. This is the distinction between research and investigation that will be used in this book, although Bergen and Cornelia Evans, in their *Dictionary of Contemporary American Usage*, indicate that this differentiation is being broken down in everyday speech.

> *Research* has become very popular in the United States since the outbreak of World War II. As Henry D. Smith has observed, the idea that the object of research is new knowledge does not seem to be widely understood and "a

schoolboy looking up the meaning of a word in the dictionary is now said to be doing research." Indeed, it has been debased even further. *Research* is frequently used to describe reading by those to whom reading, apparently, is a recherché activity, and for many a graduate student it is a euphemism for wholesale plagiarism. The word needs a rest or at least less promiscuous handling. (Emphasis in the original.)[2]

Despite the fact that the kinds of investigations for determination of fact with which this book is concerned do not usually involve scientific research, they do purport to use scientific method. The ideal is for persons involved in all kinds of investigations to be rational, non-fanatic, unbiased investigators who are aware of and can compensate for the value systems that govern their own lives.

RESEARCH AND INVESTIGATION METHODS

As indicated at the outset, determinations of fact, whether dependent upon research or investigation for generation of the necessary information, utilize a three-step process.

1. Recognition and definition of the problem
2. Development and implementation of a plan for collection of the relevant facts with ongoing organization, synthesis, and analysis of the information as it is obtained
3. Presentation of the evidence to the decision maker(s)

However, these common processes may take very different forms depending on whether the project involves research or investigation. What remains the same and what may very well be different are considered in this section.

In both settings, research and investigation, the problems are sometimes given. The assignment may be to find a way to prevent prostate cancer or to identify and gather the evidence necessary to determine the circumstances of the death of John Jones. In both settings, there is some freedom to define the focus of the activity. The assignment may be simply to conduct research on American history or to prevent crime or to come up with a story that will sell newspapers. When this kind of freedom exists, there must be criteria to guide its exercise.

In such a situation, definition of focus may begin by identifying the significant and interesting problems that remain within the field of choice. General knowledge of the field based on education, training, and experience ought to yield a fairly comprehensive list of such problems within a reasonable period of time. That list can then be further reduced by considering which of the problem areas can be narrowed enough so that it can be explored in significant depth. Isolation of the topic from its context must be possible. At that point more pragmatic considerations take over, such as whether sufficient evidence can be found to support definite conclusions and whether sufficient skills and other resources are at hand for successful conclusion of the project.[3]

It is also advisable to consider whether there are any special problems that might be encountered in research on or investigation of the defined topic.

- Can active resistance with positive attempts to conceal evidence be anticipated?
- Are the events involved so common or routine that no one will remember or have recorded them?
- Are the people involved observant and able to remember or record what they saw?
- Can the issues be defined in a neutral manner? This neutrality is important; lawyers may well be correct in saying, "Let me define the issue and I will win the argument."
- When public policy issues are involved, it may sometimes be difficult to get agreement on how their investigation should be framed.
- Another danger is that problems sometimes get redefined not by the realities of the situation but by a desire to employ a favorite research or investigative method.

Problem definition, then, not only requires knowledge of the factual situation or events out of which it grows but also may be affected by value systems associated with that context.

Once a research or investigative problem has been defined, the next step is design and implementation of an evidence collection plan. That plan may vary from the extremely complex, in which data must be collected that will later be subjected to sophisticated statistical and other analyses, to the relatively simple and straightforward observation and recording of basic facts. Behavioral and social science research falls into four principal categories, as follows:

1. *Historical* research, the patient reconstruction of the past
2. *Observation*, developing and recording additional knowledge about the present
3. *Survey* research, in which information is gathered about some population by interviewing a representative sample
4. *Experimental* research, in which one variable is changed while others are held constant in order to assess the consequences of the change

Plans for investigation are usually based on the historical method, in which the task is reconstruction of the relatively recent past. They frequently have observational components: the stakeout of a location or surveillance of individuals. The closest approach to the experimental method is provision for an opportunity to commit violations in a setting where monitoring has led to suspicion that violations are occurring. Typical of these are the "sting" operations conducted by many police organizations. These are similar to the "natural" experiments that social scientists are sometimes able to use.

There may be special jurisdictional problems in major investigations requiring the cooperation of a number of agencies or division of responsibility between general field personnel and specialists. Investigative plans may also require covert as well as overt operations. However, most investigative procedures rely on overt sources, even when the fact that the investigation is proceeding is secret. In such cases, systematic coverage of overt information sources may be covert. Covert sources are used to fill the gaps in information from other, overt sources. But remember that the information may be lacking from overt sources not because of coverup attempts but because the target of the investigation simply has not generated the information. Not even covert sources and procedures can produce information that doesn't exist.

■ WHO DOES RESEARCH? WHO INVESTIGATES? AND WHY?

Research has indeed become very popular in the United States since World War II. According to the National Science Foundation,

> In 1977, total national research expenditures, in current dollars, were $15.32 billion, compared with $8.44 billion in 1968.... In 1979, total national expenditures for all research and for research and development (measured in constant dollars) were about 8 percent above their 1977 levels.[4]

These expenditures are split among the United States government, industry, and the universities. The increased interest of the federal government is indicated by the passage of the National Science and Technology Policy, Organization, and Priorities Act of 1976,[5] which, among other things, required that the National Science Foundation periodically publish a *Five-Year Outlook* for research and technology in the United States. The first *Outlook* was published in 1980.

Universities in the United States encourage their faculty members to do basic and applied research. Both are part of the accepted mission of our universities. In addition to the intellectual reasons supporting research, the activities earn financial resources for the universities in a very practical way. For example, in the first half of the 1980s, a number of major research universities developed long-range, multimillion dollar research agreements with industry in the emerging field of bioengineering.[6]

In addition to funding university research, many of our major industrial concerns support their own in-house research divisions that conduct basic and applied research in their areas of interest. Most of that research is in the physical and health sciences, but some is also in the social sciences, mainly on economics and politics. Company management has in each case been convinced that such research, even basic research, will, in the long run, increase profits through development of new products and services.

As indicated earlier, government has also become a major supporter of research in the United States. Much of that research is defense oriented, aimed at improvement of our defense capabilities. But an appreciable amount is also public policy oriented, aimed at development of evidence for legislative and administrative determinations of fact. Here social scientists make major contributions. The primary aims of government research are, then, increasing our national security and general improvement of public policies and the processes for their formulation.

Investigation is carried out extensively in both the private and public sectors. Examples of the types of investigation are highlighted here.

Private Sector Investigations

Many persons enjoy reading novels and watching television programs depicting the activities of private investigators, the private eyes. In real life, these investigators usually spend their time in less exciting ways than their fictional counterparts. They may spend hours seeking information useful to their clients—whether individuals, associations, businesses, or industrial firms—in the conduct of their private affairs. Some are solo operators. Others are large concerns with many employees; these may offer services other than investigation, such as unarmed watchmen; armed security guards; advice about, sale, and installation of security devices; and consultation on security matters generally.

Larger business and industrial concerns frequently provide these services for themselves through in-house security divisions. In addition to the functions just listed, these divisions may conduct personnel investigations, gather organizational intelligence, carry out industrial espionage and counterespionage, and work out countermeasures against possible terrorist activity. All of these functions are designed to protect and increase profits.

Another private sector location of much investigative effort is in the mass media: print, radio, and television. It supports straight news reporting, news analysis, and in-depth investigative reports. Its justification is the public's need to know; satisfaction of that need happens also to be a lucrative enterprise.

Private interest groups do a lot of investigating in support of their efforts to enhance the interests to which they are dedicated. They keep track of and try to influence those activities of the private sector and the government that impact on the interests of their groups. Much of their investigative work is in support of efforts to initiate or influence legislation that may affect the group: the lobbying function.

Private attorneys—representing plaintiffs and defendants—frequently direct private sector investigative efforts with an eye toward using the work product in cases in court or before administrative agencies.

Public Sector Investigations

There are also many different kinds of investigations conducted in the public sector. Perhaps typical are those of the police agencies at all levels: federal, state, and local. Some of the police investigative effort is devoted to monitoring whether rules, regulations, or statutes (that is, laws of all kinds) are being obeyed. But more of the effort is expended to investigate violations when found, whether they are traditional, economic, or political crimes. The purposes are to establish who committed the violation and apprehend that person, to recover anything of value that might have been taken, and to assist the state in prosecuting any persons charged with violations.[7] Still another function of police investigators is personnel background checks.

A second group engaged in public sector investigation is that of government attorneys, both prosecutors and those who represent the government in civil cases. They must produce or supervise production of the evidence required to demonstrate that there is a violation to prosecute or a civil action to bring. Even more evidence must then be marshalled to meet the standard of proof in the case. It must also be determined whether there are potentially effective defenses to the prosecution or civil action. In addition it may be necessary to gather evidence to determine whether the background of potential witnesses and of the decision maker(s) might affect the outcome of the case.

A third group of public sector investigators is found in the military establishment. Some of these perform the same functions as do civilian government investigators: checking personnel background for security clearances, monitoring the conduct of personnel for possible violations, and detecting and proving criminal violations. But considerable military investigative effort also goes into the gathering of operational intelligence. In general, such intelligence produced by investigative effort is useful not only to military units but to other organizations as well.

A wide variety of other government personnel in the executive, legislative, and administrative branches also conduct investigations. Their activities cover a broad range and include such functions as monitoring ongoing activity; discovering and documenting violations; auditing financial programs including collecting taxes; determining whether conditions are met for conferral of government benefits (as well as for the award or denial of licenses, and for setting utility rates); and determining the need for, content, and format of new regulations or statutes to be recommended. Typical of those sometimes overlooked when attention turns to governmental employees who conduct investigations are those, usually social workers, who, in our justice system agencies, administer adult and juvenile probation and parole programs, assist prisoners with family problems, and staff juvenile court intake offices.

All of these public officials investigate matters within their jurisdiction in carrying out their mandates to serve the residents of the United States.

PREPARATION OF INVESTIGATORS AND RESEARCH PERSONNEL

Both research and investigative personnel should have as broad a knowledge base as possible. In addition they require familiarity with the techniques and skills of research or investigation. When working on a specific problem, they must also master the available information pertinent to that area. These qualifications will come from formal education, training, experience, and concentrated independent study. Career preparation is a lifelong endeavor. Continuing self-education can never stop.

In addition to a formal knowledge base, one needs imagination and intuition. Whether those traits must come naturally or can be inculcated remains an open question. A dedicated persistence to solution of the current research or investigative problem is another necessity for success. In sum, the ideal person for research or investigation has native intelligence well disciplined by the education, training, and experience that yield good judgment-making capabilities.

Preparation for a research career usually requires formal education to the Ph.D. level. University doctoral programs generally have about equal amounts of attention given to the specialized knowledge of the academic discipline involved, to the related disciplinary fields, and to research design and methods. Holders of such doctorates are called upon to design the research effort and to analyze the resulting data. Those with formal education stopping at the baccalaureate or master's level or leading to professional degrees are more apt to be employed to implement the research design or data collection plan under supervision.

Those who write history are usually holders of the Ph.D. in that discipline and employed as professors in colleges and universities. Through their research, they seek new understanding of and insight into past events that can be shared with the rest of us. Study of their method, which is called historiography, is useful for others also engaged in reconstruction of the past, such as investigative journalists and detectives.[8]

Investigative journalists, who usually are concerned with reconstruction of more recent past events than are historians, are more apt to have formal education to the baccalaureate or master's degree level. Their college major may well have been in Journalism or in English, but reporters also hold a wide variety of other undergraduate degrees, with those in History and Political Science being fairly common. Working under the protection against abridgement of freedom of the press provided by the First and Fourteenth Amendments to the federal Constitution, by some state constitutions, and by the several state-enacted "shield laws" that protect against disclosure of their sources, investigative reporters have become experts at discovering, documenting, and revealing situations and conditions that should not exist. The tradition is an old one, dating from at least the early 1800s. Upton Sinclair's book *The Jungle*, published in 1906, about scandalous conditions in the Chicago meat-packing industry, is one of the more famous examples of their work.[9] The magazine articles of Lincoln Steffens, who also wrote in the early 1900s, about corruption in government, business, and labor fall into that category as well.[10] More recently the exposure of the Watergate coverup of then-President Richard Nixon and his staff made by Carl Bernstein and Bob Woodward, reporters for the *Washington Post* newspaper, and of a wide variety of alleged evils, by Ralph Nader and his consumer advocate colleagues, are well known. The focus is usually on corruption and wrongdoing, frequently by government officials or involving government policies.[11]

Although today's investigative journalists usually have college degrees, many police detectives do not, but the numbers who are college educated, usually to the baccalaureate level, are increasing rapidly. They and other government investigators perform work similar to that of historians and investigative journalists. Again the concern is with reconstruction of the past. Basically they require the same kinds of knowledge and skills, the same dedication and persistence. Their goal frequently is to prove and bring into the open matters that others would prefer remain hidden. But there are differences. The subjects of their investigations are usually specified by law. Their object is to administer and enforce law, to prosecute as well as to publicize wrongdoing. Their freedom of action is frequently circumscribed by their superiors, and their methods may be both limited and enhanced by law. Those methods may also include authorized use of force. They work under pressing time restraints. Because of the seriousness of the charges that their evidence frequently seeks to support, the standard of proof that must be met is the very high one of proof beyond a reasonable doubt. These characteristics of police investigations make them perhaps the most well-known fact determination situations in the governmental setting.

Regardless of their formal education, persons in research and in investigative work are frequently given specific training in subject matter and techniques needed for specific projects. Practice is also a considerable asset. Experience can be a very valuable teacher to a thoughtful practitioner.

IMPACT OF THE SETTING

Historians, investigative reporters, and government investigators, as typical of the many groups engaged in the task of investigation, all must define their problems, collect the facts, and present them to decision makers. Historians pick a topic and develop a research plan. They have a great deal of freedom in defining the problem on which they wish to work, but there are limitations. Their research plan is usually well defined, frequently in a detailed proposal submitted to some funding agency. The plan is followed meticulously without much regard for time restraint until the historian decides that all the necessary information is in hand. Presentation of that information is usually directed to professional peers in an article or book or may be popularized for the general public. The judgment of their peers as to the merit of the publication is the test to be met.

Investigative reporters generally come upon topics for intensive investigation in the course of their daily news reporting. They discuss the possibility of developing a major story with their editors, and proceed only if the editors agree on the story potential. Their fact collection process will be limited by the time made available by the editor. The investigative plan is less formal than that of the historian. One lead usually results in another until a judgment is made that enough facts are available to merit publication. The story will be aimed at the general public, but will frequently be screened by the employer's lawyer for the possibility of defending against a possible slander or libel suit. The tests of the story's success will be the extent of public interest that it generates, whether it results in corrective action by those about whom it is written, and by whether it wins an award from journalistic peers.

Government investigators, in contrast, are usually assigned to well-defined problems for investigation. The problem definition function will have been performed for the investigator by a superior, although the focus of any investigation can change during its progress. The detective's investigative plan, like that of the investigative reporter, is usually much less formal than that of the historian. During collection of the necessary information, the government investigator may be simultaneously aided and restrained by specific legal guidelines. Presentation is usually to some governmental decision-making body, such as a court. Success is determined by whether the decision maker accepts the case presented as proved and takes the action recommended.

As indicated, general principles do govern the investigative function even though a specific setting may require variations in detail. Those general principles are discussed in Parts Three through Four of this book.

■ SUMMARIZING COMMENTARY

Research and investigation are very closely related processes involved in many determinations of fact. Both are useful in reconstruction of the past, which is the essential task of historians, investigative reporters, and police detectives alike. None of these types of determinations deal with absolutes, but are concerned rather with probabilities that one scholar has said can only be judged with art and a sense of responsibility.

Definitions of research involve use of the term *investigation*, which indicates that research is a special kind of investigation. It is in fact a critical and exhaustive investigation, an operation conducted with far fewer of the time and other restraints that hedge in the more practical, governmental, legal investigations with which this book is primarily concerned.

Research projects and investigations are major enterprises in today's society. Billions of dollars are spent annually in the United States by government, business and industry, and the universities on a wide variety of research projects. Even more resources both in dollars and personnel are devoted to governmental determinations of fact. With research, there are multiple possible objectives: discovery of knowledge for its own sake; discovery of knowledge whose application can raise the standard of living for all while providing profits to those making the application; and enhancement of our nation's security in an unstable and sometimes hostile world.

Investigations lead to determinations of fact that also serve a variety of purposes: protection of property, profits, freedoms, and rights; administration and enforcement of the law; and achievement of the minimal social order needed for enjoyment of freedom. For these purposes, research and investigation are widely employed in both the public and private sectors. How the purposes are interpreted, what priorities will be established, and what means will be allowed for achieving the desired ends will be influenced by community values as expressed in the work of investigators and decision makers. Uncertainty results when there is conflict among competing value systems that purport to govern specific activities. It is hoped that in such a situation, confusion can be avoided by choice of one of the value systems or by some compromise among them through the political process.

In the behavioral and social sciences there are four principal research approaches to carefully defined problems: historical research, observation, survey research, and experimental research. Investigation plans are usually based on the historical method, frequently have observational components, seldom use surveys, and can be experimental only in the sense of providing natural opportunities for violation of law in controlled settings. Investigations are frequently kept covert and sometimes use covert evidence-collection techniques, although not as frequently as fictional literature would lead one to assume.

Preparation of investigative and research personnel has the same objective: the shaping of native intelligence through appropriate education, training, and experience to use imagination and intuition to arrive at sound judgments in difficult problem situations. Intellectual capacity must be a given. Education can provide a knowledge base in both substance and technique; training can sharpen that knowledge in regard to particular problem areas. Experience can provide flexibility to meet unforeseen complications in the implementation of research designs and investigative plans. Those creating the designs or plans and analyzing the resulting bodies of information are usually more extensively prepared than are those who implement those designs or plans under supervision. There is little knowledge now available about how imagination and intuition can be developed, but specified conditions of work do seem conducive to their appearance.

Because historians, investigative reporters, and government investigators share the task of reconstruction of the past, each can learn from careful study of success among the others. The balance of this book is concerned with how they go about the collection, analysis, and presentation of evidence. But before getting into that discussion, Chapter 3 focuses on the legal and ethical restraints on investigators.

STUDY QUESTIONS

1. Why must historians, reporters, and police detectives meet different standards of proof in their investigations?
2. What are the steps preceding decision in any determination of fact?
3. What are the characteristics of an ideal investigator?
4. What is the impact of law on the work of a police investigator?

RECOMMENDED ADDITIONAL READING

- Barzun, Jacques, and Graff, Henry F. *The Modern Researcher.* 3rd ed. New York: Harcourt Brace Jovanovich, 1977.
- Rose, Louis J. *How to Investigate Your Friends and Enemies.* St. Louis, Mo.: Albion Press, 1983.

- Wilensky, Harold L. *Organizational Intelligence.* New York: Basic Books, 1967.

NOTES

1. Robert Jones Shafer, ed., *A Guide to Historical Method*, 3rd ed. (Homewood, Ill.: Dorsey Press, 1980), p. 53.
2. Bergen Evans and Cornelia Evans, *A Dictionary of Contemporary American Usage* (New York: Random House, 1957), p. 420. Because we agree with this sentiment, the authors of this text consider it to be not a research report but a contribution to teaching, despite the fact that many hours of investigation preceded its writing.
3. This discussion follows generally that in Shafer, op. cit., n. 1, pp. 43–45.
4. National Science Foundation, *The Five-Year Outlook: Problems, Opportunities and Constraints in Science and Technology* (Washington, D.C.: U.S. Government Printing Office, 1980), p. 10.
5. 42 U.S.C. §6601 *et seq.*
6. See Robert D. Varrin and Diane S. Kuckich, "Guidelines for Industry Sponsored Research at Universities," *Science* 227 (25 January 1985): 385–388.
7. See Charles R. Swanson, Jr., Neil C. Chamelin, and Leonard Territo, *Criminal Investigation*, 3rd ed. (New York: Random House, 1984), p. 2.
8. Shafer, op. cit., n. 1, and Jacques Barzun and Henry F. Graff, *The Modern Researcher*, 3rd ed. (New York: Harcourt Brace Jovanovich, 1977) are well regarded guides.
9. Upton B. Sinclair, *The Jungle* (1906; reprint, Cambridge, Mass.: Robert Bentley, Inc., 1971).
10. Lincoln Steffens, *Autobiography* (New York: Harcourt Brace Jovanovich, 1931).
11. See generally Louis J. Rose, *How to Investigate Your Friends and Enemies* (St. Louis, Mo.: Albion Press, 1983); for those particularly interested in justice systems, a good current example is *Institutions, ETC.* (published monthly), 814 North Saint Asaph Street, Alexandria, Va. 22314.

LEGAL AND
ETHICAL PRECEPTS

Not all investigative efforts are successful. At times even the recent past will escape effective reconstruction; at times it simply will not be possible to make the necessary observation of current activity. Determination of fact will fail because the facts required for decision making cannot be obtained.

The most common reason that some investigations fail is the effectiveness of the measures taken by the actors to conceal what they are doing. Most violations of law are clandestine and well planned so that they can be kept hidden. In a 1983 study of 3,360 burglary and 320 robbery investigations, about 87 percent of the burglary and about 75 percent of the robbery investigations were dropped after no more than one full day of follow-up investigation because of the considered judgment that they could not be solved with a reasonable amount of investigative effort.[1] In those cases, the perpetrators were successful in covering their tracks.

Another reason why investigations fail, even in cases in which there was hope for solution with a reasonable amount of investigative effort, is failure of a particular investigator. That failure may come because the person assigned is simply not sufficiently intelligent or interested, educated or trained, experienced or dedicated. There are persons performing investigations of all kinds who shouldn't be. Not much can be done about those not "cut out" for the task; the system does them a favor when they are identified and removed from those jobs. In contrast, those who have both the interest and capacity but not the education and training can be helped. This book is a tool for fashioning that help. Once educated and trained, capable investigators will find success increases with experience. Then, independence and responsibility can also be increased.

But sometimes even the best-qualified investigator the system can produce will fail to obtain necessary evidence because of restraints imposed by our legal system. Those restraints stem from the belief that the evidence is not as valuable to us as a society as is freedom from the intrusion by government investigators that would be necessary to obtain the evidence. The law limits what an investigator may do.

It is also true that, on occasion in a particular situation, an extremely well-qualified investigator may choose, for ethical reasons, not to push to the limit allowed by law. When that happens, the investigator is making a considered judgment that the evidence is not worth violation of a personal or professional code of ethics even when the action necessary to obtain it is legal. Needless to say, there is disagreement among practitioners and scholars on what the ethical restraints on legal action should be. In fact, some would argue that investigators are bound by their contract of employment to push the law to its limits and, if they can reasonably hope to get away with it, to go beyond those limits to obtain necessary evidence. That argument is based on the assumption that the ends justify the means. This book takes the firm position that, legally and ethically, both the ends and the means must be justified in any investigation.

The balance of this chapter is devoted to discussion of the legal and ethical limits on investigation and of why it is in the best interests of both the individual investigator and of our society to abide by those limits. The emphasis is on government investigators, and the discussion begins with a survey of some of the more important and frequently encountered legal restraints on investigation.

LEGAL PRECEPTS GOVERNING INVESTIGATION

All persons have the power to gather information through investigation. All also have the right, but only some have the duty. There are legal limitations on the right—limitations as to its objectives, its scope, and its means. Those limitations are greater for those who have only the right than for those who also have the duty; they are greater for historians and investigative reporters than for government investigators. Perhaps basic to the legal limitations on objectives is the right to privacy.

In the July 1890 issue of *Scribner's*, journalist E. L. Godkin published an article taking to task his fellow journalists and publishers who invaded the privacy of ordinary persons by publication for profit of details of their private lives in which the general public had no legitimate interest. His view was endorsed by two Harvard Law School professors, Samuel D. Warren and Louis D. Brandeis, who decided that the law ought to provide remedies for such intrusions, and argued in an article published in the November 1890 issue of the *Harvard Law Review* that, in fact, it did.[2] Whether because the authors were so prominent or their arguments so cogent, others in the law, including judges, tended to agree. A "right to privacy" was finally recognized by the United States Supreme Court in

1965.[3] Although not expressed explicitly in the Constitution, it is implied as a constitutional principle from the First, Third, Fourth, Fifth, and Ninth Amendments. Explicit statutes have also been enacted to cover particular applications of the right.[4]

Although its definition continues to expand, there are four principal aspects to the right of privacy.

1. Intrusion on an individual's solitude
2. Public disclosure of embarrassing private facts about an individual
3. Publicity that places the individual in a "false light" in the eyes of the public
4. The use by another of a person's name or image for profit

The first three of these are of obvious interest to investigators. The fourth is of more interest to investigative reporters and historians.

But the right to privacy is not absolute. It is forfeited to all, even to private persons, by those individuals who become "public personages," among whom are movie and television stars and high government officials. It is also forfeited when government investigators show probable cause to believe that the individual is involved in a crime, seeks one of certain government offices, seeks certain government contracts, seeks to be licensed by the state, seeks a government benefit, or threatens the security of the state. In all of these instances, government investigators are permitted to intrude on what would otherwise be protected areas of privacy.

That permission, however, must be used carefully. Private persons must not be motivated by malice, and the government investigator should intrude only to obtain information that is clearly relevant to the case. What is found should be kept confidential, should be distributed, even to colleagues, only on a "need to know" basis, and should not be revealed to any outside parties. It should be checked against related information and should be corroborated from independent sources if at all possible. Eventually the person involved should be given an opportunity to explain the significance or contest the validity of the information. And finally, it should be used in public proceedings only as a last resort, only if the proceedings could not go forward without it. Such professional use of the government investigator's privilege to invade privacy will protect the continued existence of the privilege. Not all the specific legal restraints on investigators can be covered here, but some of the more important follow.

One area of legal limitation on governmental investigative procedures is in search of persons, houses, papers, and effects. The Fourth Amendment to the Constitution requires that all such searches be reasonable. By specific provision in the amendment, searches are reasonable if pursuant to a judicially issued search warrant based "upon probable cause, supported by oath or affirmation, and particularly describing the place to be searched, and the persons or things to be seized." All other searches are presumably unreasonable and illegal *unless* they are an authorized part of some other lawful procedure or justifiable on the basis of emergency need. The principal circumstances in which such situations exist will be discussed in some detail here. They are important sources of information. But first the information that an investigator must gather to constitute probable cause for issuance of a search warrant will be explored.

If the information on which the warrant is to be based comes from a confidential informant, as it frequently does, two basic questions must be faced: how does the informant know that the items to be seized are presently at the place to be searched, and why should the informant be considered reliable?[5] Usually a government attorney will assist the investigator in drafting the affidavit of probable cause. In preparation for that conference, the investigator should be able to state that the informant furnishing the information speaks from personal knowledge, the date on which that knowledge was obtained, what detailed facts the informant observed, where the observations were made, and the date on which the information was passed on to the investigator by the informant.

On the issue of the informant's reliability, the investigator should be prepared to state the number of previous cases in which the informant gave accurate verified information; the nature of such information; how, when, and by whom the information was verified; the kinds of offenses involved; the period of time over which the informant has served; and the number of cases in which the information supplied led to arrest, trial, and conviction.

If the information to be relied on comes from some private citizen who can be identified, the same basic questions must be faced. The same details about the person's knowledge of the items to be seized should be available. On the issue of reliability, the investigator should have available the person's name, address, age, occupation, family situation, possible motives for reporting, and the person's apparent sobriety and demeanor when the information was reported.

If the probable cause is to be based on information from surveillance by government investigators, the investigator applying for the warrant should know who conducted the surveillance, the date and times when it took place, what exactly was observed, and how the observations support the belief that the items will be found when the warrant is executed.

When information from an anonymous informant is used as the basis for the warrant, a special problem exists as to reliability. In such a case, independent verification of some of the anonymous allegations is helpful. Indications that the informant is familiar with the situation also contributes to the sense of reliability. That the alleged criminal activity fits into the pattern known to the investigator from other cases in the area contributes as well to confidence in the tip. In 1983, the United States Supreme Court decided that the sufficiency of an anonymous informant's information for establishing probable cause depended on the "totality of the circumstances."[6]

What property may be seized by an investigator under a search warrant is usually specified by statute. That of the District of Columbia is typical.

> Property is subject to seizure pursuant to a search warrant if there is probable cause to believe that it:
> 1. is stolen or embezzled;
> 2. is contraband or otherwise illegally possessed;
> 3. has been used or is possessed for the purpose of being used, or is designed or intended to be used, to commit or conceal the commission of a criminal offense; or
> 4. constitutes evidence of or tends to demonstrate the commission of an offense or the identity of a person participating in the commission of an offense.[7]

When the warrant has been issued, it must be executed in a reasonable manner. No person is subject to arrest simply because present when the search is made.[8] If the investigators reasonably believe that such a person is armed and dangerous, a "frisk" or "pat down" for weapons is authorized.

Among the circumstances in which search without a warrant is reasonable, the following six are common enough for discussion here: plain view, consent exception, incident to a lawful arrest, automobile exception, hot pursuit, and exigent circumstances.

Seizure is reasonable without a warrant when contraband is in the plain view of an investigator who is legally present. The legal basis for the officer's presence may be quite varied. The place may be a public area, a private area to which the public has been invited, a place to which the officer has been called, or a place in which an investigation is being made of a disturbance or some other nuisance that constitutes a violation of law. Service of an arrest or search warrant in an entirely unrelated matter or hot pursuit of a suspect also may be the basis for the investigator's lawful presence.[9] This is a situation in which search is not actually involved, just a seizure authorized by the investigator's official status.

Search of an individual or an area within that person's use and control without a warrant is lawful if the individual voluntarily consents. The consent may be explicit or may be inferred from the person's statements or actions in affirmation of the search. The consent may be given by the individual involved, by a spouse, co-tenant of an apartment, parents, or by one who shares the use of a container, such as a duffel bag.[10] However, very frequently the voluntariness of the consent will later be challenged, so the investigator must carefully document the giving of consent in every case.

A search without a warrant is also reasonable if made incident to a lawful arrest, whether with a valid warrant of arrest or with probable cause to believe that a crime was committed by the person.[11] The arrest must have been made in good faith, not merely as a pretext to justify the search. The search must also be contemporaneous with the arrest. The search is limited to the person of the arrestee and the area within that individual's immediate control.[12]

A fourth situation in which search without a warrant is reasonable is sometimes called the automobile exception. In one of its applications, this doctrine is justified by the car's mobility. If an investigator has probable cause to believe that an automobile contains seizable items, that it may well be moved and the evidence destroyed unless immediate action is taken, a search is justified if executed in a reasonable manner.[13] In another application, a search of an automobile is reasonable if made incident to the lawful arrest of a person occupying the vehicle or who controls and is in the immediate vicinity of the vehicle.[14] When stopping the vehicle in either of these situations, the investigators may order the occupants to get out as a safety measure.[15] There can, however, be no lawful roving searches of vehicles.[16]

If an investigator chases a suspect, who is about to be lawfully arrested, into a building where evidence of a crime (such as a weapon or clothing) is in plain sight, the evidence may be seized and will be admissible at the trial of the suspect to whom it has been linked.[17] But, contrary to the holding of some lower courts, the pursuit must really be hot—immediate—not just warm.[18] Actually, because of the pursuit, the investigator is legally at the site where the evidence is in plain view; no search is involved, just a seizure authorized by the investigator's official status.

Exigent circumstances that will justify action without a warrant require a reasonable belief on the part of an investigator that, absent the prompt action, evidence will be destroyed, a felon will escape, or some person will be injured or killed. They involve "last chance" situations such as border searches, the report by a maid of a gun in a hotel room,[19] or a glimpse of a person with a bloody face through a half-open door.[20] These cases involve a balancing test between the Fourth Amendment protection and the societal law enforcement interest.

Wiretaps and Other Electronic Surveillance

Investigators must also consider the legal restraints when they desire to gain information by listening to the conversations of suspects with telephone wiretaps or electronic surveillance devices. These procedures are not justified unless other investigative means will not be successful. As a practical matter, a wiretap will be useful only when the suspect is known to talk regularly and freely with criminal associates over the phone.

Electronic surveillance is useful only when the suspect meets criminal associates for freewheeling discussion regularly at a specific location. The investigator usually learns about such habits of the suspect through informants or undercover agents.

Obtaining authorization from the court for a telephone wiretap is covered by both federal and state law.[21] The practice in the differing jurisdictions varies considerably, but a number of issues are involved in all wiretap situations. The first is that obtaining permission to make a tap takes time. Although it may be possible to get the order in one day, it may also take up to two weeks. From three to five days is a reasonable expectation. The delay results from two sources: first, the request to the court cannot usually be filed by the investigating officer without review of the circumstances and approval of the request by superiors; and second, discretion is vested in the court to grant or deny the request.

In some jurisdictions, the review of the request prior to submission to the court may include the prosecutor as well as superiors within the police agency. Criteria for this administrative review of the request will require that the supporting affidavit show probable cause, first, that the target suspect is committing a crime and, second, that information about that crime will be obtained through the use of the electronic means for which approval is sought and cannot be obtained through other less intrusive means. Different reviewers may use different criteria in making their assessments of those requirements. One may be satisfied to base the affidavit on the word of one informant; another may require that two or three support the affidavit. Approval by the court is not automatic. Judges are required to use discretion in determining whether the requested authorization should be granted.

If the application is approved by the court, an order is usually sent to the telephone company directing it to supply a leased extension line from the number being checked to the investigation listening post. When the line first becomes operative, several days are customarily spent listening to all calls to determine those persons with whom the suspect has crime-related conversations. After that determination is made, good practice dictates that only crime-related calls, not those that are probably innocent, are listened to and recorded. When the tap has served its purpose, the line is disconnected. Again good practice requires that the tapes made from it be inventoried and then sealed by the court. A report regarding that tape should be prepared and sent to the court that authorized the procedure. Frequently the court requires that within 90 days after termination of the procedure, letters be written to those whose conversations were overheard, outlining the circumstances in which it was done.

Similar procedures are required for operation of a pen register, a device that does not record conversations but simply numbers called, from a suspect's telephone line. Although use of a pen register without a warrant has been found by the United States Supreme Court not to violate the federal Constitution, the Supreme Court of Colorado held that the procedure did violate the constitution of that state.[22] Whether other jurisdictions will follow the lead of Colorado remains to be seen.

Evidence at Arrest or Detention

As has already been indicated, evidence may also be obtained from a search incident to a lawful arrest. Crucial to making that evidence admissible is being able to show that probable cause existed for the arrest. That standard means probable cause as seen by a reasonable, prudent government-employed investigator, not by a layperson. The expertise of an experienced investigator, such as a police officer, in interpreting the presented fact situation is respected. But that judgment must be based on objectively observable specific facts and circumstances that can be described and explained to a third person. Among the factors that can support the investigator's finding of probable cause are these: furtive movements or flight by the suspect; evasive answers to questioning; suspicious conduct (such as that customary in casing an establishment prior to burglary or robbery); lack of identification; knowledge that a crime has just been committed in the area; knowledge that the location is frequently used for crime (such as drug dealing or soliciting for prostitution); conduct unusual for the time of day or night; hearsay information about involvement of the suspect in crime; a known arrest record; and known criminal tendencies and associates. Many of these items would not be admissible at trial to prove guilt, but can be used by a street investigator in judging whether probable cause to arrest exists.

Street investigators may also take action short of arrest in some situations that will produce evidence. It is always lawful to ask for identification. Although not alone sufficient to constitute probable cause for arrest, refusal to produce identification can be considered along with other factors. However, if an investigator has a reasonable suspicion that a person is then engaged in criminal activity or has recently been so engaged in the matter under investigation, there can be a demand for identification and the suspect may be held temporarily for further checking if there is refusal. That temporary detention and a quick pat down for weapons, sometimes known as a "stop and frisk," can be made if the investigator has a reasonable suspicion based on specific facts that prompt action is necessary, and the investigator is convinced that action cannot be postponed safely and responsibly pending more detailed investigation. In such cases, the intrusion on the individual's freedom cannot be greater than the situation demands. If the temporary detention becomes prolonged, it will be considered an arrest.[23]

When an arrest is made, it yields information through the booking and associated procedures. Booking is essentially an identification process. It customarily yields the arrestee's name, address, date of birth, place of employment, and social security number. It also involves fingerprinting, photographing, and the recording of any scars or other identifying marks. It may involve the taking of hair, blood, urine, and handwriting samples as well as scrapings from beneath the fingernails if these are deemed significant evidence in the case. Stool evacuations may also be monitored and collected if necessary to recover ingested items. Should the arrested person refuse to cooperate in any of these activities, force should not be used, but an express order of the court obtained. Should the refusal then continue, enforcement becomes the concern of the judge who issued the order. The contempt power is the base for the judge's power of persuasion. If it seems necessary for body invasion to occur, it is best to obtain a written order from the court. Courts of last resort in the different states vary in the procedures that they will allow. In all booking and other associated procedures following arrest, the health and safety of the arrested person is paramount. Any special procedures must be carried out by professionally qualified persons under appropriate circumstances.

Line-up identification of an arrested person may also be conducted as part of the booking procedure incident to the arrest. Ordinarily the suspect will be asked to stand with a number of others who are approximately similar in size and appearance for viewing by victims and witnesses. Care must be taken not to direct the attention of the viewer to the suspect in any way. During the viewing, each of those in the line may, in turn, be requested to speak, gesture, put on an article of clothing, or take any other reasonable action. If the perpetrator was only heard and not seen, voice identification procedures may be followed. Similarly, photo identification procedures may be carried out with the victim and witnesses instead of an actual physical lineup. Or prior to any arrest, a witness may be asked to observe a street setting, where it is known that the suspect will appear, to discover whether identification can be made from among all of the persons observed. If any line-up identification procedure occurs after formal accusation, the defendant has a right to be represented by an attorney at the event.[74] In all cases, the identification procedure must be carefully planned, conducted, and recorded, by videotape if possible.

Overview

This summary of legal provisions governing acquisition of evidence is by no means complete, but does cover those situations most commonly encountered. It also discusses an area of the law that is still developing, so investigators must keep themselves up-to-date on the specific limitations in their own jurisdictions. An investigator ignores those limits at the risk of having the evidence declared inadmissible and perhaps, as a result, losing the case. The challenge will usually come in a pretrial motion to suppress the evidence. It will be alleged that the evidence was obtained as the direct result of illegal action, or as the result of a lead obtained from illegal action that led directly to the evidence that would not otherwise have been discovered: the fruit of the poisonous tree. In order for the motion to suppress to succeed, it must be shown that it was the defendant's personal right that was violated by the illegal procedure, not that of some third person. In legal terms, the defendant must allege *standing* to raise the issue—must show a personal interest in the items seized and a reasonable expectation that they could be kept private.

Even when all legal requirements are met, there may be occasions on which an investigator may decide a certain action that might be taken is unethical. Some of the issues raised in those instances are discussed in the next section.

ETHICAL CONSIDERATIONS

Any suggestion that an investigator not use all of the legal powers available in furthering an investigation requires establishment of criteria for exercise of that discretion. Certainly such factors as comeliness, ethnicity, race, religion, or wealth are unacceptable, just as is any kind of personal gain. What seems to be required for guidance of an investigator in the exercise of discretion is a considered, consistent ethical code. Legal provisions, such as those of the criminal code against bribery and extortion, and professional codes of ethics can help in establishing minimum requirements, but they are too basic and too general to provide for any but the most extreme situations. They cannot produce the criteria for just exercise of discretion in more subtle, borderline situations.

For assistance in thinking through and establishing a personal ethical code, investigators can call on the work of the best moral philosophers. Moral philosophy is neutral in a way that such concepts as self-interest, religion, race, and country are not, for they, in the words of Bernard Gert, "all provide reasons which sometimes support immoral action."[25] Although the need for a well thought-out personal ethical code must here be identified, it is beyond the scope of this book and the expertise of its authors to assist the reader further in its formulation. That is the task of the field of moral philosophy. The best guidance that can be given in short compass is perhaps adaptation of one of Gert's statements when dealing with a related problem: An investigator should be guided by a personal ethical rule more restraining than the legal rule only when willing to advocate that personal ethical rule publicly.[26]

The most flagrant ethical violations by investigators are also illegal. One common example is perjury. An investigator who is frustrated by not being able to find evidence to convict a suspect believed by the investigator to be a frequent and continuous violator of the law may, as a result of that frustration, lie under oath about actually seeing the suspect commit a violation. Or seriously incriminating details necessary for conviction may be added falsely to what the investigator actually did see. Such false statements under oath constitute perjury. Investigators might justify them to themselves and to their colleagues as means that are justified by the end sought. For example, during searches in cases alleging illegal sale of drugs, investigators have been known to plant envelopes of drugs seized in other cases on the person or in the room or automobile of the suspect, or to allege falsely that the suspect threw the envelopes away during a chase prior to arrest. Rather than succumb to such temptations, investigators must simply work harder to obtain the evidence necessary for conviction in a legal and ethical manner.

Illustrative of the difficult ethical questions faced by investigators that require exercise of discretion are these:

- Should an investigator instruct witnesses not to talk to opposition investigators, to hide from them, or actually personally hide witnesses away so that they cannot be located by opposition investigators?
- Should an investigator assume a false identity or resort to other subterfuges to obtain evidence?
- Is an investigator obligated to question how evidence offered by third parties was obtained?
- Should an investigator accept and offer for use evidence not known to be, but reasonably suspected to be, perjured or falsified in some other way?
- Should an investigator accept and submit for use evidence known to have been obtained illegally by third parties?

Although there is not room here for extensive argument, it is suggested that a defensible personal ethical code would require that

- Unless there is reason to believe that their personal safety would be endangered thereby, all witnesses should be made available to opposition investigators.
- Assumption of false identity and similar subterfuges should not be resorted to except in cases specifically authorized by superiors and carefully monitored in their execution.
- An investigator has an obligation to inquire into the source of evidence offered by third parties and particularly to investigate fully whether suspect evidence has in fact been falsified in some way.

- Evidence illegally obtained by third parties should not be offered for use in any case.

One source of unethical conduct by investigators is unwarranted and excessive pressure from superiors for arrests. Unrealistic organizational policies resulting in arrest quotas convey the message that the ends do justify any means that investigators may use to achieve them. Such policies demonstrate a lack of integrity on the part of the organization. An example of what happens under these conditions is the filing of false affidavits to obtain search warrants in which fictitious confidential informants are alleged to be the source of information that supports issuance of the warrants. Chief executive officers have an obligation not only to avoid such policies but to strive positively to establish in the organization a climate that requires not only lawful but ethical procedures.

The advice of Bernard Gert comes to mind: "...the fundamental reason for being moral is to avoid causing evil for others." Or, as he summarizes, the moral ideal requires going beyond the maxim, "Live and let live," to one that becomes "Live and help live."[27]

It can also be argued with justification that an investigator has a responsibility for how others use the information that has been gathered. Legitimate use is usually in a public legal proceeding that seeks to stop or punish illegal actions or to obtain compensation for financial loss incurred because of such action. Illegitimate uses include harassment, seeking to influence some person's action (official or private) by threats to make the information public, intimidation of some person, and extortion—pay for not using the information. If a sound argument can be made that the evidence is going to be or is being used unethically, the investigator may have an obligation to argue strenuously for a more ethical approach. If that effort is unsuccessful, there may develop a responsibility to protest publicly the course of action being taken. It may even require testimony for the opposition. In some circumstances, that may well be tantamount to resignation. Should discharge follow, however, it should be appealed formally to the highest level possible.

Frequently what an investigator believes to be unethical use of the evidence gathered is justified as being required by the adversary system, that an attorney must do everything legally possible to advance a client's cause, whether that client be an individual or the state. For example, it is criminal contempt and a violation of the American Bar Association's Model Code of Professional Responsibility to offer false evidence to a court knowing it to be false. But what is the responsibility of an attorney who reasonably suspects—but does not have proof—that evidence has been falsified? Some will simply close their eyes and not allow themselves to recognize the issue. Some would even argue that the adversary system requires that approach, but they are surely wrong. The question must be faced. Whoever discovered and would testify about the evidence must be closely questioned. It must be made clear that unless proof of veracity is provided, the evidence will not be used.

The position is the same whether the attorney represents the state or the defense. If the evidence is vital, the prosecutor should request dismissal of the case, or the defense attorney should withdraw. If withdrawal would leave the defendant without effective representation, the counsel should remain, making it clear that the questionable evidence will not be presented but that the state will, in every other respect, be put to its burden of proof beyond a reasonable doubt, and that every effort will be made to ensure that the state meets that burden using only legally obtained evidence. When the issue is one of defense, the presentation of evidence known to be false is not the same as representing a client suspected or even believed to be guilty. Every defendant has an absolute right to put the state to its burden of proof with legally obtained evidence; every defendant also has a right to the protection of effective counsel in that test of strength. But effectiveness does not require the use of evidence reasonably believed to have been obtained illegally.

Attorneys are also faced with the question of whether a witness believed to be testifying accurately should be cross-examined in a manner designed to make the witness appear mistaken. Another issue is whether subtle techniques should be used to appeal to nonrational processes for decision making by a judge or jury. Should the attorney appeal in sophisticated ways to economic, ethnic, racial, or religious bias; to emotion aroused by graphically portrayed injuries; or to prejudice against insurance companies, against some professional or occupational group, against out-of-state or foreign opposition parties, or against persons with different or little approved life-styles?

In this section, discussion concerned relatively mild wrongdoing by representatives of the state, but such actions are frequently precursors of much more reprehensible state oppression such as occurred in Nazi Germany. In that kind of situation, the individual is at the mercy of the state. In contrast, private wrongdoing by one citizen against another, although it can be very intimidating, is much less dangerous. Government investigators and those who present the government's case, whether in criminal or in civil matters, can also gain much in general citizen support and in cooperation in specific cases by building well-earned reputations for integrity and personal ethics. John Q. Citizen wants suppression of private predation without imposition of state oppression.

SUMMARIZING COMMENTARY

This chapter discusses the legal and ethical precepts that should guide the work of government investigators. Not all investigations will be successful. Some will fail because the violators were too clever in hiding their violations, and some because the investigators lack capacity or preparation for their task. But sometimes the failure will occur because of legal restraints on the investigative process imposed by society itself or because of ethical restraints which society expects the investigator to apply from a well-developed personal ethical code.

Investigation to produce information for determinations of fact is a power possessed by all, a right exercised by most, and a duty imposed on some by virtue of their positions as government investigators. In some respects, the law enhances the powers of those with a duty to investigate, but only within carefully defined limits. Those limitations are frequently based on the individual's right to privacy.

The right to privacy is a court-established right created in the last century. It is not absolute. Both private persons and the state may intrude in exceptional situations, the state on a much broader basis than the individual. But the state must exercise its privilege carefully, fairly, and only as a last resort.

Other legal provisions require that all searches be reasonable. Basically this means that they must be carried out pursuant to a warrant issued by a judge, but there are a number of emergency exceptions to that rule with which an investigator must be familiar. The tapping of telephone lines and the use of other electronic surveillance devices may be authorized through similar procedures. Mature judgment based on reason must be shown in using the authority, once granted. The law also authorizes and limits the collection of evidence as incident to a number of other investigative procedures, among them lawful arrest; this carries with it a right to search and to conduct identification procedures known as booking. Booking can be followed by the taking of various samples and viewing by witnesses for identification purposes. Cooperation can be enforced by the contempt power of the courts. If the legal limitations on these permitted intrusions on the right to privacy are exceeded, the evidence obtained may not be admissible in later legal proceedings.

But it is not enough for an investigator to abide by the legal limitations imposed on collection of evidence through invasion of the right to privacy. Investigators must establish for themselves well-considered ethical codes to guide the discretion they possess, discretion not to push their evidence-collection efforts to the limits that the law allows. The criteria for decision making to be built into those ethical codes can come from the work of moral philosophers who have dedicated their lives to study of the issues involved. The results are criteria more neutral, more moral, than those provided by country, race, religion, or self-interest. The resulting personal ethical codes must, however, supply criteria for guidance of discretion that the investigator is willing to advocate publicly.

And the investigator is also responsible for at least an attempt to ensure that the evidence collected is used ethically by those who present it in ultimate determination of fact procedures. That posture is not at odds with the adversary system, but is in fact demanded by it. The system simply will not work unless the opposing advocates are well balanced and fair in their methods. Building a reputation for integrity by government investigators in all of the stages of determination of fact will result in greater citizen cooperation in and support for their efforts. In sum, the goal is the minimizing of private predation without imposition of state oppression.

STUDY QUESTIONS

1. Why should a government impose legal restraints on investigation of alleged violations of law supposedly committed by its residents?
2. What are the basic arguments in favor of a right to privacy?
3. Why should individuals be allowed to have moral codes more strict than the laws that govern all?
4. At what point should general laws be allowed to limit private moral codes?

RECOMMENDED ADDITIONAL READING

- Gert, Bernard. *The Moral Rules: A New Rational Foundation for Morality.* New York: Harper & Row, 1970.
- Pennock, J. Roland, and Chapman, John W., eds. *Privacy.* New York: Atherton, 1971.
- Smith, Robert Ellis. *Privacy: How to Protect What's Left of It.* Garden City, N.Y.: Doubleday/Anchor, 1979.

NOTES

1. John Eck, "Solving Crimes," *NIJ Reports, Selective Notification of Information* 184 (March 1984), p. 6; this is a summary of John Eck, *Solving Crimes: The Investigation of Burglary and Robbery* (Washington, D.C.: Police Executive Research Forum, 1983).
2. Samuel D. Warren and Louis D. Brandeis, "The Right to Privacy," 4 *Harvard Law Review* 193 (1890); this historical sketch is based on Paul A. Freund, "Privacy: One Concept of Many," which is Chapter 10 of J. Roland Pennock and John W. Chapman, eds., *Privacy* (New York: Atherton, 1971), pp. 182–198.
3. Griswold v. Connecticut, 381 U.S. 479 (1965).

4. This statement and the discussion of the right of privacy that follows are from Robert Ellis Smith, *Privacy: How to Protect What's Left of It* (Garden City, N.Y.: Doubleday/Anchor, 1979), pp. 4–9. Smith also publishes the *Privacy Journal* from his Washington, D.C. base.
5. This discussion draws on a Search Warrant Checklist prepared by Robert Lawler, Philadelphia District Attorney's Office, 9 November 1979.
6. Illinois v. Gates, 462 U.S. 213 (1983).
7. District of Columbia Code of Criminal Procedure, Section 23-521(d).
8. Ybarra v. Illinois, 444 U.S. 85 (1979).
9. United States v. McCarthy, 448 A.2d 267 (D.C. App. 1982); Texas v. Brown, 460 U.S. 730 (1983); and Arizona v. Hicks, 40 Cr. L. 3320 (1987) (U.S. Supreme Court), which makes it clear that the officer must have probable cause to believe that the items are contraband or evidence of a crime.
10. See, for example, Schneckloth v. Bustamente, 412 U.S. 218 (1972); United States v. Matlock, 415 U.S. 164 (1974); United States v. Harrison, 679 F.2d 942, 220 U.S. App. D.C. 124 (1982); Welch v. United States, 466 A.2d 829 (D.C. App. 1983).
11. Chimel v. California, 395 U.S. 752 (1969).
12. Illinois v. Lafayette, 462 U.S. 640 (1983).
13. Chambers v. Maroney, 399 U.S. 454 (1970).
14. United States v. Ross, 465 U.S. 798 (1982).
15. Pennsylvania v. Mimms, 434 U.S. 106 (1977).
16. Delaware v. Prouse, 440 U.S. 648 (1979).
17. United States v. Minnick, 455 A.2d 205 (D.C. App. 1983).
18. United States v. Santana, 427 U.S. 38 (1976).
19. Gaulman v. United States, 465 A.2d 847 (D.C. App. 1983).
20. United States v. Booth, 455 A.2d 1351 (D.C. App. 1983).
21. See, for example, 18 U.S.C. § 2510 *et seq.* and 23 D.C. Code 541 *et seq.*
22. Smith v. Maryland, 442 U.S. 735 (1979); Colorado v. Sporleder, 666 P.2d 135 (Colo. 1983).
23. Terry v. Ohio, 392 U.S. 1 (1968); see also the discussion in Lloyd L. Weinreb, *The Law of Criminal Investigation* (Cambridge, Mass.: Ballinger, 1982), pp. 46–61.
24. United States v. Wade, 338 U.S. 218 (1967).
25. Bernard Gert, *The Moral Rules: A New Rational Foundation for Morality* (New York: Harper & Row, 1970), p. 214.
26. Ibid., p. 100.
27. Ibid., p. 208.

INFORMATION COLLECTION

In many cases, lack of knowledge is due to lack of appropriate techniques. But in some cases, lack of knowledge of facts is due to failure on the part of people to look for them.

Bernard Gert
The Moral Rules

sions of the people involved. Basic orientation may also include familiarization with a special subject matter.

When the basic orientation is complete, a plan for the investigation can be drafted. The plan will be directed at obtaining as much relevant information about the problem as is possible in view of the time and other resources available. Among the items to be covered in the plan will be sources, such as people, documents, and other physical evidence; processes to be used in tapping these sources; recording and reporting on the information as it is received; and the initial concurrent analysis necessary to ensure that the investigation is on track or that a change in direction is necessary. It cannot be emphasized too strongly that the initial plan is tentative; it will change as the investigation proceeds. Its purpose is to provide a running start for the initial investigation, to ensure that the investigative effort is well directed.

INFORMATION FROM PEOPLE

In any kind of investigation, civil or criminal, people are a primary source of information. This is why the skills of interviewing and interrogation, discussed in detail in Chapter 6, are so important. In this chapter, the focus is on the kinds of people who can assist in the fact finding necessary in a variety of settings.

In our personal lives, basic information for decision making comes from family members, friends, professional colleagues, potential suppliers of our needs, and others. The information they provide may or may not be accurate, but is usually not too difficult to check. In any event, compulsive checking is a good habit to develop. Seldom will the information from these sources be complete. It must be probed for inaccuracies, limitations, hidden and associated project costs not revealed by the information collected thus far, continuing supply and maintenance costs, and similar expanded considerations. There will usually not be anyone working actively to keep you from getting information, but others may be trying to hurry your decision, to persuade you to act before your information base is reasonably complete.

In organizational settings, the situation is not too different. There the people from whom you seek information will be your colleagues in the organization, your customers or clients, suppliers, consultants, the organization's lawyer, competitors, the trade association and government regulators, among others. Here, too, compulsive checking and cross-checking before decision making is an asset. There will also never be quite enough time for consideration. Someone will be pressing with the question, "What have you done for us lately?" In an associational setting there is, however, usually a support group responsible for assisting you to make

SOURCES OF INFORMATION

Collection of the evidence relevant to proof of a defined matter at issue must be carefully planned and directed to be effective. For the scientist, this means a meticulously worked out research design, frequently incorporated into a project proposal for funding. For a governmental investigator, the plan is usually less formal; and in routine cases of a type frequently encountered, it will follow well-known written or unwritten procedures. In unusual and complex cases, however, a great deal of preliminary planning may precede any action in the field. At the other extreme, the information-gathering process that results in an everyday personal decision may not be recognized as such at all. The entire decision-making process will be almost automatic.

Evidence collection must be preceded by a thorough understanding of the nature and scope of the issues being addressed not only by the principal investigator but by all who will assist in the project. It must also be kept in mind that the problem definition may change during the investigation as the evidence accumulates and analysis begins. The very nature of the investigation may change; it may expand or contract, or it may at some point turn out not to be worth pursuing any further.

Acquisition of initial understanding might be termed basic orientation. All of the documents and reports developed during the problem definition stage should be read. They may include the report of a triggering event, such as commission of a crime, reports of suspicions developing during routine monitoring activity, reports made during—but extraneous to—other similar investigations, complaints made by victims, and reports of preliminary investigations. When all of the available written information has been assimilated, interviews should be conducted with those who generated that basic information. They may have information not considered important enough to have been included in their reports. They may have reasonable suspicions that were not reported formally because they could not be documented. Or they may have useful impres-

the correct decision, but its effectiveness may be problematic. The situation will not be too different if the organizational setting is a governmental agency charged with civil matters.

If the investigation is aimed at detection of violations of the criminal law, new factors customarily not involved in other investigative settings come into play. The major difference is that someone wants the investigation to fail. This may happen in any case that might jeopardize vested interests, but is more common when crime is involved. The actions will have been made in secret, steps will have been taken to keep them hidden, cover-up efforts will continue, attempts will be made to lay a false trail and to divert the investigation. This setting demands a great deal of skepticism, even cynicism, cross-checking, and verification; take nothing for granted. The cast of characters from whom you will be seeking information also is different. They are complainants, suspects, acknowledged perpetrators, witnesses, and informants. For each, you must keep special considerations in mind.

For a variety of reasons, complainants may be reluctant to report what happened fully and accurately. The reported violation may in fact never have occurred. It may be alleged in an attempt to get unwarranted compensation, to satisfy a grudge, or to screen some other embarrassing event. Monetary loss may be exaggerated. There may be an attempt to protect someone: a friend, family member, or lover. There may also be reason for innocent misinformation: the person may be in shock from embarrassment or injury, may be particularly susceptible to suggestion by the questioner, or may have impaired observational faculties and memory because of the event. To meet these contingencies, the investigator seeking information from complainants must be skilled in the interview techniques discussed in Chapter 6.

With witnesses, there is another set of problems. If they are related or otherwise close to the actors in the event, the same difficulties may exist as with victims. Witnesses may be friendly or hostile. They may also simply not want to get involved, which may make them hard to find. Locating witnesses to events that are meant to occur in secret may take imagination and persistence—imagination in figuring out who might have seen the event (as well as the approach or retreat) from what vantage point, and persistence in determining whether there actually was someone at that point at the crucial moment who did in fact observe what was going on. Once a witness is located and testimony obtained, a number of background factors must be explored. Very important among these are the conditions under which the observation took place. Was the witness in a good position for accurate observation? Was the witness nearby or far away? Was the view unobstructed, or through a dirty or rain-spattered window? Was the event well lighted or did it happen in shadow and darkness? The witness's opportunity to make accurate observations must be determined.

Personal characteristics of the potential witness will also be important. Are powers of observation poor, average, or (perhaps because of some specialized training, interest, or experience) particularly acute? The same questions can be asked about memory and the ability to communicate that which is remembered. The latter may be affected by education and background. Language fluency may be a problem. The investigator must also be alert for colloquial expressions and unusual word usage. Finally, given the opportunity and the ability to make accurate observations supplemented by the capacity to remember and effectively communicate the information obtained, the potential witness must also want to portray what happened correctly. Is there any motive for not telling the truth? And even if there is none in this case, what is the person's general reputation for veracity in the community? Are there any grounds on which the witness's credibility could be attacked with success? If the person does appear later as a witness, cross-examination—which is specifically designed to test all of these factors—is sure to follow. Can you predict how the witness's credibility might stand up under cross-examination?

A very valuable human source of information for investigators in criminal cases is the informant, a person who provides information on past or planned crimes.[1] Although it sometimes occurs, use of informants is not as common in civil cases, but they are used on occasion even in social science research. In this chapter, their use in a crime setting is emphasized. An informant can be anyone with an opportunity to gain relevant information: a relative, friend, or business associate of the suspect; a delivery person, door tender, desk clerk, bellhop, waiter, elevator operator, or equipment service person; a co-conspirator or person engaged in similar crimes.

An informer can obtain the information desired in either an overt or covert manner. Pawnbrokers must make regular reports about the items placed with them; doctors may be required to report gunshot wounds; mental health therapists may be required to report cases of incest or other sexual abuse. In other cases, informants must be developed by the investigator from those in a natural position to obtain inside information. Sometimes a case is important enough to warrant an investigator working into some role in the group engaged in the criminal activity. The investigation then involves an undercover component, a complexity that will not be covered in this introductory text. More can be said here, however, about the frequent use of informants.

There are many possible motives for persons to become informants, some admirable and some not. The individual may simply want to help out the authorities through a spirit of civic mindedness; may come to respect, admire, and want to help a particular investigator; may act in fulfillment of a legal requirement; may want to stop the conduct of one of the persons involved before it gets any more serious; or may wish to escape further personal involvement in a situation that has become intolerable. But the action may also be motivated by a need to feel important, by jealousy, by a desire for revenge, to eliminate a competitor in crime, or to earn a reward. Fear may move the informant. Investigators must also consider the possibility that a volunteer informant is trying to infiltrate the investigation, to obtain information on its progress.

An investigator seeking to develop informants can play on some of these motives. For an experienced investigator, informant relationships sometimes develop quite naturally. Some person who has been helped may volunteer information. A likely prospect may be encountered in another, unrelated investigation. But frequently in a major case the investigator must seek out and persuade some individual to become an informant. Naturally, the best informants are those who are close to the criminal activity. Prostitutes and minor drug dealers are good examples. Potential can be recognized by observing and evaluating all who have contact with a suspect. They may or may not be associates in crime. In making the evaluation, the investigator considers who among the possibles is most apt to cooperate, who might provide the most information, and with whom might a deal for leniency or total immunity be most justified. When the potential has been identified, the contact is made. If a recommendation for leniency or immunity is involved, a formal arrangement with superiors and the prosecuting authority is usually required. Useful informants in serious cases are reputed to tend to be twenty-one to thirty-year-old males with felony records. This background emphasizes the caveat that investigators should never completely trust informants. They must be kept at arm's length.

Informants require careful management. Not all law enforcement agencies take that need seriously, but they should. Cases, investigative careers, and agency reputations can be ruined by mismanagement of an informant. Despite cultivation by a particular investigator, good practice requires that the informant belong to the agency, not to that investigator. To make that clear, it is frequently required that the informant be registered as such with the agency, resulting in the opening of a central file under a code name or number. Although the recruiting investigator usually becomes the control (the investigator who directs the work of the informant), another investigator may be designated as an alternate. When a formal relationship is established, a discreet but thorough background investigation is made, including a check for any criminal record. The investigation will include an interview with the informant in which the motive for cooperation, among other things, must be pinned down.

An important aspect of informant management is protection. The code name or number should always be used in arranging contact rather than the informant's real name. There should never be any mention of police during the communication. Meetings should be with one designated control investigator only, on neutral ground. The place and time of meeting should be varied frequently, and always set by the investigator, not by the informant. All information received should be regarded as privileged.

The identity of an informant should never be disclosed unless absolutely necessary, even in court. Disclosure of informant identity should be allowed only in major cases in which the informant's testimony as a material witness who saw or participated in the criminal activity is required for conviction of a major violator. In that situation, the Sixth Amendment right of the defendant to confront accusers requires disclosure.[2] Lesser cases may simply not be prosecuted or may be dismissed if already brought if disclosure becomes necessary. In such cases, continuing value of the informant must be weighed against conviction of minor violators. Even though not used at trial, information from an informant can be used in an affidavit in support of a request for an arrest or search warrant or in seeking an indictment. Once disclosure is made, special protection arrangements for the informant may be required to prevent retaliation.

Control of the informant is another important aspect of management. A new informant should be instructed by the investigator not to participate in any acts of violence, not to use unlawful techniques to obtain information, not to initiate the commission of any crime, and not to participate in the commission of a crime unless specifically instructed to do so.

Because of the difficulties of managing informants, the decision to take one on should not be made lightly. Many risks are involved. An informant may, despite instruction to the contrary, intrude on privileged communications, unlawfully inhibit free association and expression of ideas, or commit other violations of individual rights in the search for information. Such violations may compromise the entire investigation or later prosecution. Despite these risks, the nature and seriousness of the matter under investigation and the impossibility of getting the necessary information in any other way may warrant going ahead. In making that decision, the appraised character and motivation of the informant are considered. Has there been past involvement or is there potential involvement in the crime under investigation or in related crimes? Has the informant proved reliable and truthful in the past? What is the informant's motive? How does the value to the investigation compare to the potential gain to the informant? Is the investigator convinced that the informant is susceptible to reasonable control measures? Only after consideration of these factors should use of an informant be approved.

Once an informant is taken on, every effort should be made to obtain the maximum amount of information from the relationship. The individual's special expertise and familiarity with a particular locale should be exploited. For example, a gambler should be used in gambling investigations. The quality and reliability of the information contributed should be evaluated and tested periodically. This can be done by requesting information already obtained from another source, by maintaining surveillance of the informant on occasion, and by corroborating the information received if at all possible. All through the relationship, the informant's motives must be kept in mind.

If the agency has the resources for payments to the informant, such outlays should be handled with care. They should be made only for operating expenses and for verified information. Loans or advance payments based on promises should never be made, nor should the local going rate be exceeded. Do not overpay, and do keep careful payment records.

Professionalism and fairness must characterize the relationship. The investigator should be courteous to and not denigrate the informant. Never lie to an informant. Listen to the informant's problems. Follow up on all leads that are provided. Even if tips come by telephone from anonymous informants with whom there is no continuing arrangement, follow up on the leads. Try to get as much information as possible in the call; these informants will seldom call back.

When indicated, you should terminate an informant relationship promptly. The indications might be ineptitude, submission of false information, violation of instructions, jeopardizing the investigation in some way, concern that the informant's identity might become known, endangerment to the safety of the informant, commission of a criminal act, or the request of the informant for whatever reason. While the relationship persists, the legal status of the informant must be made clear. The person is not an employee of the agency, but merely a cooperating resident of the jurisdiction.

If an informant commits a crime in violation of instructions, the proper law enforcement or prosecuting authority should be notified promptly either by the control or, after discussion with the control, by a supervisor or the prosecutor involved.

In rare cases where the continued service of the informant is deemed much more important than an offense committed in furtherance of the investigation, those in charge may decide against notifying the authorities. In any event, they must also decide on use or other disposition of information from that informant. In most cases, use of the informant will be ended. If the crime is not committed in furtherance of the investigation, concern about disposition of information will not be involved. In the rare cases where decision is against notice, the following factors will have been considered: whether the appropriate authorities already know about the offense and the perpetrator's identity as an informant; the certainty of the information about commission; whether the crime is completed, imminent, or inchoate (as, for example, in an attempt, solicitation, or conspiracy); the seriousness of the offense in terms of danger to property and life; whether the offense is a violation, a misdemeanor, or a felony and whether it is against local, state, or federal law; the impact of notice on the continued use of the informant in the investigation; and the importance of the informant to success of the investigation. Suppression of knowledge about an informant's crime is such a serious step that it should be considered only at the highest agency levels. That consideration should include whether the jurisdiction honors the common law concept of misprision of felony. Not all jurisdictions do, but in those that have made misprision a part of their law, failure to report a known felony is itself a felony.[3]

In this discussion of the different kinds of people from whom information might be sought in the course of an investigation, attention has thus far been given to victims, witnesses, and informants. Interrogation of suspects and defendants is discussed in detail in Chapter 6. This leaves for further discussion here only certain knowledgeable others, experts, who at trial would be allowed to state their opinions based on alleged facts. No ordinary witness is allowed to state an opinion that the judge or jury would be able to formulate for themselves based on evidence introduced at the trial. This restriction exists because the forming of opinions or conclusions is the task of the trier of fact—the jury or the judge sitting without a jury. That province cannot be invaded by an ordinary witness, who is usually limited to testimony about personal observations that are meant to establish the brute or indifferent facts upon which ultimate conclusions will be based.

But sometimes special education, training, and experience are needed to interpret the brute or indifferent facts. The facts alone would mean nothing to a layperson, whether juror or judge. In such situations, which usually involve application of science, persons who do have the necessary education, training, and experience can qualify as experts who can then give their opinions, who can provide expert testimony. Physical anthropologists can help with evaluation of skeletal remains, dentists can identify dental work, and toxicologists can testify about poisons and their effects. Applications of science in determinations of fact are discussed in detail in Chapter 5. But another source of information on which determinations of fact can be based other than the testimony of people is documentary evidence.

DOCUMENTS AS SOURCES

Our nation floats on a sea of documents. Never before and nowhere else are papers more important and prevalent than they are in the United

States in this last quarter of the twentieth century. Almost every occupied room, apartment, and home contains many personal documentary records, among them letters, diaries, accounting and tax records, employment records, and, increasingly, genealogical records. Public agencies are even more record bound. Accountability requirements result in the creation and preservation of reams and reams of documentary records by administrative, executive, judicial, and legislative agencies. Business and industry also add prodigiously to this outpouring of paper. Records are kept by private sector firms not only for internal management purposes but also for the government: for regulatory agencies and to support tax returns. There is a paper trail leading to and from almost any organizational action that may come under investigation.[4]

Almost all of this documentary evidence is available to a skilled investigator. Much of it will be produced voluntarily upon simple request, but if the source is reluctant, legal process is available for enforced production. That process is called *pretrial discovery*. It encompasses *motions to produce, subpoenas duces tecum, interrogatories, depositions,* and *search warrants.* A bit more might be said about each.

A motion to produce, if granted, results in a directive from the judge to a party to the proceedings to produce evidence in that party's possession. The closely related subpoena duces tecum is a court order directed to a specific person to appear at a specified time and place with specified documents or other materials that are alleged to be necessary to prove relevant and material facts at issue in a legal proceeding. It is an ancient common law writ that is enforced by use of the contempt power of the court. In addition, it is now supplemented or supplanted by the use of other pretrial discovery procedures.

One such discovery procedure involves interrogatories, lists of questions submitted by one party to another requesting written answers. A deposition, another discovery procedure, is the taking of testimony under oath from an individual (with counsel present if desired) that produces a sworn written record of the testimony for possible later use. Special pretrial discovery statutes were not known under common law. Discovery procedures were provided for in civil cases very early by courts of equity, which were created to ameliorate the harshness of common law provisions. Law and equity have now generally been merged. Today discovery is permitted in most jurisdictions for both civil and criminal cases by statute or rule of court.[5] Provisions generally allow the requesting party to inspect, test, and photograph the evidence of the opposition. Because the provisions vary considerably from one jurisdiction to the next, they will be discussed here in general terms.

Formal discovery under the federal rules[6] is allowed only after a request for informal discovery has been refused. The informal request is frequently made by letter. Formal discovery is usually requested by pretrial motion, but may be ordered by the court at any time. It is provided on the theory that trials can be conducted more efficiently if both sides know the key facts in advance. But in the late 1980s, there is growing criticism of the process as used in civil cases. Two principal abuses are alleged: resort to request for massive numbers of documents as a strategy to force the opposition to settle the case, and use of discovery to learn the trade secrets of a competitor. Attempts to minimize these problems are taking the form both of amendment to the authorizing rules and of tighter judicial management of the process. Included in the latter is the use by a judge of a special master (a representative of the court, appointed for some particular act or transaction) to supervise document production in cases where discovery is used extensively.[7]

Discovery in criminal cases is much less well developed than it is on the civil side. There have been fears that allowing discovery by the defense will lead to fabrication and falsification of defense evidence to meet the case of the state. The extent to which discovery is allowed in criminal cases varies much more than it does in civil cases. There is also more difference in the authorizations to prosecution and defense than there is to the plaintiff and defendant in civil cases. There is a continuing duty to disclose requested material, once discovery has been granted. Good faith and diligence in the production of materials is required. If negligent failure of the prosecution to produce requested information can be shown to have prejudiced the defense, sanctions may be imposed against the state, including dismissal of the case. Any item of evidence in the possession of an investigative agency or any other cooperating governmental agency is deemed to be in the possession of the prosecution.

Although there is great variety among jurisdictions, the following provisions are sometimes made for discovery by the defense in a criminal case. The prosecution may be asked to furnish copies of any written statements of the accused possessed by the government. Notes on oral statements made by the defendant in response to interrogation that the state intends to offer at trial as part of its case may also be requested. Grand jury testimony of the accused relating to the charge, together with the material statements of codefendants are also covered. The defendant's prior criminal record is subject to discovery, as are documents and other tangible items of evidence and the final reports of experts who may have examined physical evidence or the defendant.

Generally not subject to discovery are statements made by the accused to private citizens who later report them to government investigators. Similarly protected are statements of government witnesses, internal government reports, memoranda, and other documents that are the work product of the prosecution. Although they may be required to be produced at trial, criminal connections of government witnesses are not subject to pretrial discovery, nor are the names and addresses of witnesses or informants.

But even in criminal cases, discovery is a two-way street. Among the discovery rights of the prosecution may be access to any documents or other tangible evidence to be used by the defense at trial, together with any reports by experts who may have tested or examined that evidence, if the defense intends to use those reports. If the defendant intends to assert an alibi, in some jurisdictions, notice must be given to the prosecution, together with the names and addresses of witnesses who will support the alibi; the location where the defendant claims to have been at the time of the offense must also be given.[8] The prosecutor must then, in turn, give to the defense the names and addresses of any witnesses to be called to refute the alibi. The accused must also notify the government if insanity is to be claimed as a defense.[9] As is the case with the government, internal memoranda and other work products of attorneys and others working for the defense are not subject to discovery. Statements made by the defendant and any prospective witnesses to the defense are also not covered by discovery. It bears reiteration that discovery, particularly in criminal cases, varies widely from jurisdiction to jurisdiction. Familiarity with the local rules is a must. The examples given are typical only, not universal.[10]

Discovery for criminal case defendants is supplemented by the United States Supreme Court decision in the case of *Brady* v. *Maryland*,[11] which held that due process requires the prosecution to provide the defense with any material information that might exonerate the accused (exculpatory evidence) or mitigate punishment, unless it is already known by or available to the defense. Any such information in the possession of any government agent cooperating in the prosecution is deemed to be in possession of the prosecutor whether that official has actual personal knowledge of it or not. It must be passed on to the defense in time to allow its effective use. Failure to abide by the *Brady* doctrine can result in a new trial if the information is considered to be significant in view of the other evidence at the trial.

Yet another supplement to the criminal defendant's right of discovery in federal cases is the Jenck's Act.[12] That act requires the prosecution to turn over to the defense any statements by government witnesses that might be useful to the defense in impeaching the testimony of those witnesses on cross-examination. To be effective, the production of the statements must be timely; it must give the defense adequate time to analyze them and plan their use. Similarly, the prosecution may require that statements made by the defendant and prospective defense witnesses be produced as "reverse" Jenck's material. A number of local jurisdictions have adopted rules that correspond to the provisions of the Jenck's Act.

A third court process, in addition to the subpoena duces tecum and that available under special pretrial discovery statutes, which is sometimes useful to investigators in obtaining documents from uncooperative sources, is the search warrant. Although its use for this purpose in criminal cases is limited by the defendant's right against self-incrimination, the search warrant may be used to obtain instruments of a crime (such as documents in a fraud case), proceeds of a crime (stolen stock certificates), and contraband (counterfeit government bonds) that may also be useful in proof of the defendant's guilt. Federal and some state statutes now allow issuance of search warrants to obtain general evidence of a crime (weapons, stained clothing, and so on).[13]

Once documentary evidence has been obtained, it must be evaluated on two levels: its authenticity as the document that it purports to be, and the credibility or worth of the statements that it contains. On the first issue, as much information is collected as is possible about the circumstances in which the document was made and in which it has since been kept. This is the question of external validity. That having been determined, attention turns to appraisal of the statements contained in the document, which are subjected to the same verification process as any other statements. This is the question of internal validity. These two aspects of a document—external and internal validity—are separate, although the content of the document is sometimes useful in determining its external validity.[14]

Under the best evidence rule, the original rather than a copy of any document central to an issue at trial must be produced unless its absence can be explained.[15] Confidence in a document's external validity will also be enhanced by a showing that it was created routinely as a part of an ongoing activity and that it was made at or about the time of the events with which it deals.[16]

OTHER PHYSICAL EVIDENCE

Much information about past events can be obtained from items of physical evidence other than documents. But such items of evidence must be discovered and their significance recognized before access to the information they bear can be obtained. In civil cases, a search of the scene of the event (such as an automobile collision, industrial chemical leak, or explosion) will frequently yield such physical evidence. It may also reveal conditions important to the case such as open ditches or other unfenced dangers. In criminal cases, the crime scene search is standard operating procedure for the officers first on the scene or for designated crime scene search officers, sometimes called evidence technicians. They seek the instruments and other evidence of the offense, fruit of the crime, contraband, and other items and aspects of the event that might identify the perpetrator, such as the modus operandi used. Searches may also be conducted away from the scene: on the probable routes of approach and escape, of an automobile that may have been used, and of the home or office of the victim or a suspect.[17]

The evidence will frequently be subjected to scientific examination. If the result of the examination is positive, the item of evidence and the test results will be offered at the trial. In order for the evidence to be admitted, its origin must be documented and a chain of custody from discovery to trial must be established to ensure its original authenticity and that it has not been tampered with since found. Much more will be said later in Chapter 5 about scientific examination of physical evidence.

REFERENCE SOURCES

In almost every community there is a vast amount of information available from local reference materials. Such information is routinely sought in scientific investigations, sometimes sought in investigations leading to civil proceedings, and much less frequently sought by criminal investigators. That neglect weakens the investigation of many criminal cases. Although the amount varies from place to place, there is always some such reference material available.

Because it is richer in such information sources than most communities, the District of Columbia metropolitan area provides a good example for detailed discussion. Among its resources are libraries, government agencies, private associations, commercial information search firms, data banks, and think tanks.

There are over 30,000 libraries in the United States; more than one-sixth of the total library resources in the country are located in the District of Columbia metropolitan area. It has public lending libraries; libraries of local schools, colleges, and universities; and a vast array of special libraries, both government-operated and private. They can be located, as can similar institutions in any community, through library directories available for the locality or for the area. It behooves investigators to cultivate directors and staffs of the libraries they find most useful. It is usually the reference librarian who is most useful. Librarians *can* help; that help *should* be sought; the extent to which they *will* help may depend on the attitude of the investigator. Be appreciative, and show it.

Paramount among library resources in the District of Columbia area is the Library of Congress, which ranks among the greatest in the world. Among its many special features are a computer catalogue of all books published in English since 1968; legislative information files since the 93rd Congress; copies of all United States Government Printing Office publications; all United Nations documents; over three million technical reports in its Science Reading Room; a collection of doctoral dissertations on microfilm with an index; a National Referral Center that furnishes names of organizations willing to provide information on specific topics. The library sells copies of Central Intelligence Agency reference reports on the economic and political structures of other countries. It is well worth a visit for a tour and to obtain brochures describing what is available there. In suitable cases, the library's holdings can be exploited by investigators thousands of miles away through the interlibrary loan program of local libraries.

But great as it is, the Library of Congress is not the only such resource in the District of Columbia metropolitan area. There is also the library system of the Smithsonian Institution, which has thirty-six branches. There are 185 private, academic, and governmental law libraries, all listed in a guide published by the Law Librarian's Society of Washington, D.C. There is the National Library of Medicine with over three million items and a user's guide to facilitate access. There are also a number of photo libraries; that of the Library of Congress alone has over ten million photos, illustrations, maps, cartoons, and similar items. All of the special libraries are listed in a publication entitled *Library and Reference Facilities in the Area of the District of Columbia*.[18] For researchers, there are the Scholars' Guides published by the Smithsonian's Woodrow Wilson International Center for Scholars; they list archives and libraries with holdings on particular subjects. There are also the libraries of the major federal executive departments and other agencies. All of these supplement the usual public lending library system. Although the District of Columbia library resources are exceptional, every community has at least a start on its own special collection.

Government agencies are another source of information. *The United States Government Organization Manual* (available from the Government Printing Office) and its state and local counterparts are good places to start looking. When you have identified the agency most apt to have the information sought, contact its public information office. Sometimes your local legislator can provide a shortcut and obtain faster service. Almost every agency has its legislative liaison office. Congressional representatives, for example, can also call on the Congressional Research Service, the Congressional Budget Office, the reading and legislative history files of the Library of Congress, LEGIS (a computer data base on legislative history), and prepared packets of information (called "Issue Briefs and Information Packs") about currently popular topics. They can also assign their own and committee staffs to special information-gathering tasks. Anyone can have access to the *Catalogue of United States Government Publications* in which the Superintendent of Documents lists 1,000–2,000 new titles every month.

Also useful is the *Subject Bibliography Index* published by the United States Government Printing Office, a list of subject bibliographies frequently carrying several hundred items. For information on Congress, the *Congressional Record Index* lists debates by name and subject; the *Record* comes out every two weeks. For the executive branch, there is the *Weekly Compilation of Presidential Documents* (speeches, news conferences, messages to Congress, personal appointments, and so on) published by the Office of the Federal Register of the Government Printing Office. The *Federal Register* itself is a source for executive agency documents, all proposed rules and regulations, legal notices, and even agendas for scheduled meetings. *Federal Regulations* contains all rules and regulations having the force of law. For the judiciary, all routine court documents are open to the public unless sealed by specific court order, rule, or statute. Court opinions in specific cases are published regularly. And for the federal court system, there is a court newsletter, *The Third Branch*. Information not published can frequently be obtained through use of the Freedom of Information Act.[19] There are also commercially available sources, such as the newspaper, *Federal Times*, and books such as Matthew Lesko's *Information U.S.A.: The Ultimate Guide to the Largest Source of Information on Earth—The U.S. Government*.[20] Much similar information on foreign governments and countries can be obtained through their embassies in Washington, D.C.

Most state and local governments have parallel information sources, even though they may not be as extensive. At the state level, the records in the office of the Secretary of State on businesses incorporated in and doing business in the state and the records of the Motor Vehicle Department are frequently useful, as are those kept by the Commissioner or Department of Insurance. At the county level, the county clerk, recorder, register of deeds, and others have information on births, deaths, marriages, divorces, property ownership, and almost all aspects of an individual's life, as do similar offices at the city level.

In addition to libraries and government agencies, private groups of various kinds are also excellent sources of information. The trade association is one such group. Statistics and other information in the trade, industry, or business represented are gathered by and available from such associations. In fact, lobbyists employed by trade associations reach out aggressively for opportunities to convey that information. Not only do they attempt to reach government leaders and others actively making decisions directly affecting their interests, they also wish to educate the general public about their groups. They may be advocates tainted by self-interest, but they also build their reputation as useful information sources by maintaining credibility. They supply background information on the industry, the history and current status of its regulation, the industry position on proposed new regulations and other laws affecting the business. They will frequently refer interested persons to independent outside experts and other sources for information on issues. If your opinion is important to them, they may volunteer research, writing, and analysis of matters relating to their interests about which you may inquire. These groups can be found at the state and local levels as well as at the federal level.

There are also private firms that will supply information for a price. They may be called information retrieval services, investigative services, consulting firms, market research firms, or survey firms. Many specialize in particular kinds of information. In some instances, similar services are available from government or government-funded agencies at all levels.[21] Extremely useful are city directories, both the conventional telephone books indexed by name and the crisscross directories indexed by addresses and by telephone numbers.

A number of government agencies maintain special data banks in areas of their interest to which individuals can be given access by computer. There are also a number of well-known research organizations in the Washington area, sometimes known as think tanks. Perhaps the best known is the Brookings Institution, which is primarily interested in economics, foreign policy, and domestic government policies. It publishes a quarterly magazine as well as reports, monographs, and books. Rightly or wrongly, it has earned a reputation as a liberal organization. Its principal rival, the American Enterprise Institute for Public Policy Research, is generally thought of as conservative. It is concerned with economics, energy, health, legislation, and national defense. It publishes newsletters, magazines, and books. It also runs a legislative analysis service which puts out summaries of the provisions of pending federal legislation, the history of its development, and arguments in favor of and against the bills. That service is free to members of Congress and sold to the general public. The Heritage Foundation in Pennsylvania, a think tank that has been labeled ultraconservative, is getting considerable attention in the late 1980s. And there are many more of lesser renown. Although fewer in number, think tanks also exist at the state and local levels.

SUMMARIZING COMMENTARY

Much of the information necessary for determinations of fact can be obtained only by the personal observation of an investigator, but there are also other important sources to be tapped. To be sure that no potential source is overlooked requires a research design for the scientist, an investigation plan for the investigator. That plan will make sure that all possible information is obtained from people, documents, other physical evidence, and from a variety of reference sources, including offices that maintain official records.

In major investigations, persons to be questioned may include complainants, suspects, acknowledged perpetrators, witnesses (including experts), and informants. As will be emphasized more in Chapter 6, each category presents special considerations; an interview with a given individual in any of these groups requires special preparation. Investigators who are not well prepared for interviews will not ask the crucial questions, will not be able to spot significant statements during the conversation for further development, and will not be as able to break down resistance.

The use of informants presents special management problems. They must be registered with the agency, their background investigated, their safety protected, their activity controlled, their payment documented, their performance monitored, and their services terminated if not satisfactory. Given the many problems involved with informants in major investigations, one should not be taken on unless important information cannot be obtained in any other way. Any relationship with an informant must be professional and fair.

Documents of many types are a common source of information. Frequently they are available to the investigator for the asking. When not, the legal processes of pretrial discovery, and in limited circumstances, the search warrant, can be used. Discovery is available to both sides in the case. Its purpose is to prevent surprise and to promote efficient progress at the trial.

Physical evidence other than documents is also frequently available. It sometimes requires scientific examination. Its identity and circumstances of discovery must always be established. Then the chain of custody must be kept intact as insurance against tampering.

Tremendous amounts of information useful both as background and as evidence in its own right are also available from standard reference sources in most cities, counties, and states and at the federal level. These include libraries, government agencies, private associations, commercial information search firms, data banks, and think tanks. Directories and other guides for access to these resources are usually available. If a government agency is reluctant to cooperate, the Freedom of Information Act can be used. Careful cultivation of these sources will further many investigations.

STUDY QUESTIONS

1. Why is a well-prepared research design or investigation plan important in any search for information?

2. What skills are important in obtaining information from people?
3. What are the two aspects of a document's validity that must be probed before information from that document can be relied on?
4. Why are expert witnesses sometimes used in the presentation of physical evidence?
5. How many ways can library resources be useful in an investigation?
6. What are the ways in which an informant can be useful?

RECOMMENDED ADDITIONAL READING

- Gardner, Thomas J. *Criminal Evidence: Principles, Cases and Readings.* St. Paul, Minn.: West Publishing, 1978.
- Jennings, Margaret S., ed. *Library and Reference Facilities in the Area of the District of Columbia,* 12th ed. White Plains, N.Y.: American Society for Information Sciences, 1986.
- Lesko, Matthew. *Information U.S.A.: The Ultimate Guide to the Largest Source of Information on Earth—the U.S. Government.* New York: Viking Press, 1983.

NOTES

1. This section on informants relies on a memorandum dated 15 December 1976 from Edward H. Levi, Attorney General, to Clarence M. Kelley, Director, Federal Bureau of Investigation, entitled "Use of Informants in Domestic Security, Organized Crime, and Other Criminal Investigations."
2. See Rovario v. United States, 353 U.S. 53 (1956).
3. See, for example, Misprision of Treason, Fla. Stat. § 876.33 (1974).
4. For a detailed discussion of the use of records in the investigation of economic crimes, see Leigh Edward Somers, *Economic Crimes: Investigative Principles and Techniques* (New York: Clark Boardman Company, 1984), pp. 86–109.
5. See, for example, Florida Rules of Civil Procedure, Fla. Admin. Code §§ 1.280–1.390 and Florida Rules of Criminal Procedure, Fla. Admin. Code § 3.220.
6. See Federal Rules of Civil Procedure §§ 26–37 and Federal Rules of Criminal Procedure § 16.
7. See Daniel B. Moskowitz, "Jurists Attack Abuses of Right to Pry into Opponents' Secrets," *The Washington Post* (30 January 1984): Washington Business, p. 28, c. 1; and "Workshop on Curtailing Discovery Abuse Sponsored by Center," *The Third Branch* 16, No. 1 (January 1984): 1.

8. Federal Rules of Criminal Procedure, § 12.1.
9. Federal Rules of Criminal Procedure, § 12.2.
10. For a general discussion, see Andre A. Moenssens, Ray Edward Moses, and Fred E. Inbau, *Scientific Evidence in Criminal Cases* (Mineola, N.Y.: Foundation Press, 1973), pp. 29–58.
11. Brady v. Maryland, 373 U.S. 83 (1963).
12. 18 U.S.C. § 3500 (1957).
13. William E. Ringel, *Searches and Seizures, Arrests and Confessions*, 2nd ed. (New York: Clark Boardman Company, 1979), pp. 2–12; see also Warden v. Hayden, 387 U.S. 294 (1967).
14. Robert Jones Shafer, ed., *A Guide to Historical Method*, 3rd ed. (Homewood, Ill.: Dorsey Press, 1980), pp. 127–170.
15. But see Federal Rules of Evidence, § 1002, which does make duplicates admissible.
16. Thomas J. Gardner, *Criminal Evidence: Principles, Cases and Readings* (St. Paul, Minn.: West Publishing, 1978), p. 649.
17. Charles R. Swanson, Jr., Neil C. Chamelin, and Leonard Territo, *Criminal Investigation*, 3rd ed. (New York: Random House, 1984), pp. 15–44.
18. Margaret S. Jennings, ed., *Library and Reference Facilities in the Area of the District of Columbia*, 12th ed. (White Plains, N.Y.: American Society for Information Sciences, 1986).
19. 5 U.S.C. § 551 (1966); this act is discussed at some length in Chapter 10.
20. Matthew Lesko, *Information U.S.A.: The Ultimate Guide to the Largest Source of Information on Earth—the U.S. Government* (New York: Viking Press, 1983).
21. An example is the National Criminal Justice Reference Service maintained by the United States Department of Justice.

INFORMATION FROM SCIENCE

5

Knowledge comes from experience, both personal and vicarious. Since no individual in one lifetime can have enough personal experience to learn all that life requires, learning from the experience of others is a necessity. The most efficient way to obtain this experience is through well-organized education and training programs. Self-study is a possibility, but few have the resources and the discipline to use that method.

Even using vicarious experience to the limit, no single individual can acquire all of the knowledge that may be useful in a lifetime. The result is specialization, with the extensive particular knowledge of one individual being made available to others when needed. Some knowledge and skills can be picked up rather quickly, but other fields require long, intensive, and expensive periods of education, training, and practice before proficiency in them can be achieved. Among them are the sciences, which can contribute a great deal of information useful to determinations of fact. Investigators other than specialized laboratory personnel do not customarily have scientific educations. They must rely on those who do for the scientific information needed in their investigations.

This chapter is concerned with how that scientific information can be obtained. First it discusses some general considerations, and then a few of the more frequently used scientific specialties. Because of time and space restraints, the discussion is necessarily introductory. Entire books are available on various aspects of this topic.[1] This chapter draws on that literature and on the personal knowledge of the authors gained over many years of education, training, and experience.

GENERAL CONSIDERATIONS

Scientific evidence is useful in both civil and criminal cases. On the civil side, it is used, for example, in patent infringement cases, in manufacturer's liability suits, in worker's compensation cases, and in automobile accident and other *tort* cases (cases of legal wrongs done to other persons not based on contracts). Its need can be recognized in almost any kind of criminal prosecution. The more that is at stake in either kind of case, the more frequently will scientific evidence be called upon. It can be helpful in a number of significant ways. Scientific processing of trace material found at the site of an event can result in the discovery of brute facts that would otherwise not become known, and scientific knowledge can interpret facts whose significance would otherwise not be apparent to laypersons. As James Osterburg points out, its use in criminal cases can result in linking the crime scene and the victim to the criminal, corroborating or disproving an alibi, inducing admissions or confessions, and exonerating the innocent.[2]

Among other purposes, scientific evidence could also be used to identify victims, identify substances such as drugs, and establish the authenticity or falsity of documents.

In civil cases, the use of scientific evidence can result in identifying the reasons for failure of materials used in manufacture or construction; establishing cause of injury or death; establishing the cause of an explosion; and establishing whether an airplane accident was due to human error, some failure of the plane, abnormal weather conditions, or some combination of these factors. The list could be made much longer, but these illustrations demonstrate the pervasive importance of scientific assistance in formal determination of fact.

Osterburg further points out that scientific evidence could and should be used much more widely in criminal cases but is not for some very basic reasons: investigators' lack of knowledge of how it can be of help, and of what to look for and preserve for identification; disillusionment with laboratory results caused by unrealistic expectations; and unavailability of quick service from convenient facilities. In another context, he emphasizes what may be the most basic limitation of all in routine criminal cases: cost. Similar factors are at work in civil cases, but there the amounts at stake and the possibility of recovering costs from opposition parties make expense less of a deterrent.

Scientific evidence is different in that the facts by themselves cannot be understood by the usual decision maker, whether judge or jury. The facts are such that they must be interpreted for laypersons before their significance becomes apparent. That interpretation comes in the opinion of the scientific expert based on the facts of the case. Lay witnesses cannot express opinions except in very limited circumstances. They must testify only to basic facts from personal knowledge unless those underlying facts registered with the witness in such a subtle way that they are not actually observed as isolated components of the situation, and unless the overall impression testified to by the witness is one encountered in everyday experience. Examples of such situations include testimony as to speed of vehicles, distance, identity of persons, and color of an object. An impression of speed, for example, is based upon so many facts observed because of experience that recitation of them would be impossible. Scientific evidence requires interpretation not because the underlying facts cannot be stated but because they are meaningless to laypersons even when stated.

There are a number of useful purposes that expert scientific opinion can serve in determination of fact. One is *identification*. A given object or substance can be placed in a clearly defined category: a powdery substance can be identified as heroin, or a substance obtained from a corpse can be identified as strychnine. A second is *individuation*. A fingerprint on a gun can be established as having come from John Doe's right forefinger, or a bullet can be shown to have been fired from Doe's pistol. In these cases, the fingerprint and bullet are not only identified as belonging to a certain category, but are shown to be different from all others in their category, to be individual or unique. In criminal cases, identification can disprove guilt or can establish the possibility of guilt. Individuation can show possibility and, in some cases, proof of guilt. It is most frequently used to associate two objects, such as a bullet with a gun, or to associate an individual with a scene by demonstrating, for example, that the person's fingerprints were found at the scene. When this is the case, the testimony is often referred to as *associative evidence*. These are common applications, but scientific evidence also has many more applications in governmental proceedings.

Different types of investigators tend to call on different kinds of scientists. Historians most frequently use scientists from the following fields: linguistics (the study of language); paleography (the study of ancient handwriting); epigraphy (the study of inscriptions); diplomatics (the critical study of official or business documents); chronology (the measurement of and placing of events in time); and specialists in seals, heraldry, genealogy, and numismatics (study of coins and medals).[3] Investigative reporters tend to rely more on economists, political scientists, and public policy experts, although they may also call on a much wider range of experts as the subject matters of their stories vary. Government investigators are most apt to use, among others: accountants and auditors; fingerprint experts; document examiners; experts on firearms and ammunition; pathologists; chemists, toxicologists, and serologists; physical anthropologists and dentists; and psychiatrists, psychologists, and neurologists. As a group, scientists whose work product is routinely used in legal proceedings are called *forensic scientists*. If they work primarily on criminal cases, they are frequently called *criminalists*. In the next section, the use of each of these kinds of experts by government investigators is considered in more detail.

UTILIZING SCIENTIFIC EXPERTS

Government investigations can be assisted by scientists in a wide variety of situations. As noted in the previous section, objects and persons can be placed into categories, their uniqueness can be determined and demonstrated, they can be associated with one another and with specific places, cause and effect can be determined, and clinical diagnoses can be made. When the examinations have been completed and conclusions reached, the results can be testified to in the relevant proceedings.

But none of this can happen until a capable investigator recognizes the need and makes the appropriate arrangements. For those engaged in criminal investigation, obtaining the services of the necessary experts is not usually a problem. Many of them will be available at a crime laboratory maintained by the local, state, or federal government. Such experts are on the government payroll. With others, such as forensic pathologists, there may be a standing arrangement with a private practitioner in the jurisdiction, if there is none on the staff of the coroner or medical examiner. For government investigators seeking less frequently utilized experts and in all cases for private investigators who cannot draw on government resources, experts can be found locally in commercial laboratories, in hospitals, and in colleges and universities. Some advertise their expertise and availability in professional journals and magazines. Most are listed in professional directories and may be reached through professional associations.

Once a likely candidate has been located, there must be a careful check of suitability. Usually basic information can be obtained from the candidate, who will probably have a professional résumé emphasizing education, training, experience, research and publications, and membership in professional societies. All of these factors must be checked to determine the professional scientific standing of the prospect. It must also be determined that the expert is willing and able to serve within the time frame imposed by the pending proceedings.

But for this special purpose, the individual's general background and character must also be investigated. Credibility is particularly important in an expert witness. A personal interview should be arranged to allow the investigator to assess the scientist's ability to communicate. Will the proposed expert make a good first impression on the decision maker? Will the testimony on direct examination be believable? Will the expert be able to perform credibly on cross-examination? Previous experience on the witness stand will obviously be important for these considerations.

Need for the services of the scientific witness must be established by previous investigative effort, frequently at the scene of a triggering event, such as a crime. That means recognition, collection, and preservation of the material to be examined, in many cases. Not only the chain of custody but the purity of the material must be ensured. The employed expert must be briefed on these previous procedures and their appropriateness for scientific purposes established. The expert will need to know the nature and source of the sample, the procedures necessary for protecting and preserving the sample to ensure admissibility of test results in the later legal proceedings, exactly what questions about the sample are to be answered, and when the answers are needed. The attorney responsible for presenting the testimony of the witness will also wish to brief the expert on the demands of the particular proceedings involved. (See Chapter 14.) The investigator should obtain as much information as possible about the qualifications of any expert to be used and about those of any experts who will be called by the opposition. This responsibility holds for all experts; to avoid repetition, we will not reiterate it in our discussion of specific experts.

With all of these factors in mind, attention can now turn to the work of investigators with specific scientific experts.

Accountants and Auditors

With the increasing importance of economic crime, accounting and auditing have become more relevant to the investigative function. Financial management is based on bookkeeping, which is essentially the clerical function of recording financial information. Accountants are more concerned with its analysis. As Leigh Edward Somers points out, accountants perform six principal functions.

> Accountants *observe* events and *identify* those events that are considered evidence of economic activity, such as the purchase and sale of goods and services; they *measure* these selected events in financial terms; they *record* these measurements to provide a permanent history of the financial activity of the organization or unit; they *classify* their measurements of recorded events into meaningful groups; they *summarize* and *report* their measurements; and last, accountants may be asked to *interpret* the content of their *statements* and *reports*.[4] (Emphasis in original.)

Until about the turn of the century, auditing was done primarily to detect financial fraud. Now detection of fraud is incidental. Management itself has been assigned "the primary responsibility for the safeguarding of assets and for the prevention and detection of errors and fraud."[5] The primary purpose of a normal audit is to establish whether the financial statements and records of a company fairly reflect the current financial condition and operations of the company. A complete examination of accounting books is a bookkeeping audit. The normal audit is concerned with whether the financial position and operating results are being presented accurately by management. It is not concerned with revealing employee fraud. Bookkeeping audits are concerned with stealing *from* the company; normal audits, stealing *by* the company through misrepresentation of financial condition.

Accounting and auditing are central to many investigations leading to civil legal proceedings growing out of business and industrial operations. Investigators must learn to work closely with these specialists, who are accustomed to establishing bases for civil suits or application of administrative sanctions, but not with preparation for criminal prosecutions. The financial experts must learn to modify their evidence-gathering techniques to make their work product acceptable at criminal trials; must become sensitive to the special needs in such cases for identification and preservation of evidence; and must develop a consciousness of when a witness, by becoming a suspect, requires different legal treatment. Criminal investigators must realize the usefulness of civil sanctions and how to gather the evidence needed to justify their imposition.

There is a great future for investigators who include accounting and auditing in their education and training. Within the last ten years, almost all federal executive departments have been required by Congress to establish an office of Inspector General. Some states and major cities have followed suit. Under this concept, the accountant/auditor is not merely a consulting expert but actually becomes an investigator colleague. Until more recruits with dual capabilities become available, investigators and auditors must work together as teams, each learning from the other. It is in that capacity, rather than simply as expert witnesses, that accountants and auditors are most useful in investigations.

When accountants and auditors who are not fellow investigators are used, it is the responsibility of the investigator to obtain the necessary documents, books, and other records for examination, using legal process if necessary.

Fingerprint Experts

Fingerprints are frequently used to identify individuals, to tie individuals to objects, and to tie individuals to places. Fingerprint evidence is not just acceptable to the courts, but is given great weight by judges and juries alike. The general public is convinced of the reliability of properly prepared and presented fingerprint evidence. It is frequently used in criminal cases and sometimes in civil cases.

It is the investigator's responsibility to recognize that fingerprints may be important in a given case. The necessary search of the scene may be done either personally or by some other member of the investigative team. In many departments, specially trained evidence technicians will be immediately available, perhaps working out of a mobile laboratory designed and equipped for that purpose. The development, lifting, and analysis of latent fingerprints is a skill that requires training and experience that the investigator may not possess or may not have the time to exercise in the circumstances. Programs and equipment are now available for the use of computers in comparing fingerprints found at the scene of an event with known fingerprints in agency files. This specialized use of computers makes the identification of a single print found at the scene a practical possibility for the first time.

Although fingerprint evidence is common, there are factors, other than purposeful avoidance through using gloves or wiping handled surfaces, that may preclude their deposit in usable form. If the tips of the fingers are too clean and free of natural oils and salts, no prints will be left. There are surfaces that are simply not suitable for acceptance of prints, and the exact manner in which the object is touched will also determine whether a clear, unsmudged latent fingerprint will be left. Development of new techniques and processes to meet those problems in fingerprint technology is an ongoing activity. An investigator must know as much as possible about such matters to be able to recognize when a search for latent prints is indicated.[6]

It is also the responsibility of the investigator to obtain the known prints of suspects and of persons legitimately at the scene for comparison with prints found there. The elimination prints of those legitimately there can usually be obtained by request, and sometimes the suspect may also cooperate freely. Then too, the suspect's prints may already be on file because of a previous arrest, or because taken in connection with a job application, or in similar circumstances.

Government investigators will customarily have free access to government-employed fingerprint experts. Defense attorneys and those representing clients in civil suits will have to hire independent experts, of whom there are many. Such experts will frequently have resigned or retired from a public agency where they obtained their training and experience. In any event, as with other experts, their qualifications must be confirmed.

Document Examiners

As was pointed out in Chapter 4, documents are a tremendously important source of information in many investigations. Their mere existence as objects is sometimes of vital importance and their contents can provide the information for successful conclusion of the matter involved. In civil cases, documents are central to suits based, for example, on promissory notes, contracts, and wills, among many other types. Similarly, documentary evidence may crop up in any criminal case and is frequently central to investigations of forgery, kidnapping, confidence games, embezzlement, and policy gambling operations. But the use of documentary evidence presents two basic problems: Is the document itself authentic? Is the information it contains accurate? Experts in document examination can be helpful in answering both of these questions.

On the question of authenticity, the examiner can tell whether a document was handwritten by a given person or produced by a particular typewriter. Analysis of the ink and the paper itself can reveal whether they were available at the time the document is supposed to have been prepared. Study of rubber stamp and seal impressions can be helpful. Regarding the content, erasures, interlineations, other additions and interpolations can be revealed. Charred and water-damaged documents can be restored, as can erased and otherwise obliterated contents. These services are quite useful.[7]

Once again, it is the responsibility of the investigator to recognize the importance of the document and to collect and preserve it. No special skill is needed except with burned or otherwise damaged documents. In addition to the originals, the investigator frequently must obtain known authentic specimens of hand- and typewriting for comparison purposes. These are known as standards or exemplars. Sometimes they will be produced voluntarily upon request. When that is not so, known authentic samples can frequently be found that were prepared for some unrelated reason, such as application for a driver's license or for employment. If the suspect is arrested, a handwriting sample can be taken as part of the booking process. However obtained, the genuineness of the standard must be established by the investigator.

Firearms Experts

Information that an investigator can obtain from an expert on firearms and ammunition includes whether a particular bullet was fired from a specific handgun or rifle, whether a particular cartridge was fired in a given gun, how far a gun was held from the victim when the shot was fired, and what an obliterated serial number on a gun was. It might also be shown that a bullet taken from the body of a suspect was fired from a police officer's gun, thus placing the suspect at the scene of a crime. The once highly publicized diphenylamine paraffin test of hands to determine whether a suspect has recently fired a gun has been abandoned as nonspecific. Instead, a suspect's hands may now be swabbed and the residue subjected to neutron activation analysis.

Firearms evidence has application in a wide variety of cases. In civil matters, it is important in hunting or other gun "accidents," in suspected suicide cases, and in the increasing number of suits against manufacturers over alleged defective guns and ammunition. Although it may be important in any criminal case in which a gun is used, it is frequently central in assault and homicide cases.

Material for examination by a firearms expert is usually found at the crime scene or in the body of a victim. It is the obligation of the investigator to make certain that nothing is overlooked, that what is found is properly collected and preserved, and that it is delivered to the examiner in its original condition. Standards for comparison can come from a weapon found at the scene, one seized on arrest of a suspect or under search warrant. It may also be possible to locate bullets and cartridges known to have been fired from a suspect's gun that has since vanished.

Forensic Pathologists

Medical doctors who specialize in study of the changes that occur in a human body from other than natural causes (usually in organs such as the liver or kidneys) are called forensic pathologists. They customarily work on cases of injury or death that are expected to result in legal actions. Their work can aid in establishing the identity of a deceased person, the cause and manner of death (whether from natural causes or violence), the approximate time of death, whether sexual assault was involved, the impact of violence on the bodies of persons already dead, whether a death was suicide or homicide, and the type of weapon probably used to inflict wounds. Their services are useful in civil cases of wrongful death, in criminal homicides, and in cases of unexplained death.[8]

When an investigator encounters a case of apparent suspicious or unexplained death, the first responsibility is to establish that death has in fact occurred, that the person is beyond medical aid. The scene must then be secured and photographed, and the office of the medical examiner or coroner notified. Until that official arrives, the crime scene search should not disturb the body in any way. If at all possible, a complete autopsy should be ordered, which may include toxicological and serological examinations.

Every jurisdiction has a medical examiner or coroner who is responsible for investigating cases of suspicious death for the state. Other government investigators work closely with that officer, who sometimes employs chemists, serologists, and toxicologists in addition to pathologists. Although such government services are generally not available to defense and civil case investigators, directories listing pathologists are available, and a diligent investigator will usually find one willing to cooperate.

Chemists, Toxicologists, and Serologists

This group of scientists, who are usually employed either in police crime laboratories or the laboratories of coroners or medical examiners, can provide a very wide range of information to investigators, given the opportunity. Their work usually involves "wet" and instrumental chemistry and microscopy, with physical chemistry coming to play an increasing role.[9] They can frequently answer questions such as the following:

- Was a person intoxicated at a given moment and, if so, to what level?
- Was a person poisoned and, if so, by what poison?
- Is a substance found at a crime scene blood? If so, is it animal or human? If human, of what type is the blood and how old is the stain?
- Is the person from whom a sample of saliva, tears, vomitus, perspiration, semen, gastric content, or fecal matter is available a "secretor" whose blood type can be determined from the sample? (Some 80–85 percent of persons are.) If so, what is the type?
- Is a stain semen? Are sperm present? If so, are they human?
- Is the blood of a suspect of the same type as that in samples from the scene?
- Has a person engaged in sexual intercourse recently?
- Is a chip from the scene of an event paint? If so, is it from an automobile or some other source?
- Do materials from the scene of a fire contain accelerants?
- Is a given substance a drug? If so, which one?

There is no limit to the kinds of cases, both civil and criminal, in which these and similar questions may crop up. Any civil matter that may result in a tort suit could involve such evidence. Among criminal cases, it is common in assaults and homicides, sex offenses, burglaries and robberies, drug abuse cases, motor vehicle cases, and unlawful burning cases, among others. One new technique recently developed in this area is DNA (deoxyribonucleic acid) analysis or fingerprinting. It makes individuation possible in cases in which a small amount of blood, hair, or semen is found at the scene of an event and in which similar samples can be obtained legally and ethically from suspects. If the DNA pattern from the sample found at the scene matches that of a suspect, scientists assert that a positive identification has been made. The suspect has been associated with the scene. The test is also useful in paternity cases because an infant's DNA pattern is inherited from its parents in a definite way.[10]

It is obvious from the list of questions just given that an investigator must be alert for a wide variety of physical evidence at crime and other event scenes if the services of this group of scientists is to be exploited fully. Unfortunately, cost considerations preclude even looking for the evidence in many routine cases.

Physical Anthropologists and Forensic Odontologists

Identification of the unknown dead is usually made from physical appearance, clothing and personal effects, or from fingerprints. With only skeletal remains or isolated bones, those means of identification are not available. Then the investigator can call on the physical anthropologist and the forensic odontologist (dentist). Given a skeleton, the physical anthropologist can usually tell the investigator the race, sex, approximate age, and approximate height and weight of the person. With patience, a reconstruction of facial features can be made.

Because teeth are very hard to destroy, they are more frequently available than bones. From them, the dental specialist may be able to tell age (up to about 20 years old), sex, and facial characteristics to corroborate the physical anthropologist's findings. But the dental expert may also be able to tell race; socioeconomic background; occupation; and some habits, such as pipe smoking, from the teeth and jaw. If given predeath dental records, the dentists can also verify or disprove a suspected identification with a high probability of accuracy. Those predeath records might be written notes, charts, or most positive of all, X rays. The dentist can also on occasion identify teeth marks made in human flesh, in an apple, a piece of cheese, or some other item left at the scene of an event as having been made by a particular suspect.

Needless to say, this information from physical anthropologists and forensic odontologists is useful in many kinds of cases, both civil and criminal. In civil matters, identity may be a problem in wrongful death suits, in insurance cases, and in inheritance cases, to name just a few. In criminal cases, such information is of obvious use in homicides, may be useful in sex offenses in which the victim was bitten, may solve burglaries in which bite marks are left in food, and, if false teeth are left behind during commission of the offense, in almost any other kind of crime.

Psychiatrists, Psychologists, and Neurologists

These three groups of specialists are all involved with mental health problems, problems of the brain and nervous system. Psychiatrists may testify whether, in their opinion, a person is, for legal purposes, sane or insane—healthy or mentally ill. Among the civil cases in which this may be an important issue are those involving wills, ability to contract, responsibility for *tortious* wrong, imposition of guardianship, and involuntary civil commitment to a mental institution. In criminal cases, insanity may become an important issue in at least four situations: where it is alleged to preclude formation of the specific intent required by a statute under which the accused is charged; where it is alleged that the accused was insane and hence not responsible at the time of the conduct for which the charge is laid; where insanity of a type that would preclude trial is alleged at the time of the trial; and where it is alleged at the time punishment is to begin, which may preclude the punishment. An insanity plea may be entered in any criminal case. Psychiatrists may also testify to mental problems short of legal insanity and, although it rarely happens, as to the competence or credibility of a potential witness.

Clinical psychologists frequently serve as consultants to psychiatrists, who testify as to the role the psychological information played in the forming of their opinions as to sanity. In some jurisdictions the psychologists may testify if there is also psychiatric evidence in the case. In other states, a psychologist may testify whether or not any psychiatric evidence has been introduced. Psychologists usually testify as to a person's intellectual ability, perception, behavior, personality, or emotional response to certain stimuli. Neurologists similarly frequently serve as consultants to psychiatrists in determining whether a person's brain or nervous system has been impaired by disease or injury.[11]

In 1985, the United States Supreme Court, in the case of *Ake v. Oklahoma,* granted Glen Berton Ake a new trial after conviction of murder and sentence of death because the state of Oklahoma denied his request for an independent psychiatrist to be furnished at state expense to help formulate his defense of insanity. Prior to that decision, forty-one states and the District of Columbia held that indigent defendants must be furnished psychiatric assistance under certain circumstances. Justice Thurgood Marshall wrote for the Court that fundamental fairness required that defendants must have psychiatric assistance as part of the "raw materials integral to... an effective defense."[12]

A psychiatric examination will usually include general clinical observations (such as the circumstances of the examination, the general appearance of the person being examined), the taking of the patient's family and personal history, the results of psychological testing and of physical and neurological examinations. The psychological examination may include personality, intelligence, and psychomotor tests of retention, memory, and conceptual thinking. The neurological examination is a clinical assessment of the status of the patient's nervous system, which generally includes a search for general neurological disorders, a specific search for epilepsy, and the taking of an electroencephalogram (EEG). When a psychiatric examination is indicated, a request for voluntary cooperation is made through the person's attorney. If that request is not successful, a pretrial motion will be filed, stating what is desired, why it is believed necessary, and why the results will be relevant and material to the proceeding.

USING LIE DETECTION TESTS AND HYPNOSIS

Courts of the United States have not yet accepted the polygraph (lie detector) as being well enough established scientifically to be the source of admissible evidence. The polygraph is a machine that measures and makes a graphic ink record of as many as four bodily reactions made by a person hooked up to the machine to the answering of specific questions. In 1980, twenty-two jurisdictions allowed the results of polygraph tests to be admitted by stipulation of the parties. Fifteen allowed admission by stipulation after one party withdrew from the agreement and objected to admission. Thirteen jurisdictions would not allow it to be admitted even after stipulation, and there was no case law on the issue in one jurisdiction. In no jurisdiction will polygraph results be admitted over objection where there has been no stipulation. Grave doubt about the accuracy of the results remains among scientists. Even its supporters admit that the results are ambiguous in about 10 percent of the cases in which it is tried. Those who criticize its use point out that the impact of mistaken results would be very high and assert that there is great danger of abuse of the machine. The so-called truth serums, Pentothal (often referred to as sodium pentothal) and similar drugs, have also failed to achieve acceptance.[13]

After initial acceptance, courts are now holding that witnesses other than defendants in criminal cases cannot testify to "facts" remembered only after their memory has been "refreshed" during hypnosis.[14] This result is approved by a 1984 report which, after careful review of research on hypnotism, concluded as follows:

> We believe that hypnosis should not be allowed to form the basis of testimony in court. The testimony of witnesses who have been hypnotized is not more accurate than that of unhypnotized witnesses. However, it is almost certain to have been made more convincing regardless of accuracy. Further, a very real risk exists that pseudomemories have been created in hypnosis which the witness cannot distinguish from...original recollections.[15]

The study does conclude that hypnosis can, in some cases, produce useful leads.

> This use can be justified, however, *only* for investigative purposes where it is recognized that the use of hypnosis may substantially decrease the reliability of the witness's memory, and *only* in cases where a suspect has not been identified to the subject, where there has not been widespread publicity involving speculations about the perpetrator, and where law enforcement officials do not have strong beliefs about what actually transpired.[16] (Emphasis in original.)

In a 1987 case, the United States Supreme Court decided that, despite the problems just discussed, defendants in criminal cases must be allowed to testify to recollections supposedly refreshed through hypnotism. The decision was based on the constitutional right of a defendant to testify in her or his own behalf, which was deemed to outweigh the state's interest in excluding possibly unreliable evidence. Thus the decision does not apply to testimony by other witnesses.[17]

UTILIZING TECHNOLOGY

All forensic scientists who assist investigators use technology, which is applied science or science put to work, in their scientific procedures. In addition, investigators use technology directly in their field work in many ways. Four products of modern technology frequently used by investigators—cameras, sound recorders, transmitters, and personal computers—are described in the following sections.

Cameras

Investigators use cameras in many situations. Among them are to record a scene; to photograph documents and other physical evidence; to record the identity of persons participating in some event; to record activity of certain individuals (for example, to document their presence at a particular place at a given time, to show them doing things that they should not be doing or that they allege they are unable to do, and to show them associating with other identified persons); and to prepare exhibits. For these and other purposes, a wide variety of cameras are used. Among the most popular now for general use are 35 mm cameras that are practically automatic in their operation. Polaroid cameras that produce instant pictures are also quite useful. Very small cameras are available for use when the investigator wishes to be unobtrusive in picture taking. Video recorders are useful to record interviews, but their cost is too great for use in any but the most serious cases.

To become expert in using a camera requires training and practice with available equipment. Two major concerns focus on the processing of the film: preservation of confidentiality of the information in the pictures and making sure that the film is not tampered with during development. The best answer for both problems is to have the film developed in an official laboratory or to develop the film personally.

Sound Recorders

Recorders can be used in a variety of situations. They are very helpful in open recording of interviews. They can also be used to record conversations surreptitiously in appropriate cases, particularly those intercepted by telephone taps. Many kinds, sizes, and shapes of recorders are available. Special microphones designed for use in particular circumstances (such as the parabolic microphone used to record conversations from a distance) are also available, as are various kinds of filters and sound enhancers that make the recordings easier to understand.

Naturally, special knowledge about what equipment is available coupled with training and practice in its use are important to success. It is also imperative that the investigator know when the consent of those whose conversation is being recorded is necessary, how to get that consent, and how to prove later that the consent was in fact voluntarily given. It may be necessary to get a specific legal authorization—a court order or written authorization from a superior, such as the Attorney General—to use the recorder in some situations. As is the case with film, special procedures must be followed to ensure that the recordings, once made, are not later tampered with.

Transmitters

Transmitters are used both in communication and in tracing and locating moving persons and things. In general communication systems, there is usually a fixed base transmitter and smaller units in moving vehicles or on moving persons. Small transmitters (bugs) can also be used surreptitiously to listen in on and to record conversations. They can be concealed in a room, in a vehicle, or on the person of an investigator or informant (the person is "wired") who is going to have a conversation that will be useful to have overheard and recorded. Specially designed transmitters can also be used to track those on probation or parole and indicted persons released pending trial, if, in all cases, such tracking has been declared a condition of release.

There are many different kinds of transmitters available for different situations. Training is central to success in their use. Among the concerns of the investigator are whether the equipment will really work in a given situation, whether its use there is lawful and authorized, and whether its use is ethical. The basic legal question is whether the use is an unwarranted invasion of privacy.

Personal Computers

Cameras, recorders, and transmitters have been available for investigative uses for many years. Personal computers are much newer; their use is much less widespread. However, they can be invaluable in complex investigations. They can be used to facilitate keeping names, dates, and locations straight. They can also be used to record and show linkages among persons, groups, and organizations. In the investigation of economic crimes, they are useful in recording, analyzing, and displaying financial data. Special knowledge and training are required for their use. The use of personal computers in many kinds of investigations is expected to increase dramatically as investigators become more familiar with them.

These four examples of the direct benefits of technology in field investigations are illustrative of a much broader range of their use. As science progresses, the new knowledge will continue to be applied in practical ways that are helpful for investigators seeking information for use in determinations of fact.

SUMMARIZING COMMENTARY

This chapter describes the utility of science as an information source for investigators. When requested, scientists are allowed to state their opinions in legal proceedings because the underlying facts would be meaningless to the judge, jury, or other decision maker. Their testimony is useful in a wide variety of both civil and criminal matters. Its primary uses are to identify items and substances, to demonstrate their uniqueness, and to demonstrate relationships among them. For a variety of reasons, cost being an important one, scientific evidence is not used as frequently as it might be.

Different types of investigators use different kinds of experts. Among those most frequently used by government investigators are accountants and auditors; fingerprint experts; document examiners; experts on firearms and ammunition; pathologists; chemists, toxicologists, and serologists; physical anthropologists and dentists; and psychiatrists, psychologists, and neurologists.

It is the investigator's responsibility to recognize the need for expert advice, to obtain and submit the materials and persons required for examination, to obtain the services of the expert, to brief the expert on the nature and circumstances of the examination, to specify exactly what is required and when, and to include in the case file an appraisal of the expert as a potential witness, including professional qualifications and standing.

Two areas once regarded as promising have proved to be disappointing: lie detection and hypnosis. Although polygraph results are admissible by stipulation in some jurisdictions, they are nowhere admissible over objection without advance stipulation. A similar fate has befallen testimony by witnesses whose memory has been "refreshed" by hypnosis; such testimony is now not usually admitted. Although hypnosis can be used to obtain leads in strictly circumscribed situations, the cases in which that is advisable are rare. Testimony of a criminal defendant refreshed by hypnosis, however, must be admitted.

Scientific examinations are a valuable source of information in many investigations. Their greater use would improve the quality of many determinations of fact. Technology or applied science is also useful to investigators, as is demonstrated by the routine use of cameras, sound recorders, and transmitters in a variety of ways. Personal computers, a relatively new technological advance, are rapidly being brought into play in complex investigations. Determinations of fact are being made more accurately because of these applications of technological progress.

STUDY QUESTIONS

1. Why are expert witnesses allowed to state their opinions when lay witnesses are not?
2. What is the difference between the concepts of identification and individuation?
3. What are the responsibilities of an investigator with respect to a prospective expert witness?
4. What, other than psychiatric assistance, might be considered as "raw materials integral to...an effective defense" under the *Ake* case?

RECOMMENDED ADDITIONAL READING

- Moenssens, Andre A., Inbau, Fred, and Starrs, James E. *Scientific Evidence in Criminal Cases*, 3rd ed. Mineola, N.Y.: Foundation Press, 1986.
- Osterburg, James W. *The Crime Laboratory: Case Studies in Criminal Investigation*, 2nd ed. New York: Clark Boardman Company, 1982.
- Somers, Leigh Edward. *Economic Crimes: Investigative Principles and Techniques.* New York: Clark Boardman Company, 1984.

NOTES

1. Andre A. Moenssens, Fred Inbau, and James E. Starrs, *Scientific Evidence in Criminal Cases*, 3rd ed. (Mineola, N.Y.: Foundation Press, 1986) and James W. Osterburg, *The Crime Laboratory: Case Studies in Criminal Investigation*, 2nd ed. (New York: Clark Boardman Company, 1982).
2. Osterburg, op. cit., p. 3; the later discussion of Osterburg's findings relies on pp. 3, 4, and 31.
3. Robert Jones Shafer, ed., *A Guide to Historical Method*, 3rd ed. (Homewood, Ill.: Dorsey Press, 1980), pp. 138–147.
4. Leigh Edward Somers, *Economic Crimes: Investigative Principles and Techniques* (New York: Clark Boardman Company, 1984), p. 70.
5. Yoshihide Toba, "A General Theory of Evidence as the Conceptual

Foundation in Auditing Theory," *The Accounting Review* 50, no. 1 (January 1975): 411–412.
6. Osterburg, op. cit., pp. 21–23.
7. Moenssens, Inbau, and Starrs, op. cit., pp. 548–549.
8. Ibid., pp. 270–271.
9. Ibid., pp. 324–414.
10. Philip J. Hilts, "New Crime Identification Tool Devised: DNA Analysis May Be More Accurate Than Checking Fingerprints," *The Washington Post* (20 September 1987): A3, c.1.
11. Andre A. Moenssens, Ray Edward Moses, and Fred E. Inbau, *Scientific Evidence in Criminal Cases* (Mineola, N.Y.: Foundation Press, 1973), pp. 60–111; this discussion is omitted from the 1986 edition cited earlier.
12. Ake v. Oklahoma, 407 U.S. 68 (1985); see Al Kamen, "High Court Expands Trial Rights," *The Washington Post* (26 February 1985): A1, c.3.
13. Moenssens, Inbau, and Starrs, op. cit., pp. 539–571; see also State v. Valdez, 91 Ariz. 274, 371 P.2d 894 (1962) and State ex rel. Collins v. Superior Court, 132 Ariz. 180, 644 P.2d 1266 (1982).
14. See Harding v. State, 5 Md. App. 230, 246 A.2d 302 (1968), overruled in State v. Collins, 296 Md. 670 (1983).
15. Martin T. Orne, David F. Dinges, and Emily Carota Orne, "The Forensic Use of Hypnosis," *Research in Brief* (National Institute of Justice, December 1984): 4.
16. Ibid.
17. Rock v. Arkansas, _____ U.S. _____ (1987); Al Kamen, "Court Rejects Ban On Use of Hypnosis," *The Washington Post* (23 June 1987): A6, c.1.

TALKING TO PEOPLE   6

Most investigators get much of the information required to build their cases from talking to people. In addition, investigators can and should purposefully expand their general knowledge through directed conversations, conversations directed by the investigator to draw out the special knowledge and expertise of others. This means that investigators must have or develop an interest in people.

In society today, there are many occasions on which each of us must spend appreciable amounts of time with persons met casually in a social setting. Indeed some of these exposures are frequent and continual. For many, these events are either boring or painful or both. For others, these occasions are pleasant and valued. Some of us have a natural interest in other people, seem to enjoy social conversation. The rest of us, however, can school ourselves to make such conversation more pleasant to both parties and more valuable to us. The result can be a growing interest in others, a conscious seeking out of others with a wide range of interests, and an increasing sensitivity to the emotions, moods, interests, and intellects of those around us. Investigators must train themselves to enjoy talking to others both to build their general knowledge base and to be able to get specific information from others when required by a current investigation. Four techniques you might use to become a more successful conversationalist are outlined here.

1. One crucial skill is to discover the area about which the other person has special knowledge and expertise and then direct the discussion to that topic.
2. Practice effective listening. Concentrate on what the other person is saying. Do your best to learn about the topic. You never know when the knowledge you gain will become important to you.
3. Shape the discussion about the other's special area of interest to fit your judgment as to which facets of that interest might be most useful to you or are naturally most interesting to you. Make comments and ask questions that nudge the exchange in that direction.

4. To obtain maximum profit from the conversation make sure you follow up; do some reading about the topic so that the content of the discussion jells and is stored in your memory rather than forgotten. You can and should develop your memory in this way. Frequently the other person will be delighted to send you something to read, either self-written or from the general literature. And it may well be that, once sensitized to the area, you can focus on material related to it in your routine reading of the daily newspaper, magazines, and the professional literature that crosses your desk.

In short, make your conversations with others learning experiences for you. Although this may initially seem to be selfish, you will actually be giving others considerable pleasure. Most people enjoy discussing matters about which they have special knowledge. You will soon earn a reputation in your social circle as being a brilliant conversationalist, which in reality means that you are a good listener.

Preparation for successful talking to people fortunately also leads to what most of us would consider to be an interesting life: doing a lot, reading a lot, and talking a lot. The goal is development of wide-ranging personal interests and knowledge that will lead to greater personal and professional success. For an investigator, knowing something about many things is more important than knowing a lot about a few things. The in-depth knowledge required by a current investigation will, of necessity, be developed in the initial stages of that investigation. Building your general knowledge base will give you a head start on every new investigation. Varying your non-professional activity will serve that end. The motto "I'll try *almost* anything once," is a good one for investigators.

What you won't try, you can read about. Vicarious experience is frequently easier to obtain than actual, and can be just as valuable. For this purpose, scan at least one good newspaper every day. Never get caught in a waiting room or similar situation without a book of your choosing. Of course, if you can strike up a conversation with another person who is also waiting, that is even better. Learn and practice conversation-opening gambits, and then shape the discussion as outlined previously. For most of us, reading time is easier to build into our daily lives than is conversation.

Once you have developed the skill of talking to people about meaningful topics, you must also learn to remember the content of the discussion until you can later outline and expand it in writing. But you cannot retain something you have not understood. As an aid to understanding, learn to summarize and reiterate what you have heard. Try beginning by saying, "As I understand it, this is what happened" or "What I understand is that. . . ." This process, sometimes called active listening, gives you an immediate accuracy check and helps you to remember facts and ideas. It requires an ability to articulate orally, to plan and make an organized statement quickly: to think on your feet. Do this frequently during the conversation. Don't let too many points pile up. Nail down every three or, at the most, four points made by repeating the summarizing process.

Obtaining information by talking to people is basic to the art of investigation. It is an art that can and must be learned. Its learning requires practice. That practice can enrich the personal lives of investigators as well as enhance their professional skills. In this context those skills are usually referred to as interviewing and interrogation techniques. But it is well to remember that they are essentially the more general art of successful conversation, applied in a special setting.

TALKING TO WHOM?

Talking to people as part of an investigation must be focused on those who can provide information about basic facts and events. Because there is never "enough" investigative time available, priorities must be established among those to whom it would be desirable to talk. Generally speaking, the more important the case, the deeper into the list of priorities the resources made available will reach. All other things being equal, the order of interviews might well be as follows:

1. Initiator of the complaint that resulted in the investigation
2. Actors in the event or events being investigated
3. Eyewitnesses to the event
4. Witnesses to related occurrences happening prior to or after the principal event
5. Persons who are familiar with the actors, the general nature of the event, or the context in which it occurred

But all other things are seldom equal. There are many possible complicating factors that may change this logical interview sequence. One of them, which would eliminate the initiator of the complaint, might be interruption of the event in process by enforcement investigators, rather than learning about it by report after the fact.

A second complicating factor might be the condition of the actors after the event. If one is injured, in an obvious state of shock, or emotionally upset, the interview might have to be postponed. Because these conditions affect different people differently, the investigator must judge whether the actor is in condition to cooperate effectively. Obtaining as much information as possible immediately is important, but accuracy is also. The investigator must be both realistic and humane in deciding whether to postpone the interview. If the actor is not available, is undergoing treatment at the scene, or has been removed to a distant hospital, the decision to postpone the interview has in effect been made for the investigator.

Still a third factor might be a judgment on the part of the investigator that an actor, witness, or other knowledgeable person has an interest in the event that might make that person hostile to the investigator, that might lead to noncooperation and falsehood. In such circumstances, the investigator may wish to postpone the interview until as much information as possible has been obtained from other sources. Again, judgment by the investigator is called for.

Yet a fourth upsetting factor may be the circumstances in which the event occurs. If it happens outdoors during a pouring rain, a blizzard, or in subzero temperature, the investigator may wish to conduct the interviews later in more comfortable surroundings. Special surroundings may also be required when interviewing certain persons, such as children, invalids, or those who are feeble because of advanced age. Common sense based on study and experience will make it possible for the investigator to set the priorities for whom is to be interviewed when and where.

FINDING PERSONS TO INTERVIEW

Usually there will be no difficulty in locating an initial group of persons to be interviewed about the matter under investigation. The initiating complaint will contain the names of at least some of the actors or the investigating officers will hold persons at the scene upon discovery of the event requiring investigation. At the close of the first and all succeeding interviews, the investigator should ask the interviewee for the names, addresses, and telephone numbers of any other persons who might have information about the event in question. You can also leave your card with the interviewee, requesting that you be contacted if any additional relevant information comes to mind.

If one or more of the parties to the event seem to have disappeared, you can follow routines for tracing them that have been developed by experienced investigators. As Charles O'Hara points out, a record of change of address may be available from the post office, Board of Education, Board of Elections, the Motor Vehicle Bureau, or a local mover.[1] If the person is charged with a crime, the police department will have established procedures that can be followed. These will include circulation of wanted notices; checks with a wide variety of local, state, and federal agencies; and checks of facilities that the suspect may use, such as hotels and racetracks.

In addition to locating and talking to the actors in the event, the investigator will be interviewing eyewitnesses. Their identities may be available from the complainant or initial investigating officers. If not, they can sometimes be located through a canvass of the area. In addition to those who live in the area, an attempt should be made to talk to those who work there, visit there, or pass through on a regular basis. The police officer on whose beat the event occurred should not be overlooked. The records of taxicab companies serving the area may produce leads. A check should also be made as to what else was going on in the vicinity at about the time of the event under investigation and who was involved. The canvass might also be expanded to include possible approach and departure routes to and from the scene.

Important information may be obtained from persons who know well the parties to the event. They may be helpful in establishing motives, with information about the moods and conduct of the parties before and after the event, and with information about any changes in the routine of the lives of the parties at about the time of the event.

The number of persons who might have pertinent information to whom an investigator can talk will depend on the importance of the events under investigation. It may also depend on the probability of bringing the investigation to a successful conclusion, as will be explored in Chapter 8, where discussion turns to management of criminal investigations. If experience shows that events with certain characteristics are typically not investigated successfully, resources will not be devoted to them.

INTERVIEW VERSUS INTERROGATION

Particularly in criminal cases, conventional wisdom has sharply differentiated between *interview* and *interrogation*. The latter is frequently defined as "the questioning of a suspect, perpetrator, or individual who is reluctant, or refuses, to cooperate with the interviewer."[2] As a taught technique for use with persons known to be hostile to the investigation, interrogation has emphasized greater "control" over the person being questioned, through the use of an austere setting from which the person can draw no comfort, through a manner of questioning that seeks to dominate and intimidate, through lying to the person about what is already known about the events or about what others have said about them, and through other elements of bluff and bluster. Attempts are made to exploit any perceived weaknesses in or special concerns of the one being questioned. Lie detector, or polygraph, machines are used. In short, interrogation procedures are just one step away from the use of force—or at least a strongly implied threat to use force—to get the answers desired by the interrogator. The goal is to obtain an admission that would tend to prove some required element of an offense or a confession to the entire offense.

During the last fifty years, the courts of the United States, including the United States Supreme Court, have largely eliminated the use of physical or psychological abuse to obtain admissions and confessions by making the resulting statements inadmissible in later criminal trials. The key United States Supreme Court case is *Miranda v. Arizona,* which held that a suspect in a criminal case must be "read his rights"[3] prior to being questioned in a custodial situation (any situation in which the suspect feels restrained not to leave). The suspect must be told the following:

- You have a legal right to remain silent when questioned.
- Any statement you make may be used against you in a court of law.
- You have a right to counsel now and during any questioning.
- If you want counsel now but can't afford one, the court will appoint one at no expense to you.

The *Miranda* warning is not required for a simple noncustodial interview. Although the exact breadth of *Miranda* is still being established,[4] the net effect has been to eliminate most of the differences between interviewing and interrogation.

However, investigators do face two practical problems in interviewing hostile persons. The first is determining whether *Miranda* applies, whether the person to be interviewed is in fact a suspect being held in a "custodial situation." Frequently a person who is interviewed simply as a prospective witness in what might be perceived as custody may, either during the interview or later, become a suspect. If that occurs during the interview, questioning should be stopped and the person informed of the rights provided by *Miranda* before the interview may continue. If the change in status occurs between interviews, the *Miranda* warning must be given before the second questioning proceeds in a custodial setting.

The second practical problem for the investigator is whether an interview with a suspect should be conducted any differently than an interview with a friendly prospective witness. Although there are differences of opinion on this issue, the authors believe that the same basic techniques should be used in both situations. Because the suspect will frequently be in custody, the room in which the interview will be conducted will probably of necessity be austere. Interview rooms that have the comforts of home are not generally available in police stations and jails. There will also be an atmosphere of security, with barred windows and doors and persons in uniform (perhaps with sidearms) in evidence on the way to the interview room, even if not in it. The setting, then, may well be dominating and intimidating by its very nature, but that need not affect the conduct of the investigator in the interview room.

Generally speaking, the investigator should be polite and respectful to the subject during the interview. When that subject is a disreputable person with a criminal record against whom there is strong evidence of having committed yet another crime, politeness may be hard to come by. But the investigator should regard the person as a citizen, not as a suspect, just as in a courtroom respect must be shown for the role of judge regardless of the person occupying that position. The authors believe firmly that, in the long run, a reputation for polite and respectful handling of all persons will gain an investigator more useful information than a reputation for abuse of some.

This does not mean that the investigator cannot be firm and persistent in the questioning of an unwilling suspect, but it does mean that there must be special effort not to become angry and emotional when admissions or a confession are not forthcoming. In fact, it is detrimental to an investigator even to give the appearance of losing control. Keeping your temper is imperative. Keep your voice down; don't speak any louder than is necessary. Don't begin to speak more rapidly than normal. Don't interrupt the suspect and don't ignore attempts by the suspect to interrupt you. It is more important that the suspect talk than that you do so.

This does not mean that the interview cannot be directed. Ask the suspect to get back to the matter at hand; ask probing questions; point out inconsistencies and ask for clarification. Remember, because of the *Miranda* warning, the person in a custodial situation knows that there is no requirement to answer your questions. To be able to direct the conversation, the investigator must have *in mind* as much information as possible about the case. There should be no need to consult the file during the interview. And remember that you may obtain useful facts even though there is no admission or confession from your hostile subject.

Specific types of conduct that courts will not tolerate during the questioning of a suspect are outlined here.

1. There should, obviously, be no physical abuse.
2. There should be no threat of physical violence, either openly or by implication.
3. There should be no warning that dire consequences will follow if the person does not talk.
4. There should be no threat to arrest the suspect's significant others if he or she doesn't talk.
5. There should be no promise of release or of reducing or dropping charges in return for admissions or confessions.
6. There should be no promise to intercede with other authorities for leniency in return for a statement.
7. There should be no promise not to prosecute for other known or suspected crimes.
8. There should be no use of illegally obtained evidence to break down the person's resistance.

9. The subject should not be arrested on some trumped up charge in order to create an opportunity for questioning.
10. The person should not be held incommunicado.
11. The questioning should not be prolonged unduly.

Any of these practices may result in any admission or confession obtained being held inadmissible at a later trial.

The literature on investigation is full of what the authors consider to be unethical tricks for use with suspects. They are not recommended here. The result is not worth the cost. Cases are solved by good investigation and without admissions and confessions. Statements by accused persons are notoriously unreliable. Some countries forbid their use in trials. A reputation for fair, honest, scrupulous treatment of all persons, friendly or hostile, will bring more useful information to an investigator than any other approach. Our society has moved toward approval of such ethical action. Perhaps the best way for an investigator to achieve the state of mind that will make it possible to conduct successful interviews with hostile persons is to remember that every citizen is innocent until proved otherwise in a court of law.

CONDUCTING THE INTERVIEW

Once the need for an interview has been established, it should be undertaken as soon as it can be done effectively. There are a number of circumstances, however, that may call for temporary postponement. Among them are the condition of the person to be interviewed (injury, shock, emotional upset); lack of immediate availability; lack at the moment of an appropriate place for conducting the interview; and a belief that more information about the event from other sources will make a later interview more productive. The need for the investigator to be both realistic and humane in assessing whether conditions require postponement of an interview has already been discussed. The postponement decision might well be determined by the availability of alternate potential witnesses for interview, which would mean that the investigator's time would not be wasted by the postponement.

Generally speaking, the investigator should use the most appropriate available setting for the interview. An expressed wish of the subject not to be seen talking at length with the investigator should be honored. At least a modicum of comfort is also important for effective communication. In any event, the need for privacy is paramount. Interruptions, whether by telephone or by persons coming into the room, stop the flow of information at least temporarily and may destroy a carefully established rapport with the person being interviewed. If it is believed important to have a witness present to allay later accusations of improper conduct or to provide some support for a fragile subject, that third person should sit or stand in as unobtrusive a spot as possible. Remember the adage "out of sight, out of mind," and be sure that the witness's attention is not drawn to the third party. Agency policy may dictate whether an observer is to be used and how the information obtained during the interview is to be recorded. Unless crucial admissions or a confession result, the investigator might well wait until after the interview before making notes about what was covered. If some kind of recording is to be used during the interview, even if only note taking by the investigator, the process should be discussed with the person being interviewed at the outset. An interview should not be filmed or taped without permission. To do so may well violate the subject's right to privacy, and may alienate prospective witnesses.

Every interview really has four parts: a beginning, a middle, an end, and, once the investigator is again alone, an assessment of the information obtained. At the outset, the investigator must present identification credentials, state the matter to be discussed, and ask for the cooperation of the other person. Identifying information must also be obtained from the interviewee, together with telephone numbers, addresses, and other means through which the person might later be contacted again if necessary. This beginning should be a settling-in process, interspersed with small talk, during which the individuals become comfortable with one another.

Once rapport has been established, the investigator should direct attention to the event under investigation, asking for a narrative statement of what the subject knows about that situation. Recent research aimed at increasing the completeness and accuracy of reports by eyewitnesses recommends that the victim or witness be asked to relive the experience mentally prior to making the narrative statement. The investigator should say something like:

> Try to reconstruct in your mind the circumstances that surround the incident. Think about what the surrounding environment looked like at the scene, such as rooms, locations of furniture, vehicles, the weather, lighting, any nearby people or objects. Also think about how you were feeling at the time and think about your reactions to the incident.[5]

The researchers also recommend that the witness be asked to mention every detail remembered even though it might seem unimportant. The researchers call their approach the "cognitive interview."

When the subject begins to talk, the investigator must concentrate on listening to and watching the other person. Note taking, if done at all, should be done as unobtrusively as possible. Be patient; let the person wander a bit as long as the diversion has some relationship to the matter at hand. Unexpected connections among seemingly unrelated events may be revealed. When the narrative is complete, begin probing with comments and questions needed for clarification or to bring out more detail. The developers of the cognitive interview recommend that the investigator begin this process by asking the witness or victim to try to rethink and describe what happened from some new perspective: as if located at some different vantage point for describing the scene, or as if he or she were some other person present describing what that person saw, or even what one of the principals must have seen during the event. They also recommend that the person being interviewed recall and relate the event in reverse order, or both backward and forward from some critical act in the events.

In addition, the researchers recommend specific probes about physical appearance, names, numbers, speech characteristics, and conversation. Regarding appearance, the investigator is urged to ask whether there was anything unusual about the appearance or clothing of the participants, whether a participant reminded the witness of anyone and, if so, why. The observer should also be asked if any names were spoken and what they were. If the observer says, "Yes, but I can't remember what the name was," urge the witness to run through the alphabet thinking of names starting with each letter. Ask about how many syllables there were in the name. Probe whether a number was involved and, if so, how high or low it was, how many integers there were in it, and whether there might have been a letter in with the numbers.

As to speech characteristics, the investigator should ask whether a voice reminded the witness of anyone and, if so, why. If not, was there any unusual quality about the voice? If conversation was involved, what were the reactions of the observer and others present to what was said? Were any unusual words or phrases used?[6]

Also check any apparent internal inconsistencies in the story, and statements that are inconsistent with information from other sources. Be sure that you understand everything that the interviewee sought to tell. For that purpose, summarize the important points in your own words, then ask if that summary is correct.

In probing the story of the interviewee, keep your comments and questions short; tackle one topic at a time. Use clear and easily understood language. Ask questions that call for simple answers, but still for something beyond yes or no. Use bland language that does not stir up emotions. Do not use questions that suggest the desired answer, that assume something not yet established to be fact, or that embody the fact and require only a yes or a no. In developing the discussion, move from the known to the unknown, from the general to the specific.

In closing the interview, ask about any others who may have information about the event. Be sincere in thanking the person, stressing the importance to the investigation of the cooperation of knowledgeable persons. Remember that the continued cooperation of this person and others similarly situated is crucial to your continuing success as an investigator. Investigators also find that, at this point when the person believes the interview is over, important additional information may be revealed without prompting.

As soon as the person is gone, record your understanding of the gist of the conversation or reorganize, expand, and analyze any record made during the talk. Try to fit any new information obtained with that available earlier. Make a written evaluation of the sincerity of the person; note the probable value as a witness in court, including how well the subject would probably stand up under cross-examination. This report should be completely professional in tone and content. Remember that it might later be subpoenaed by the opposition. And then, before moving on to the next task, make at least a private personal evaluation of your own performance during the interview. Did you make any mistakes? If so, how can you avoid them in the future?

Both during and after the interview, there will frequently be doubts about the accuracy and truthfulness of the information elicited. Important in those assessments are a number of factors. One is the physical opportunity of the person to obtain the information reported.

> Could she really see what she describes as having happened from her reported location?
> How close was he to the events as they were taking place?
> Was it a dark, rainy, foggy night or a bright sunshiny day?
> Was the observation made right on the spot or from some distance through a rain- or mud-spattered window?
> Is the vision or the hearing of the subject impaired in any way?
> Is the one reporting conversation fluent in the language used?
> Could there have been idioms or colloquialisms used that were misunderstood?

A myriad of such factors might have influenced the accuracy of the account that the person wished to convey.

But even assuming that the person does have an accurate knowledge of what happened, there still might be warping of the information during the telling, either accidentally or purposefully. Accidental distortion can occur through the language problems just mentioned, with the misinterpretation being either on the part of the investigator or the subject. Purposeful distortion comes from omissions, half-truths, and outright lies, which may be very difficult to detect. As yet, the art or science of lie detection is not accurate enough to be accepted by the courts. Some individuals like to believe that they can detect lying in others, but they are consistently unable to do so when tested under controlled conditions.

Simple nervousness on the part of the subject is not a good indicator. The process of being interviewed is stressful in and of itself for many, more so for the simple innocent than for the confirmed wrongdoer. Some who are very self-assured and straightforward are skilled liars. It is well for the investigator to keep the level of sophistication of the subject in mind. But the best defense against deception is an awareness that it might be attempted. The possibility that the person has a motive to lie should always be considered.

> Is there some self-interest (monetary or otherwise) at stake in the events?
> Might there be a desire to protect some third person?
> Could a grudge against one of the actors or against the investigator or a colleague be involved?

Once alert to the possibility of deception, the best protection is not accepting new information as truthful until it has been verified. Check it against information from other sources; check its plausibility, given what is known about the actors involved; and check its internal consistency. Until verified from at least one independent source, every item of information must be regarded as only tentatively established.

There is no substitute for preparation in achieving successful interviews. Do your homework first, both about the events in question and about the person to whom you will be talking. The self-assurance that comes from being prepared makes it easier to establish rapport at the beginning and quickly earns the respect of the other person. Tie your self-introduction to persuasion to cooperate, stressing the importance of the individual's help in getting the facts straight. Listen well to what is said, even at the expense of some additional time. Probe, and summarize what you are told to check the accuracy of your understanding. Get to know something about the person, particularly the communication skills demonstrated. Assess the probability that the person is sincerely trying to give you accurate information. If the interview is important enough, ask the person to check your written report of it later. Be sincere in your expression of appreciation for cooperation, and ask about other possible sources of information.

PROBLEMS IN SPECIAL CASES

Not all interviews can be conducted in the same manner. Persons of different ages and in different positions in life must be approached in different ways. Different kinds of cases may require consultation with varying sets of experts. Adaptability and versatility are necessary in an investigator who is responsible for a variety of cases.

Child abuse and neglect cases pose a particularly broad and difficult set of interview situations for both social workers and police officers.[7] In addition to talking to the child and any siblings and playmates of tender age, there must be discussion with the adult members of the household and other adults who have contact with the child and family. Assessment of the damage to the child resulting from the abuse or neglect will frequently require interviews with physicians, psychiatrists, and other professionals. In many situations, the caretaker of the child will regard the mere fact of initiation of the investigation as a personal accusation of incompetence if not of neglect or abuse. Few situations require greater skill and sensitivity than these.

Investigation of such cases is usually begun by social agencies. Contact with the family by the social work investigator should start with an interview with the child's caretaker. After the initial introduction, that interview should begin with a statement of the agency's responsibility to families, its intention regarding procedures to be followed in discharging that responsibility, the possibility that criminal charges may result, and a statement of the rights and responsibilities of the caretaker. There should be no mention of the source of the complaint initiating the investigation. The cooperation of the caretaker should be sought as tactfully as possible, but it should be made clear that the investigation will proceed in any event, whether with or without that cooperation. It will probably take all of the investigator's skill to establish a cooperative rapport with the caretaker. Not infrequently, even that best effort will fail; in such cases, the police must be contacted and the investigation continued with the aid of their authority.

Discussion with the caretaker should focus first on the general atmosphere in the family, with emphasis on child-rearing practices, moving then to relationships with each of the children, including the one or ones alleged to have been abused. If the alleged abuse and neglect are aggravated, it may take considerable self-control for the investigator to remain objective, but doing so is imperative. The caretaker will be under no such restraints, and may well become emotional and quite angry. Skilled interviewers will develop techniques for comforting and allaying the fears and anger of the caretaker, but should never ignore threats of physical injury. Any and every threat must be taken seriously and a judgment made whether or not to postpone continuation of the interview until after the caretaker has cooled down. Sometimes the situation can be sidestepped by moving on to talks with the children or with other adults in the family with a view to returning to the caretaker later. But there will also be times when the investigator assesses the threat of personal injury to be so great as to require departure, contact with the police, and return to the scene under police protection. When in doubt, the investigator should leave.

When the decision is to leave, the investigator should consider the effect the pause may have on the child's safety, the possibility that the caretaker might try to cover up the truth during the investigator's absence, the likelihood that the family might flee with the child, or the time frame for completing the investigation.

These considerations will frequently require that the investigator call the police from the nearest public phone, requesting their immediate assistance on an emergency basis. Pending their arrival, the house should be kept under observation. With the police on the scene, the investigation should continue to completion. In such a situation, the children might well be put into protective custody when the interviews are completed. However, the seriousness of that step must be kept in mind.

When the interview process moves on to young children, the investigator faces a particularly difficult task. It may turn out that a child is too young for verbal communication. In that case, inspection for signs of physical abuse or neglect by an investigator of the same sex may be required. If possible, any session with the child should be private, without the caretaker or others present. If the child is too nervous or upset when alone, a sibling or some other person trusted by the child may be present. Choice of that person requires judgment by the investigator that there will be no obstruction of the interview.

There are many special considerations when conducting an interview with a child. One is use of a play setting and play equipment. Special materials are available for guidance in the use of that technique.

Others in addition to very young children require special interviewing techniques. Older children and teenagers, young adults, the middle-aged, and the elderly may have special information-holding characteristics because of their age that could be tapped by an alert interviewer.[8] Such special considerations as native intelligence, language abilities, degree of cooperativeness, motive for falsification, and tendency to exaggerate must also be taken into account.

In general, an extensive personal knowledge base, practical experience in talking with a wide variety of people, and an interest in the psychology and sociology of human relationships will make it possible for an investigator to become skilled in obtaining information from conversations with others.

SUMMARIZING COMMENTARY

In most investigations, much of the crucial information comes from talking to people. Even where documents and other physical evidence are important, testimony by people is necessary to verify their discovery, their preservation pending trial, and their significance to the case. Investigators must therefore become expert in obtaining information through conversation. That skill can be practiced and the investigator's general knowledge base expanded by taking every available opportunity for directed conversation with those contacted in daily life.

There are four principal skills that guarantee success in directed conversation: discovering the other's area of expertise, effective listening, shaping the discussion of the topic to your interest, and follow-up reading after the discussion. Preparation for such directed conversation should include doing, reading, and talking. Directed conversation with others develops excellent background knowledge in an interviewer.

Shortage of investigative time requires that interviewing be done on a flexible priority basis. Flexibility is required because a variety of circumstances can require departure from your ideal schedule. Although in most cases those you wish to interview are readily available, it sometimes takes imagination to identify and locate the persons who possess the information you need. Well-developed procedures are available for locating persons who seem to have disappeared.

Court cases setting out the legal rights of those suspected of violations of law have placed severe limitations on the intimidating interview process called interrogation. In addition, there is good cause to believe that a reputation for fair, honest, and scrupulous treatment of all persons in interview situations, whether friendly or hostile, will bring to an investigator more information than will trickery and intimidation.

Special thought should be given to when, where, and how a prospective interview should be conducted. Each of these factors will vary from one interview to another. Privacy and comfort are two important considerations. Agency guidelines may well cover the mechanics of the interview, such as the kind of record to be made. All four parts of an interview, the beginning, middle, end, and recapitulation, should be carefully planned. Attention should be given not only to the information needed but also to the person's potential as a witness in later legal proceedings. All of this requires preparation, which is the secret of success in obtaining information from people just as it is in most other investigative procedures. Research is now being done on a new kind of directive interview called the cognitive interview.

Some interviews present problems. Talking to very young children can be particularly difficult, but each age group requires its own approach. Persons with different roles in the events under investigation as well as with different positions in life also require variations on the basic approach.

At times, the physical safety of the interviewer may be threatened. Such threats should always be taken seriously. The investigator must make a considered judgment whether to break off the interview and return later with the protection of police officers. But on the whole, obtaining information by talking to people can be a pleasant as well as profitable way to spend investigative time.

In the next chapter, an overview is presented of the peculiar attributes of one common type of investigation, that in a police setting.

STUDY QUESTIONS

1. How does the scope of an investigator's general knowledge base impact on success as an interviewer?
2. What is meant by directed conversation with others?
3. How can an investigator decide the order in which several persons should be interviewed?
4. How does one find a person to be interviewed who seems to have disappeared?
5. Why is there now less difference between interviewing and interrogation than there was fifty years ago?
6. Why is it important in a criminal investigation to note when a prospective witness becomes a suspect?
7. What are the important aspects of the four successive stages in any interview?
8. What special techniques are useful in interviewing young children?

RECOMMENDED ADDITIONAL READING

- Dexter, L. A. *Elite and Specialized Interviewing.* Evanston, Ill.: Northwestern University Press, 1970.
- Gerber, Samuel R., and Schroeder, Oliver. *Criminal Investigation and Interrogation.* Cincinnati, Ohio: W. H. Anderson and Company, 1962.
- Larson, J. A. *Lying and Its Detection: A Study of Deception Tests.* Montclair, N.J.: Patterson Smith Publishers, 1969.
- Royal, Robert, and Schutt, Steven. *The Gentle Art of Interviewing and Interrogation.* Englewood Cliffs, N.J.: Prentice-Hall, 1976.

NOTES

1. Charles E. O'Hara, *Fundamentals of Criminal Investigation*, 4th ed. (Springfield, Ill.: Charles C Thomas, 1976), pp. 188–198.
2. Richard H. Ward, *Introduction to Criminal Investigation* (Reading, Mass.: Addison-Wesley, 1975), p. 108.
3. Miranda v. Arizona, 384 U.S. 436 (1966).

4. See Al Kamen and Ed Bruske, "*Miranda* Exception is Created," *The Washington Post* (5 March 1985): A1, c.1.
5. See R. Edward Geiselman and Ronald P. Fisher, "Interviewing Victims and Witnesses of Crime," *Research in Brief* (National Institute of Justice, December 1985).
6. These techniques of the cognitive interview have proved successful in experiments and in 1987 were being tested in a field project supported by the National Institute of Justice. The institute monitor is Anne Schmidt, National Institute of Justice, 633 Indiana Avenue, NW, Washington, D.C. 20531.
7. This discussion draws on *Child Abuse and Neglect Investigation Decisions Handbook,* prepared under the direction of Gregory L. Coles, Department Director, with the assistance of Data Management Associates of Albany, N.Y., and Springfield, Ill. (Illinois Department of Children and Family Services, 1982).
8. Ward, op. cit., pp. 103–107.

A POLICE INVESTIGATION OVERVIEW

7

Police investigations are a particularly important kind of investigation. They are typical of the most difficult investigations possible; they are of crucial importance both to the target individuals and to the community at large; and there are so many of them that they create a large number of jobs for investigators. For these reasons, this and the next two chapters consider their nature.

Organization for and management of police investigations is, in the United States, primarily a local function. There is a national commitment to keeping this governmental activity as close to the people as is possible, which is implemented by the Tenth Amendment to the Constitution of the United States. The general responsibility for administration and enforcement of the criminal law is in our city and county governments. Despite that fact, state governments do have a role to play which stems primarily from the need for some statewide coordination and for the financial need to regionalize some scarce resources. Many of our states operate a state police agency that has concurrent jurisdiction with city and county agencies for enforcement of the traffic laws (with primary emphasis on major highways in rural areas) and that handles those aspects of some investigations (such as in drug abuse and organized and economic crime cases) that stretch across county lines.[1] They will generally assist in more routine investigations without broad geographic ramifications only at the request of the local city or county authorities.

The state police also frequently furnish crime laboratory and sometimes radio communication services to local law enforcement agencies. They occasionally contract to furnish police services to smaller municipalities and rural areas. They also have come to act as a substitute for the militia or national guard units in labor unrest, racial conflict, and other situations where riot conditions are threatened. In some states, there is not a unified state police. Instead there is a highway or traffic patrol and one or more separately organized investigative offices such as a state bureau of investigation or a state insurance fraud investigation unit.

Although of growing importance, state investigative units generally supplement rather than replace local agencies.

There are also important investigative agencies at the federal level. Their responsibilities include

- Protection of federal officials
- Investigation of attempts to harm federal officials
- Investigation of crimes against the federal government such as espionage, sabotage, treason, theft and destruction of federal government property, and fraud against the government
- Protection of our borders
- Enforcement of the revenue laws
- Enforcement of the laws against drug abuse
- Relief of state and local law enforcement burdens through such devices as investigation of interstate flight to avoid prosecution[2]

A tremendous amount of federal investigative effort goes into background checks on prospective federal employees. Federal agencies also coordinate official liaison of United States agencies at all levels with Interpol, the international police organization. As a result of increased concern over drug abuse, the Central Intelligence Agency and our military departments are also being assigned new special responsibilities to aid civilian law enforcement agencies.[3] But the fact that law enforcement agencies do exist at all levels of government does not change the fact that primary reliance is placed on thousands of local law enforcement departments.

TRADITIONAL CRIMINAL INVESTIGATION

When the detective function was first recognized in police departments of the United States, the investigators tended to be generalists working alone or with one other on a wide range of cases. In larger cities, they were frequently assigned to a specific neighborhood. They developed close ties to their communities, cultivated sources of information that kept them aware of what was going on there, and kept their information to themselves. They did not develop specialized knowledge and skills about particular kinds of investigations, and were eventually found to be corruptible by the communities with which they had become so familiar.[4]

But in some cities, there were elements of centralization and specialization at very early dates. By 1980, those characteristics had become typical. In a 1975 survey of 152 police departments, the Rand Corporation found that detectives were centralized at headquarters in 63 percent, assigned primarily to districts in 22 percent, and mostly in headquarters but with some in the districts in 15 percent.[5] Centralization went hand in hand with specialization. In larger cities, separate squads were assigned to homicide, assault, sex crime, burglary, robbery, auto theft, and fraud cases. In smaller departments, the specialization might be limited to crimes against the person and crimes against property. In the smallest cities, the specialization might well be informal based on the special interests of individual investigators.

A number of advantages have been claimed for specialization. Among them are the definite fixing of responsibility for specific kinds of cases, development of higher levels of skill in handling a narrowly defined group of cases, facilitation of training in the newest techniques and procedures, creation of a strong sense of identity in a detective with the unit, growth of pride in accomplishment with resulting high morale among unit members, development of public interest in and support for the investigative units, and the freeing up of the uniformed force to spend more time on crime prevention efforts.

However, there are also a number of recognized disadvantages. One important drawback is the delay in response time caused by the referral of cases by patrol officers to detectives, with a resultant resentment on the part of victims of that delay. Denying patrol officers any meaningful role in the investigation of serious crimes also lowers their morale, which exacerbates difficulties in maintaining communication between patrol and investigative units. Specialization also leads to increased administrative and clerical work loads. These disadvantages led to federally funded research on whether the investigative function of police agencies might not be better organized and managed. The result was a new concept in the *management of criminal investigation* (often abbreviated as *MCI*).

MANAGING CRIMINAL INVESTIGATIONS

At the heart of the new MCI concept is assignment of more investigative responsibility in a wide range of cases to patrol officers on whose beats the violations occur. Those officers are assisted in complicated cases by investigative specialists assigned to the patrol areas. A centralized departmental investigative unit is retained for investigation of major crimes against the person and for check fraud cases. That unit is also given the responsibility for obtaining and serving warrants. Adaptation of the model to specific departments does result in variations, but most adopting cities maintain the essential components.[6]

Among the advantages claimed for the new approach are more thorough initial investigations by patrol officers, immediate follow up of leads in a continuing investigation by detectives, greater efficiency in the solving of property crimes, and better communication between patrol and detective officers. But difficulties in implementing the new approach have also been noted. As with any change, there is deep-seated resistance by many who defend the traditional way. Their primary arguments are that allowing a patrol officer to take on investigative tasks will tie up that officer for too long and result in the officer leaving the beat area to track down leads, two circumstances that will weaken patrol of the beat. The short answer to these critics is that, in either situation, the patrol officer will call in the available investigative specialist and turn the case over to that detective, returning then to patrol of the beat. For effective implementation of MCI, patterns of activity and firmly held assumptions about how crimes can be solved must be changed. This change requires full commitment to the new approach by all concerned. To be fully effective, the new methods require strong support services such as effective retraining of the experienced personnel involved and a flow of useful information from a crime analysis unit.

A somewhat fortuitous convergence of a number of factors led to development of the new concept of managing criminal investigations. One was the development of a new generation of police managers with college and university educations who not only saw the disadvantages of the previous approach but allowed careful research on its perceived weaknesses and then heeded the results of that research. Another important factor was the availability of federal financial support for the research through the Law Enforcement Assistance Administration of the United States Department of Justice. Federal funds supported the required research, the publication and other dissemination of the research results, as well as their experimental field testing. During that testing process, better educated and better trained patrol officers were able to meet the challenges of their new initial investigation responsibility with greater success than would have their less well prepared predecessors. Each of these factors made a major contribution to the development and success of the new approach.

Early studies by the Rand Corporation and the Stanford Research Institute documented the shortcomings of the traditional procedures. More than half of serious offenses were never thoroughly investigated. Investigators spent much of their time reviewing reports, documenting files, and locating and interviewing victims in non-solvable cases. In cases that were solved, they spent more time in post-clearance processes than in identifying perpetrators. It became apparent that if victims could not identify perpetrators to patrol officers during the initial interview, in most cases no identification would be made later. If perpetrator identification did occur later, it would be through routine police procedures, not through investigative effort. In very few cases did investigative effort provide the proof on all elements of a criminal charge necessary for conviction after trial or for successful plea bargaining.[7] Dissatisfaction with this situation led to a search for a new approach.

Assessment of the goals for the investigation of crimes identified four needs for each category of crime.

1. Increases in the number of arrests
2. Increases in the number of clearances (One arrest may clear several cases but, in another situation, several arrests may clear only one case.)
3. Increases in the number of cases accepted for prosecution
4. Increases in the number of convictions

The first two of these success components or criteria are obviously under the control of the investigators. The second two are also influenced by the ability, dedication, and preparation of the case prosecutors. The last is affected by the functioning of judges and juries. But as any new approach was implemented, these variables of prosecutor, judge, and jury action would be expected to remain relatively constant, which justifies attributing any resultant changes to the new approach.

Design of the new approach led to emphasis on five components: initial investigation, case screening, management of the continuing investigation, police–prosecutor relations, and a system for continuous monitoring of investigative performance. Each of these components deserves further discussion.

Performance of a directed initial investigation by the responsible patrol officer is a key element of the new approach to management of criminal investigations. Its purpose is twofold: to obtain the information necessary as a basis for closing those cases that cannot be solved with available resources, and to obtain all of the information available at the scene so that the same work need not be repeated later by a detective to whom a solvable case is assigned for continuing investigation. In other words, the initial investigation is aimed at obtaining information on "solvability factors" necessary in case screening. Among the solvability factors in a typical case would be whether there was a witness to the crime, whether a suspect can be named, whether a suspect can be described, whether a suspect vehicle can be identified, whether property stolen is traceable, whether significant physical evidence is available, and whether there was a definite, limited opportunity for anyone other than the suspect to commit the crime.

If the answer to all of these questions is no, the case will be closed as not solvable. No more resources will be wasted on it. When there is positive evidence on some of these factors, a judgment must be made whether to assign the case for continued investigation or to close it. If the decision is in favor of additional investigation, the report of the patrol officer constitutes a solid basis for the additional effort.

This process of decision making is called case screening. It eliminates unsolvable cases from the work load, thus saving resources for cases involving leads that do promise solution and for better preparation of solved cases for prosecution. Departments vary in their reliance on the initial patrol officer for making the screening decision. In minor cases and even in serious cases where no evidence of solvability exists, the case may be closed by the patrol officer. Where there is solvability evidence but its strength and weight are debatable, review of the patrol officer's recommendation by a more experienced supervisor will be required. There may even be a second review of all decisions to close serious cases.

Management of investigations in which additional expenditure of resources is deemed merited requires systematic assignment of the cases and periodic review of progress in the continued investigations. The two are related. Together they lead to three desirable results: more equitable investigator work loads, better use of individual investigator talents, and more expeditious closing of cases. This function requires a supervisor with a knowledge of the investigative intricacies of different kinds of cases, of the talents of the available investigators, and of the indicia of a case that further effort will not solve. That kind of knowledge comes with experience, with maturing through investigation of large numbers of a variety of cases.

The relationship of investigators with prosecutors who will later present the cases that are solved is important at a number of decision points. The first is determination of the initial formal charge to be lodged. A single substantive criminal law statute dealing with one kind of criminal conduct can create more than a hundred separate and distinct but closely related offenses. The offense charged must comprise the peculiar set of elements provable by the evidence available from the preliminary investigation. Isolating that charge from all of the other related offenses created by the statute is no simple task. And the detailed evidence produced by the continuing investigation may well require a change in the initial charge prior to formal arraignment, a second point at which investigator-prosecutor collaboration is essential. And as will be documented in Part Four of this book, the investigator is an essential aid to the prosecutor during presentation of the case in court. In addition to the collaboration at these three crucial decision points, a positive police–prosecutor relationship can be of help to the investigator during the investigation when legal process is necessary in the search for information, when pretrial discovery, a subpoena duces tecum, or a search warrant is sought. Effective collaboration will result in an increase both in the percentage of solved cases accepted for trial and in the percentage of tried cases that result in conviction.

Last among the discrete components of the new approach to management of criminal investigations is a formal system for monitoring progress. The system chosen must provide the manager with continuous feedback not only on the progress of the investigation but on the performance of the individual investigators. The former is necessary for running adjustments that may be required during the investigation and the latter for identification of strengths and weaknesses in the work of the investigator. Exploitation of the former will result in better use of the available resources. Pinpointing the latter can result in tailored retraining of the investigator. Without such information from a case-monitoring system, usually a combination of written reports and face-to-face conferences, the case manager is severely handicapped.

Together these five components of modern criminal investigation management (initial investigation, case screening, management of the continuing investigation, police–prosecutor relations, and continual monitoring of investigative performance) can considerably improve the productivity from available investigative resources. To achieve that goal, however, certain conditions must be created both within the investigative units and in the department generally. First of all, top management must be firmly committed to the new approach. Furthermore, that commitment must be conveyed effectively to key command personnel and to the supervisory subordinates. It must also be conveyed effectively to patrol officers and investigative specialists alike. Unless there is genuine internalization of the norms of the new approach by all persons involved in its implementation, its potential will not be achieved.

Second, there must be training and retraining at all personnel levels on the new approach to management of criminal investigations. This training must challenge the basic assumptions that underpinned the old, ineffective investigation strategies and must teach the new MCI assumptions and strategies.

Third, there must be enforced adherence to all screening procedures that increase patrol time available for initial investigations. Those procedures will eliminate patrol response to noncrime events and permit the planned scheduling of nonemergency patrol services to free up blocks of patrol time for initial investigations. Without explanation, the new procedures may be politically unpopular with local residents. A carefully designed educational program explaining the new procedures must therefore be carried out in the community before the procedures are implemented.

A fourth requirement for effective implementation of the MCI concept is development of procedures for data generation and analysis. Included must be generation of the management information necessary for ongoing assessment of investigative performance. Also included must be policy analysis that can detect need for change from the data collected. This provides both the operating fuel and the running repairs needed to keep the system going.

A fifth necessity is a reward and promotion system within the department generally that recognizes the performance important to management of criminal investigations. Without tangible rewards for excellence, the department will be seen as giving only lip service to the new method.

In addition, the new approach must be ensured continuity by being written into the formal rules and procedures governing investigations. The MCI philosophy and practical application must be integrated into the basic recruit training program and into the initial investigative training program for those assigned to detective duty. Incumbent patrol and detective officers must be encouraged in every available way to make the changes in their work habits required by MCI.

FINE-TUNING THE MCI CONCEPT

Once the new model for management of criminal investigations had been accepted by the United States Department of Justice, it was field tested. On the basis of that experience, the model was revised and expanded but without any basic changes to the five original components.

Assignment of initial investigation responsibility to patrol officers was, for example, not just retained but strengthened. Responsibility for detection of solvability factors was reemphasized, as was the role of the patrol officer in recommending—and in some cases deciding—case closure or continuation. In addition, an increased role, within time available, in the continuing investigation was recommended. To gain more time for that continuing role, a call-screening system was recommended that would set priorities among demands on patrol officers' time, diverting some calls from patrol response to a telephone report taker, to reporting by mail, and to referral to some other agency capable of response. It was also recommended that the patrol officer's initial investigation be guided by a report form designed as follows:

- It uses color coding to highlight the requirement of evidence on solvability factors.
- It lists the factors to be checked in the order in which they should receive attention.
- It lists the factors that require a response on their presence or absence.
- It provides a space for recording the time spent in searching for them.

A patrol supervision system is recommended for return of reports judged to reflect inadequate search for the factors or inadequate documentation of a statement of their presence.

Continued reliance on case screening is also recommended in the revised model. However, it is recognized that decisions on case closing will be affected by local investigative priorities as well as by political and other situational factors. Under the revised model, use of the screening process to audit patrol investigative performance and supervision is advocated as is departmentwide coordination of the screening process. Special attention is paid to improvement of communication with victims by providing a mechanism by which they can forward new information to the police and by a procedure for advising victims in a sensitive way that investigation of the crimes against them has been suspended.

Actual management of continuing investigations is strengthened by a review procedure that limits both the duration of individual investigations and the total degree of effort expended on them. Delegation of responsibility for the continuing investigation to the initiating patrol officer is provided for when success is probable and the officer has time available. Investigator time thus gained can then be used to detect possible links among inactive cases, on major case investigations, for service on special task forces and for establishment of special units such as an anti-fencing squad.

Additional techniques are also recommended for strengthening police–prosecutor relationships by demonstrating the commitment of the department chief to that end by encouraging informal chief–prosecutor communication as well as formal meetings. The chief should, if possible, involve the prosecutor in the design of a new approach to management of criminal investigations. Case preparation procedures should be devised that are consistent with the prosecutor's requirements for initial charging, formal accusation, and conviction of defendants. At a lower level, one officer should be made responsible for liaison with the prosecutor's staff. This officer should be charged with fostering cooperation between the two agencies through such actions as communicating the prosecutor's standards to investigators, assisting in submission of cases for prosecution, assisting investigators in the preparation of specific cases, and obtaining the cooperation of the prosecutor in the training of investigators in case preparation and court procedures. The liaison officer should also try to persuade the prosecutor to provide feedback to investigators about what happened to submitted cases both through informal contacts with investigators and through completing a more formal case disposition form.

Regarding incorporation of an investigations-monitoring component, the revised model recommends a system that provides feedback on how the entire new approach to criminal investigation management is working and how individuals are working within that system. This requires that program and personnel performance measures that reflect stated goals and objectives be devised. It also requires the service of analysts who can suggest needed policy changes. Periodic assessment of the impact of screening and review processes on investigative efficiency will be a central concern of the analysts.

In sum, there has been a new approach to management of criminal investigations widely adopted in the 1980s. Its design was based on empirical research; it was tested in the field. The result has been enhancement of the role of patrol officers by vesting in them important investigative responsibilities. The time of specialist investigators thus saved has been used to improve their role in continued investigations. As pointed out by John Eck, both facets of the new model have proved successful: patrol officers can perform initial investigations well and can also, where time is available, be used effectively in some continuing investigations; specialized investigators can solve cases through effective continuing detective work where success was not preordained. For even greater success, Eck recommends that, in initial investigations,

- Less reliance be placed on victims as a source of information.
- Greater emphasis be put on physical evidence collection when such evidence can be used.
- Greater effort be devoted to canvassing neighborhoods for witnesses.
- Patrol officers use department records more extensively and make greater use of informants.

His recommendations for continuing investigations are that

- Law enforcement agency records be used more effectively.
- Detectives make more extensive use of informants.
- Agencies have policies defining how informants are to be handled.[8]

Although there is continued resistance, particularly among smaller police departments with less well educated officers, the adoption of the MCI concept by larger departments seems to ensure its continued spread.

PORTABILITY OF THE MCI CONCEPT

Given the success that the new model for management of investigations has had with police cases, can it be applied as well to nonpolice investigative settings? Outside the police setting, there will be few investigative units that maintain a patrol force that makes it possible to split the initial and continuing investigations. In such units, the investigator initially assigned to the case now usually carries it through. There is no reason, however, that the initial phase of every investigation should not focus on solvability factors as a basis for screening out unsolvable cases, for pinpointing cases that will be solved with little additional investigative effort, and for selecting those cases in which effective use of additional investigator time may well result in solution.

There also would seem to be every reason in any investigation for the investigator to work closely with whomever will present the information obtained to the decision maker. The case presenter should know better than anyone else what kind of information is needed for a successful presentation and should be willing, if properly approached, to assist in every way possible in the gathering of that information.

By the same token, an effective case-monitoring system would seem to be important in investigative programs of all kinds. The need by supervisors and managers for information both about the progress of individual investigations and about the performance of individual investigators is not unique to the police field.

In short, the MCI concept does seem applicable to investigations in a wide variety of settings other than criminal investigations.

SUMMARIZING COMMENTARY

In the last decade, there has been a major change in the way progressive police departments handle criminal investigations. A new generation of well-educated police managers fostered research on traditional criminal investigation, devised a new five-component approach to meet the weaknesses discovered, field tested that approach, and now uses it widely. At the core of the new method is the assignment of significant investigative responsibilities to the patrol officer first at the scene of the crime. That initial investigation is focused on obtaining evidence regarding specified solvability factors, information that will allow screening of cases into three categories, as follows:

1. Cases that cannot be solved with a reasonable assignment of investigative resources.
2. Cases whose solution is almost guaranteed by information produced by the initial investigation with very little additional effort.
3. Cases that can be solved in a reasonable period of time by the expenditure of reasonable additional investigative resources.

Under the new system, most specialized investigative effort will be devoted to the third category of cases. Management of that effort is a central concern. Its goal is systematic assignment and periodic review of cases. To keep those investigations on track and producing the information required for prosecution, managers must focus on building effective relationships between the police and the prosecutor and his or her staff. The guidance and assistance of the staff is some assurance that the investigative work product will fill their needs. Such management should also assure that the case investigator will be an effective assistant to the prosecutor in preparation for and in presenting the case at trial.

For managers to be effective in their control of the investigative caseload, they must be supported by a case-monitoring system that will allow evaluation of progress on individual cases and of performance by individual investigators.

To be most effective, the new approach to management of criminal investigations requires a supportive environment in the department. Central to this is a strong commitment by top management. Given that commitment, effectively conveyed, the other necessary support elements will follow.

Several of the elements of the MCI concept will apply to investigative units operating in nonpolice settings. Its success thus far merits the necessary adaptation and trial. For better understanding of the kinds of investigative problems with which it must be effective, read Chapter 8, which explores the nature of investigations of street crimes.

STUDY QUESTIONS

1. What is at the core of the difference between the traditional and the new approaches to management of criminal investigations?
2. What is the basis for the claim that the new approach will improve morale in police departments?
3. Why are major crimes against the person and check fraud cases essentially excepted from handling by the new approach?
4. Why are effective training and retraining crucial in any departmental shift from the traditional to the new approach?
5. What is the essential role of top departmental management in adoption of the new approach?
6. What is the greatest difference between municipal police investigative units and those functioning in other settings?

RECOMMENDED ADDITIONAL READING

- Eck, John E. *Solving Crimes: The Investigation of Burglary and Robbery.* Washington, D.C.: Police Executive Research Forum, 1983.
- Greenberg, Ilene, and Wasserman, Robert. *Managing Criminal Investigations.* Washington, D.C.: U.S. Department of Justice, U.S. Government Printing Office, 1979.
- Ward, Richard H. *Introduction to Criminal Investigation.* Reading, Mass.: Addison-Wesley, 1975.

NOTES

1. Georgette Bennett-Sandler, Robert L. Frazier, Donald A. Torres, and Ronald J. Waldron, *Law Enforcement and Criminal Justice: An Introduction* (Boston: Houghton Mifflin, 1979), pp. 36, 51–53.

2. Ibid., pp. 39–51.
3. George C. Wilson, "New Police Powers for Military Weighed," *The Washington Post* (25 June 1985): A6, c.1.
4. See Richard H. Ward, *Introduction to Criminal Investigation* (Reading, Mass.: Addison-Wesley, 1975), pp. 5–7.
5. Ilene Greenberg and Robert Wasserman, *Managing Criminal Investigations* (Washington, D.C.: U.S. Department of Justice, U.S. Government Printing Office, 1979), p. 15, citing Peter Greenwood and Joan Petersilia, *The Criminal Investigation Process*, vol. 3, "Observations and Analysis" (Santa Monica, Calif.: Rand Corporation, 1975).
6. See the initial publication of the model as a "prescriptive package" written by Peter B. Bloch and Donald R. Weidman, *Managing Criminal Investigations* (Washington, D.C.: U.S. Department of Justice, U.S. Government Printing Office, 1975). After testing of the model, the 1975 edition was revised by Greenberg and Wasserman, op. cit. A more recent research project evaluating the model as applied to burglary and robbery was reported in John E. Eck, *Solving Crimes: The Investigation of Burglary and Robbery* (Washington, D.C.: Police Executive Research Forum, 1983).
7. Greenberg and Wasserman, op. cit., pp. 2–3; the discussion that follows also draws on this text.
8. Eck, op. cit., pp. xxiv–xxvii.

TRADITIONAL CRIME INVESTIGATIONS

8

Violations of the traditional criminal law are what many persons regard as the common grist for the police investigation mill. Such crimes have a focused impact. Many of us have been hit personally; those who have not probably have relatives or friends who have been. Fear of traditional crime has an obvious, detrimental impact on the quality of our lives. Most people at some time modify their preferred actions because of that fear. But given that impact, traditional crime—with rare exceptions such as the current problem of traffic in narcotics—remains a minor national problem when compared with issues relating to the economy, national defense, health care, and destruction of our environment. Even in that national context, however, traditional crime is frequently an important local issue. Because it is their primary responsibility, local and state governments must give it their day-to-day attention.

Our substantive criminal law sets the outer limits on acceptable everyday conduct. Clearance rates (measures of how many cases are solved by the police) are low and the rate of perpetrator incarceration for most kinds of offenses are so minuscule as to be almost negligible, but a little bit of enforcement seems to go a long way. Public demand also has little relationship to aggregate statistical information about crime. It is more related to isolated dramatic incidents highlighted by the media and then taken up by those seeking political office. The demand, once apparent, must be met by effective criminal investigation of representative cases that result in prosecution and conviction. On occasion, that demand tips the balance in local elections and results in prosecutors and other law enforcement officials with reputations for having done a good job being elected to high office. The position of public prosecutor has always been an initial stepping stone in successful political careers.

Although coping with traditional crime is an important item on the agendas of municipal police agencies, it is not their only concern. To keep the law enforcement effort against traditional crime in perspective, it must be remembered that the police must also cope with white-collar crime, organized crime, and public corruption as well as maintain minimal public order on a day-to-day basis.

White-collar crime is a relatively new concern. Much of the business and professional conduct that is now prosecuted was regarded, in an earlier day, simply as sharp business practice. "Let the buyer beware" was the slogan of the times. Besides, how could the pillars of the community who were involved be considered criminal? Even if the citizenry had the desire to prosecute, those who would have had to initiate the prosecution were probably under the control of the perceived wrongdoers. But seldom were the white-collar abuses seen at all, much less seen as criminal. Their impact on most people was very indirect in most cases: just a rise in prices that, if noticed, could be attributed to other causes. Whistleblowers, investigative reporters, and other muckrakers have made the public much more aware of the scope and seriousness of white-collar crime. Consumer and environmental protection agencies are now common in both the public and private sectors. Our awareness levels have been raised about the significance of the diffuse and indirect effects of white-collar crime; this has, in turn, led to demands for investigation and prosecution.[1]

Law enforcement must also focus on organized crime, which the public most commonly thinks of as the product of an ethnic Mafia engaged in gambling, loan sharking, narcotics traffic, and prostitution. Its true nature is, however, considerably broader. As Dwight C. Smith, Jr., has pointed out in *The Mafia Mystique*,[2] the term *illicit enterprise* is a better descriptor. Enterprise, all of which is organized, ranges on a continuum from the completely legal to the completely illegal. Illicit enterprise is not limited to any particular ethnic group. It's as American as apple pie. It's also European, Asian, African, and Latin American. Its specialty is sometimes called victimless crime, crime in which the victim is society at large rather than individuals. The individual consumer is usually a willing customer, one who is voluntarily seeking a service or commodity that society believes should not be available.

Public corruption is another serious concern of law enforcement in the United States in the late 1980s. At least an attempt is now being made to meet some aspects of that challenge. More resources are available at all levels—federal, state, and local—for renewed efforts to hold public officials accountable for their stewardship.[3] But the fight is a difficult one, with powerful interests working against its success. However, there does seem to be broader public support now than ever before for the law enforcement effort. Perhaps the Watergate scandal drove home to the public the importance of corruption as seriously undermining the effectiveness of government. As a result, the Federal Bureau of Investigation is devoting an appreciable segment of its resources to the investigation of public corruption. Within the last ten years, offices of inspectors general have also been created in almost every major federal executive department, a move that is now spreading to the states and larger cities. One of the primary responsibilities of the inspector general is the investigation of corruption within the agency of which the office is a part.

It is in this context of competing demands for investigative resources from other areas of law enforcement responsibility that the following general discussion of enforcement against traditional crime is presented. More detailed information is given to all police officers in their initial recruit training and in advanced in-service training courses that focus on criminal investigation.

COMMONALITIES AMONG STREET CRIME INVESTIGATIONS

Fortunately there are many investigative procedures that are common to most investigations of traditional crimes. Several of these have been mentioned earlier in this book in connection with other topics. What follows is a comprehensive outline of an investigative plan suitable for most traditional crimes.

Successful investigations begin with a careful approach to the crime scene. When the investigator, whether a patrol officer or specialist, first receives the assignment, all the then-available information must be obtained.

Is the event still in progress?
How many perpetrators are involved?
Are they known to be armed?
Have shots been fired?

If the crime is in progress, approach to the scene should be coordinated with the backup unit also assigned. Possible approach and retreat routes to and from the scene should be considered. When the vicinity is reached, a careful lookout should be kept for potential witnesses and possible fleeing suspects. No unnecessary noise should be made. All sides of the site should be covered as soon as possible after arrival.

First attention on the scene should be given to any victims, aiding them if injured and obtaining from them information about the event and its perpetrators. If suspected or identified perpetrators are still present, they should be secured and their questioning begun. The scene itself should be secured and all unnecessary persons removed. Potential witnesses should be identified and, as soon as the personnel are available, a canvass of the area, including approach and escape routes, begun to locate and identify additional witnesses. Exercise of the investigator's interviewing skills is important even at this early point.

With the scene secure, the search for physical evidence should begin, either by the investigator or by assisting evidence technicians. Everything done and learned in these preliminary procedures must be recorded as soon and as completely as possible. This is the routine generally followed in reactive investigations, whether made in response to a report or on discovery by patrol officers of crime in progress.

If the investigation is proactive, initiated by the agency rather than in response to a report or complaint by others, it will usually be based on information from a crime analysis unit that has identified what is believed to be a pattern among past crimes in the jurisdiction. That information will include the kinds of targets that are currently the object of criminal attack locally as well as the method (modus operandi) or methods (modi operandi) being used by criminals who are currently active in the jurisdiction. That kind of information gives the investigating officers a specific reason for being where they are and for doing what they are doing. Without that kind of information, the officers can only circulate through the jurisdiction in random patterns hoping that the next crime will occur when they are nearby.

Some of the information on which proactive police work is based may be fed into the crime analysis unit as the result of intelligence. As noted earlier, intelligence (clear, timely, reliable, valid, adequate, and wide-ranging) is the kind of information specifically sought for proactive policing. It may be gathered by a unit of the city police department, by a city crime commission, by a state unit such as the California Bureau of Criminal Identification and Investigation or the New York State Identification and Intelligence System, or by the voluntary National Law Enforcement Intelligence Unit, which was organized in 1956 for the sharing of intelligence information.[4] Important information might also be from the National Crime Information Center operated by the Federal Bureau of Investigation.[5] But there has been considerable disenchantment with police intelligence operations. It is alleged that over-zealousness led to unwarranted invasions of privacy and to attempts to suppress legitimate political criticism and dissent.[6]

At least some of the information obtained by intelligence programs is from covert operations. Their purpose is multifaceted: to discover past, current, or planned wrongdoing; to identify all parties to the events; to identify organizational, operational, or physical weaknesses that facilitate the wrongdoing so that they can be corrected; and to obtain the evidence necessary for prosecution and conviction of the wrongdoers. A method frequently used in such covert, undercover investigations is placement of some person not known locally as a law enforcement officer among the suspected wrongdoers. That person may be a new police recruit who is not yet identified with the department, an investigator borrowed from another department, or a professional undercover agent hired from outside law enforcement.

An undercover investigator sometimes can be inserted into the necessary position with inside cooperation. In other situations, the undercover officer can be put in place, without the knowledge of anyone involved in the enterprise, through the personnel department or other normal channels. Once in, reporting methods and schedules must be worked out. Possible problems that must be avoided include use of procedures by the agent that could result in a defense of entrapment in later criminal prosecutions, the possibility that the agent might join the wrongdoers and furnish them with information about police knowledge of and attempts to suppress the illegal activity, and the possibility that inexperience or lack of professionalism might lead to inappropriate actions by the agent.

When the investigation is complete, the agent might surface and testify against the wrongdoers or might be arrested with them and then released if not required to testify in later legal proceedings. Or, if prosecution is not possible or desired for some reason, the agent might simply be fired or otherwise removed from the scene along with the principal alleged wrongdoers without being identified as an undercover agent.

SPECIAL CONSIDERATIONS OF SPECIFIC OFFENSES

In addition to the commonalities among traditional crime investigations, there are special considerations applicable to the investigation of several separate categories. It is these unique features that lead to pressure for investigators to specialize in certain kinds of investigations. Line managers of the specialists must be well-informed generalists capable of utilizing effectively the varied talents of investigators who have special interests, knowledge, and skills. The specialists, in turn, must also have a broad base of general information that serves as a foundation for this specialized work. When the demand for a particular kind of investigation becomes great enough to take all of the time of an investigator, allowing one to specialize in meeting that demand becomes feasible.

In the balance of this section, discussion focuses on special considerations that must be kept in mind when investigating assault and homicide, sexual assault, larceny, burglary, robbery, arson, drug abuse, and rural crime.[7]

Assault and Homicide

In these cases, one particular source of information is the nature of the wounds suffered by the victim. Those that were inflicted by others must be distinguished from wounds that may have been self-inflicted. Some can be identified as self-defense wounds. Scrapings from beneath the victim's fingernails or blood on the victim's person that is not of the victim's type may indicate that the perpetrator was injured during the assault and the kind of injury probably suffered. Attendance at autopsies and conversations with forensic pathologists, both in formal training sessions and informal discussions, are possible sources of information about wounds. Specialized knowledge about various kinds of weapons that can inflict certain kinds of wounds is also useful for investigators in these cases.

Precautions must be taken and techniques to be used in exhuming and preserving bodies should be learned. When and under what conditions persons at various stages and in different walks of life will commit suicide should also be explored. For example, elderly persons will frequently kill themselves on Monday mornings after one more weekend without a visit from any friend or relative.[8]

Investigators specializing in assault and homicide should also be acquainted with the kinds of assistance that can be obtained from pathologists, psychiatrists, forensic laboratories, and a wide range of nonmedical scientists. Because conviction for assault or homicide can result in a long period of incarceration or the death sentence, investigators specializing in such cases must be well educated and trained for their work to prevent miscarriage of justice. Advanced training is available to assigned officers on an in-service basis.

Sexual Assault

Investigators specializing in sexual assault cases must use an impersonal, professional, clinical approach to the conduct involved while maintaining a sensitive respect for the human dignity of the victims. In most cases of sexual assault, the victims will be women or children, but assaults against men, particularly homosexuals, are becoming more common. Rape of male prisoners by other prisoners has become a serious problem in our jails and prisons.

The victim of a sexual assault frequently will be in psychological shock that may well be more serious than any physical injury suffered. Because of the psychological and physical problems involved, and to make talking easier, victims are increasingly being given the option of talking to either a female or a male investigator.

In these cases, investigators must be particularly knowledgeable about recognition and preservation for scientific examination of body fluids, hair, stains on clothing, and what may appear to be simply debris at the scene of the event. An understanding of human relationships and skill in exploring them during interviews is also important. It is sometimes extremely difficult to persuade the victims to talk about the assaults on them.

Special resources are available for assistance in these cases. The scientific laboratory is important for examination of physical evidence. Psychologists, psychiatrists, psychiatric nurses, and social workers may be helpful.

Specially trained clinic and hospital personnel knowledgeable in the handling of sexual assault cases may be available. Local women's organizations may have special programs of assistance for female victims of rape and other sexual assault. With increasing frequency, female prosecutors will be assigned to such cases.

If a rash of sexual assault cases remain unsolved, community anger and fear may well put significant pressure on the investigators involved. To meet the many demands of these cases, particularly stable and dedicated investigators are required.

Larceny, Burglary, and Robbery

Cases involving theft of personal property have a set of requirements that are different from those of crimes against the person. Larceny can generally be defined as theft that does not involve entering a building (statutory burglary) and that does not involve violence or threats against the person (robbery). (This definition and discussion is of the narrow, traditional offense of larceny; there is a trend in modern statutes toward a broader offense known simply as theft.) Sometimes property reported as stolen has merely been misplaced or lost. On the other hand, recovered stolen property was sometimes never missed or was simply considered lost by the owners. In larceny cases, access to the property alleged to have been stolen is very important. Who was in possession of the property when it disappeared? When and where was it last seen?

Insurance plays a special role in all theft cases. Articles otherwise disposed of may be reported stolen or the extent of an actual loss may be inflated in an attempt to defraud the insurance company.

Negotiable instruments and other documents are frequently involved in larceny cases. Machines such as those used to write checks and to prepare other such documents are important; investigators assigned to these cases should have knowledge about them. Knowledge about systems used by manufacturers to identify automobiles, sound system equipment, boats, motors, bicycles, business machines, and construction and farming equipment is also very useful. Mass-produced items (such as clothing), without identifying serial numbers or other marks, present difficult problems of proof of ownership to theft investigators. Sometimes owner or owner-employee complicity will be involved in theft from warehouses or shipping docks, or by maneuvers such as hijacking shipments.

Computer crime frequently involves theft of money, information, or simply of processing time. The variety among theft cases is almost endless.

Another special aspect of theft investigations is the required knowledge of distribution channels for the stolen goods. Receivers of stolen property (fences) are necessary for the continuation of large-scale thievery.[9] In recent years, police agencies have caught many thieves by setting up fencing or "sting" operations. Such approaches are effective against professional thieves, the presence of whom is another characteristic of the various theft offenses.[10] Assault, sexual assault, and homicide are seldom professional activities. Larceny, burglary, and robbery frequently are. Unless the object stolen is money, there must be a ready market where the loot can be converted into cash. Too little attention has been paid to investigation of fencing operations in the past, but in recent years advances have been made.

Common law burglary is the breaking and entering of the dwelling house of another in the nighttime with an intent to commit a felony therein by the defendant. The intended felony is usually theft. Silver, jewelry, cameras, art works, audio and video equipment, and cash are often targets. Statutes have commonly expanded the definition of burglary to include places other than dwelling houses (such as offices, stores, and warehouses), as well as to modify other requirements of the offense.

This expansion should not be interpreted to mean that residential burglaries have ceased; many still occur. In them (more so than in other burglaries), there is always the danger of simple or sexual assault if the burglar happens to encounter an occupant of the premises. For that reason, and because of the psychological trauma that frequently accompanies violation of one's personal space even in the absence of a face-to-face encounter, residential burglaries result in a high level of anger and fear on the part of householders.

Burglars are frequently professionals and are often armed. Investigators should pay special attention to the means of entry and exit. Tool marks at such locations can be shown to have been made by tools later found in the possession of a suspect. Articles such as clothing, food, and tools may be left at the scene. Insurance also plays a special role in burglary cases. Crime-pattern analysis will sometimes provide information that makes the surveillance (staking out) of a particular location a feasible procedure. There is also, as with larceny, the necessary relationship with a fence or another reliable channel for the disposition of the stolen goods.[11]

Robbery is basically theft through the use of violence or threat of violence. Perpetrators are usually armed and frequently dangerous. They are quite often professionals. Crime-pattern analysis can, as with burglaries, sometimes suggest possible targets that can be staked out. Banks and some other commercial establishments where robbery is a serious risk may have cameras that can produce pictures of the perpetrators. Robbers may choose their targets on the basis of information from persons doing business there. On occasion, they can be identified from equipment such as guns or automobiles used in the robbery and then abandoned. They may be given "bait" money that is marked or a packet of bills that will explode and mark the perpetrator with a dye.

There is always the possibility that hostages will be taken in a robbery attempt that goes wrong. If hostages are taken, negotiation for their release and for surrender by the perpetrators will almost always be conducted by officers who have been specially trained for that purpose.

In all three of the theft offenses described here, assistance can frequently be obtained from special private investigators who are full-time employees of the insurance companies involved or of insurance company trade associations. Such investigators are frequently retired from law enforcement agencies; they are mature, well educated and trained, experienced investigators who have become very skilled in the investigation of certain kinds of thefts. Police investigators should get to know those assigned locally just as they should become acquainted with state and federal investigators who may be of assistance. Even with that help, solution rates in theft cases are very low.[12]

Unlawful Burning

Arson and other unlawful burnings make up another category of crimes that present special problems. Increasingly, those who wish to burn a house or business establishment for the insurance proceeds can hire professionals who burn buildings for profit.[13] Although arson-for-profit is a significant problem, other motives for unlawful burnings by amateurs are also common. Settling a grudge, revenge, and malicious mischief are among them.

Investigators of unlawful burning should know a great deal about how fires get started, whether by accident or on purpose. Electrical origin and spontaneous combustion of oily rags can be detected by characteristic remains. The patterns of how a fire spreads can also be indicative of source. A fire that seems to have started in several locations at once may well have been set. If chemical accelerants were used, traces usually remain. In some fraud cases, the ashes and other remains may indicate that claims about loss of building contents are false. Sometimes an insurance fraud case can be established as a preliminary to conviction for an unlawful burning. Again, specialists in the employ of insurance companies and associations can be most useful. In fraud cases, many of the considerations discussed in Chapter 9 regarding economic crime are relevant.

Drug Abuse

Investigators who specialize in cases of illegal manufacture, possession, distribution, and use of drugs must have knowledge of a wide range of regulations, ordinances, and state and federal laws that attempt to control abuse of drugs. They must also know something of the chemistry of drugs and their impact on the human body. How illicit manufacturing operations are established, how illicit drugs are smuggled into the country, patterns of distribution, and the culture of drug abuse are important to investigators as well. Ways in which legal drugs are diverted to unlawful uses, what steps are necessary to ensure that supplies of drugs seized by law enforcement officers do not find their way back out to the street, and what kinds of persons (such as doctors and nurses) are particularly subject to misuse of drugs are additional areas of interest to drug abuse investigators.[14]

Traffic in narcotics is a police problem that has largely been created by the laws passed to control drug abuse. That means that changes in the law, which occur with some frequency, have a major impact on illicit drug flow patterns. Informants and undercover agents are widely used in drug investigations. Because of the high profits involved, the traffic in drugs draws professionals who are frequently armed and dangerous, a fact that must be kept in mind by investigators specializing in drug cases.

Rural Crime

Automobiles, modern highway systems, and the mass media have made outlying areas much less rural than they were in the past. As urban comforts and services have spread throughout the countryside, they have brought with them much of the wide range of crime that plagues our cities and towns. But in addition, there are offenses that are peculiarly rural. They include theft of farm animals, theft of timber, theft of farm machinery, and illicit cultivation of marijuana.

Animal theft, a modern version of the rustling common in the Wild West, can be by amateurs for private use or by professionals systematically organized on a commercial scale. With professional theft, the method of operation and possible marketing and distribution systems are important to the investigator.

Timber theft is also of increasing importance. In addition to amateur theft for firewood, theft of high-value individual trees, such as black walnut suitable for veneer, takes place. In remote areas, illegal logging operations of considerable scope are possible. They frequently occur on government forest holdings. A relatively new rural crime is the illegal cultivation of marijuana in remote areas, also frequently on government land. Both general and special knowledge and investigative techniques are important to rural crime investigators.[15]

■ SUMMARIZING COMMENTARY

Investigation of traditional crime absorbs the time of a great number of police investigators. One basic common approach can be used in almost all such investigations. It includes getting complete information when the assignment is taken, coordinating with the backup support provided as the vicinity of the offense is reached, aiding the victims, taking suspects and perpetrators into custody, recording information from the parties and witnesses at the scene, securing the scene for search for physical evidence, and beginning the canvass for witnesses.

When the investigation is proactive rather than reactive, it will usually be based on intelligence from a number of sources that, when studied by a crime analysis unit, reveals a pattern in some criminal activity. Knowledge of the pattern makes it possible to anticipate a criminal act, which can then be interrupted as it gets underway. Some of the necessary intelligence will be from informants and undercover agents.

In addition to the commonalities shared by most traditional crime investigations, those of different categories of offenses will have their own unique aspects. Special knowledge, techniques, and skills are useful in the investigation of assault and homicide, sexual assault, theft offenses (larceny, burglary, and robbery), unlawful burnings, drug abuse, and rural crime. Special resources can be called upon in each different type of traditional crime investigation, and differing groups of experts are available for assistance. This need for specialized handling of different offense types leads to specialization among investigators.

As is the case generally, investigators of traditional crimes must be prepared for their tasks. The goal is development of mature judgment-making ability in the investigator. Education and training, learning from the experience of others vicariously, are the most efficient methods for shaping that required ability. Background knowledge comes from a broad education and general life experience; the necessary specific information comes from focused training. Learning how to learn in the formal education and training experience permits lifelong, ongoing professional self-education—a necessity for keeping up-to-date.

In Chapter 9, consideration moves on to police investigation of the economic white-collar offenses that impose such a serious financial burden on residents of the United States and other developed nations.

STUDY QUESTIONS

1. Why have police investigations focused so sharply on traditional crimes?
2. What are some of the factors involved in the shift in recent years to investigation of other kinds of offenses in addition to traditional crimes?
3. What is the basic difference between reactive and proactive criminal investigation?
4. What should be the focus of basic entry-level training for police detectives?
5. How can investigators acquire the knowledge, techniques, and skills required for specialization in specific categories of traditional crimes?

RECOMMENDED ADDITIONAL READING

- David, Pedro R., ed. *The World of the Burglar: Five Criminal Lives.* Albuquerque: University of New Mexico Press, 1974.
- King, Harry. *Box Man: A Professional Thief's Journey.* (As told to and edited by Bill Chambliss) New York: Harper & Row, 1972.
- Klockars, Karl B. *The Professional Fence.* New York: Free Press, 1974.
- Schultz, Donald O., and Norton, Loran A. *Police Operational Intelligence.* 3rd ed. Springfield, Ill.: Charles C Thomas, 1973.
- Wilson, James Q. *The Investigators: Managing FBI and Narcotics Agents.* New York: Basic Books, 1978.

NOTES

1. As representative of the growing literature, see Harold F. Russell, *Foozles and Frauds* (Altamonte Springs, Fla.: Institute of Internal Auditors, 1977); Colin H. Goff and Charles E. Reasons, *Corporate Crime in Canada: A Critical Analysis of Anti-Combines Legislation* (Scarborough, Ont.: Prentice-Hall of Canada, 1978); August Bequai, *White-Collar Crime: A 20th-Century Crisis* (Lexington, Mass.: D.C. Heath & Company, 1978); Leonard I. Kraus and Aileen MacGahan, *Computer Fraud and Countermeasures* (Englewood Cliffs, N.J.: Prentice-Hall, 1979); and Albert J. Reiss, Jr. and Albert D. Biderman, *Data Sources on White-Collar Law-Breaking* (Washington, D.C.: National Institute of Justice, U.S. Government Printing Office, 1980).

2. Dwight C. Smith, Jr., *The Mafia Mystique* (New York: Basic Books, 1975), p. 335; see also National Advisory Committee on Criminal Justice Standards and Goals, Task Force on Organized Crime, *Organized Crime* (Washington, D.C.: U.S. Government Printing Office, 1976); U.S. Congress (Senate) Committee on Government Operations, Permanent Subcommittee on Investigations. *Organized Crime: Stolen Securities*, Parts 1–4. 92nd Cong., 1st sess., 1971; Gay Talese, *Honor Thy Father* (New York: World Publishing, 1971); Vincent Teresa, *My Life in the Mafia* (Garden City, N.Y.: Doubleday, 1973); Norman W. Philcox, *An Introduction to Organized Crime* (Springfield, Ill.: Charles C Thomas, 1978); August Bequai, *Organized Crime: The Fifth Estate* (Lexington, Mass.: D.C. Heath & Company, 1979).
3. Regarding the basic nature of the problem, see Susan Rose-Ackerman, *Corruption: A Study in Political Economy* (New York: Academic Press, 1978), passim. Both management and labor have been corrupters of government officials. On the role of management, see John M. Johnson and Jack D. Douglas, eds., *Crime at the Top: Deviance in Business and the Professions* (Philadelphia: Lippincott, 1978); regarding labor, see Joseph E. Finley, *The Corrupt Kingdom: The Rise and Fall of the United Mine Workers* (New York: Simon & Schuster, 1972).
4. See Robert G. Caldwell and William Nardini, *Foundations of Law Enforcement and Criminal Justice* (Indianapolis: Bobbs-Merrill, 1977), pp. 141 *et seq.*
5. For an early police-oriented view, see Donald O. Schultz and Loran A. Norton, *Police Operational Intelligence*, 3rd ed. (Springfield, Ill.: Charles C Thomas, 1973), passim.
6. See generally Alan F. Westin, *Privacy and Freedom* (New York: Atheneum, 1967). For particular problems in federal and local settings, see James Q. Wilson, *The Investigators: Managing FBI and Narcotics Agents* (New York: Basic Books, 1978), pp. 154–158, and James F. Ahern, *Police in Trouble: Our Frightening Crisis in Law Enforcement* (New York: Hawthorn Books, 1972), pp. 49–55.
7. More detailed information is available in a wide selection of training manuals and textbooks used in the in-service training of police officers in criminal investigation. See, for example, Charles R. Swanson, Jr., Neil C. Chamelin, and Leonard Territo, *Criminal Investigation*, 3rd ed. (New York: Random House, 1984).
8. Information volunteered to the senior author (Richard A. Myren) by active investigators during informal discussion of their cases.
9. See Marilyn E. Walsh, *The Fence: A New Look at the World of Property Theft* (Westport, Conn.: Greenwood Press, 1977), and Karl B. Klockars, *The Professional Fence* (New York: Free Press, 1974).
10. Harry King, *Box Man: A Professional Thief's Journey* (As told to and edited by Bill Chambliss) (New York: Harper & Row, 1972).

11. See Pedro R. David, ed., *The World of the Burglar: Five Criminal Lives* (Albuquerque: University of New Mexico Press, 1974).
12. John E. Eck, *Solving Crimes: The Investigation of Burglary and Robbery* (Washington, D.C.: Police Executive Research Forum, 1983), pp. xvi–xvii.
13. Clifford M. Karchmers, Marilyn E. Walsh, and James Greenfield, *Enforcement Manual: Approaches for Combatting Arson-for-Profit Schemes*, Vols. 1 and 2 (Washington, D.C.: U.S. Department of Justice, U.S. Government Printing Office, 1981).
14. See Samuel F. Levine, *Narcotics and Drug Abuse* (Cincinnati: W.H. Anderson and Company, 1973).
15. See Swanson, Jr., Chamelin, and Territo, op. cit., pp. 520–556.

ECONOMIC CRIME INVESTIGATIONS   9

Economic or white-collar or suite crimes are not as dramatic as individual street crimes may be, but they cost residents of the United States over fifty billion dollars annually.[1] Their investigation presents challenges even to the best intellects among the nation's investigators. They are particularly difficult because they present special legal problems, complicated accounting and auditing problems, and a need for the investigator literally to live with a complex case for a long period of time. This has meant the development of a specialized group of investigators and a specialized group of defense attorneys.[2] Concentrated concern on the part of law enforcement agencies across the nation with economic crime is relatively recent. It may well be part of the same attitudinal shift away from blind encouragement of entrepreneurship at any price that, in this century, has led to manufacturers' being held increasingly liable for dangerous and defective products and to the consumer and environmental protection movements.

SPECIAL LEGAL PROBLEMS

Investigators working on economic crime cases must deal with very complex areas of the law, both criminal and civil. On the criminal side, understanding and differentiating among such concepts as embezzlement, larceny by trick, and obtaining items of value by false pretenses have plagued generations of law students. Some states have attempted to simplify this area of their law by merging these offenses into a single offense of "theft," but courts continue to have problems with the interpretation of those statutes.[3] In addition, statutes proscribing different kinds of fraud have become many, varied, and complicated.

Much of the relevant law is civil, basically regulatory, given teeth by civil penalties and criminal sanctions as well. It concerns such areas as securities, real estate, false advertising, insurance law, and corporate law, to which most criminal investigators are never exposed. There are frequently alternatives to criminal prosecution: civil remedies that are administrative or regulatory, one of which is the injunction against future undesirable conduct.

When criminal prosecution is sought, it is frequently difficult to frame the charges properly. And legal techniques unfamiliar to investigators of more traditional crimes are often used to obtain the necessary information. Discovery is widely used both by the state and the defense; the subpoena duces tecum is also often relied on. Included among the charges is apt to be one of conspiracy, perhaps laid under one of the modern continuing criminal enterprise statutes, such as the federal Racketeer Influenced and Corrupt Organization Statute (commonly referred to as RICO) discussed in detail later in this chapter. Asset seizure and forfeiture have become important tools. All of which means that investigators frequently find themselves intimate bedfellows with lawyers, a relationship that all involved sometimes find difficult to sustain. Several aspects of this close relationship bear further discussion.

As is the case with organized crime, there is no single statute or small group of statutes in the criminal code that defines economic crime.[4] It comprises all kinds of deception, guile, and trickery engaged in for economic gain. Fortunately the conduct that the law seeks to control is easier to describe.

Most economic crimes have five components.

1. A wrongful intent
2. Disguise of purpose
3. Reliance on victim ignorance and carelessness
4. Voluntary victim cooperation
5. Concealment of the violation

The wrongful intent may be to commit an unlawful act, to achieve a purpose inconsistent with the spirit of the law, or to achieve a purpose inconsistent with public policy. Intent may be admitted by the perpetrators in statements to colleagues or, more rarely, to investigators. Or intent may be implied by a course of conduct that includes the other four usual components of economic crime.

Disguise of purpose is usually achieved through misrepresentations either in oral statements or in documents, often both. Proof of this component requires testimony of witnesses to the making and the falsehood of the documents and oral statements.

Offenders prey on victims who they know or have reason to believe have little knowledge about financial matters and dealings. Such persons also frequently fail to protect their financial assets. The combination of ignorance and carelessness sets them up as ideal targets for those who specialize in economic crime.

White-collar thieves move in on the prospective victim with a deceptive setup that leads the victim to believe that inaccurately presented facts are true and will lead to a substantial financial profit. As a result, the victim cooperates voluntarily in the scheme that leads to substantial economic loss.

Once the scheme has run its course, the offender seeks to conceal the fact that fraud has occurred. In many cases the concealment is so skillful as to be permanent; the victim may never realize that it was crime rather than a streak of bad business luck that led to the loss. Or the concealment efforts may seek to achieve only a temporary coverup, to gain enough time for flight and disappearance.

These five basic components are generally crafted by white-collar criminals into four basic categories of economic crime.

1. Personal crime; the individual makes purchases on credit with no intent to pay for them, or is involved with tax evasion schemes.
2. The crime individuals commit in the course of their occupation or profession; common examples are embezzlement or accepting bribes to act in a certain way.
3. Business crime where the illegal action is incidental to the main course of the business; examples might be violation of antitrust or food and drug regulatory laws.
4. Business crime in which fraud is at the heart of the business; fraudulent home improvement schemes and bankruptcy frauds are of this type.

Although investigators may gain insight into the complex legal issues involved in the prosecution of economic crime cases through specialized training and experience, they will also work closely with lawyers who are co-investigators or who are assigned by the prosecutor's office to guide the investigation of cases that they will later prosecute in court.

Those lawyers will be able to determine the precise charges eventually to be lodged. They will be cognizant of administrative and civil actions that can be taken against perpetrators as alternatives or supplements to criminal prosecutions. Their experience both in terms of numbers and types of economic crime cases on which they have worked may well be broader than that of police-based investigators. The lawyers may have been more specifically educated and trained to work with accountants and auditors.

Their influence on the investigation may make it easier to convince the prosecutor that the completed case is viable. This requires a soundly prepared case that highlights the available evidence on each element that must be proved in order for conviction on the offense to be charged. It may also highlight legal action that might be required to obtain missing evidence on a required element or that will strengthen some facet of the case.

Lawyers can also organize presentation of the case to the prosecutor or other prospective presenter in a persuasive manner that convinces the presenter that the desired action (whether administrative, civil, or criminal) can be obtained and that the case is important enough to merit the time and energy necessary for effective presentation to a decision maker. The ideal presentation for that purpose will usually combine oral and written components.

SPECIAL ACCOUNTING PROBLEMS

Accounting involves the recording of financial transactions; auditing involves the analysis of those records, the preparation of summary statements based on the analysis, and certification that the summary statements present an accurate picture of the financial status of the enterprise engaged in the financial activity. Accountants and auditors are accustomed to preparing materials for use in a wide variety of administrative and civil legal proceedings, some, but not all, of which concern alleged violations of law. In the past they have not often been involved in investigations looking toward criminal prosecutions, but that involvement is increasing with the recent emphasis on prosecution of economic crimes.

Frequently their work involves interpretation of ambiguous contract clauses that can result in the shifting of very large costs from one party to the contract to another or among a group of contracts under each of which those costs are treated differently. Such issues may involve amounts that dwarf losses due to outright criminal violations on the part of a contractor or the contractor's employees. In such situations, little concern may be shown for lesser incidental criminal violations that may surface during the audit.

Because they have not generally focused on criminal investigations, accountants and auditors are not usually familiar with the procedures for obtaining and safeguarding evidence in a manner that will ensure its admissibility at a later criminal trial. Even government auditors are not accustomed, for example, to noting when a witness in a custodial situation becomes a suspected criminal violator and, at that moment, to administering a *Miranda* warning. They may also not be aware of how much more evidence must be obtained in criminal cases to meet the state's burden of proof beyond a reasonable doubt than is necessary to prove some element of a civil case by a preponderance of the evidence or even by clear and convincing evidence.

On the other hand, criminal investigators are not usually as skilled as accountants and auditors in discovering and documenting the paper trail that leads to and from every financial transaction. Criminal investigators also lack knowledge of how to document violations of civil law and administrative regulations that may carry a sanction more effective in changing a course of activity than would any criminal penalty provided.

At this writing, there are few persons available who are educated and trained both as accountants or auditors and as criminal investigators. Consequently, teams made up of individuals with one or the other of these backgrounds and a lawyer work together in the investigation of economic crime. Each team member contributes unique expertise to the team capability.

An Office of Inspector General has been established in almost every major federal department since 1970. Preexisting separate auditing/ accounting units and criminal investigation units have frequently been put together in that office. Some of these "marriages" have suffered almost irreconcilable conflict without the possibility of divorce.

Auditors and accountants are heard to say that their required new concentration on criminal fraud as opposed to other important aspects of financial transactions has set their professions back to earlier, less sophisticated and less productive times. Criminal investigators, on the other hand, find themselves swamped with books and documents that bury them for years in one complex investigation. Both speak with some contempt of the "audigator" who is supposed to result from crossbreeding of the two kinds of specialists. But the marriage is slated to endure; perhaps it will become happier when the two specialties can be combined in each team member through appropriate preservice education and training.

Persons with the combined dual background are now appearing, albeit in very small numbers. These people, graduates of special college and university programs that are interdisciplinary in nature, are very much in demand.

INVESTIGATIVE APPROACHES TO ECONOMIC CRIME

Investigation of the five common components of economic crime requires a combination of general and specialized knowledge, techniques, and skills. Intent, for example, must usually be proved by a combination of statements and of inferences drawn from behavior. The investigator must have some specialized knowledge to know what to look for. More general investigative procedures can then be used to obtain evidence of the statements and to document the existence of the behavior.

Statements about criminal intent will usually be made to associates.

They, or persons who overheard the statements being made, must be located and persuaded to testify. Sometimes intent can be inferred from statements of fact that are conflicting or from statements known clearly to be false. An apparent organized program of dissemination of false or misleading information either in documents or by word-of-mouth may justify an inference of criminal intent. The inference of intent may also be made legitimately from activities for which no lawful motive can be discerned, or from repetition of apparently unlawful activity. Actions taken to impede the investigation may also lead to an inference of criminal intent.

Once again, general investigative procedures can be used to show misrepresentation and disguise once the investigator is aware of the kinds of misrepresentations that are necessary to achieve the required deception of the victim. Documents and testimony about oral misrepresentations can be obtained from associates, victims, intended victims who were not deceived, and others who may have been present when the misrepresentations were prepared or made. The use of symbols, names, or language very similar to those of legitimate business operations may be available as evidence of intent to disguise the activity as being engaged in by the legitimate firm.

The component of voluntary victim assistance to the offender also requires that the investigator be familiar with how the scam works. This is necessary to question victims and intended victims about their roles in the proceedings and how they were persuaded to take those roles. Frequently the victims will be reluctant to talk about the ignorance, carelessness in financial matters, or touch of greed that led them to assume the necessary cooperative role. All the interviewing skills of the investigator may be needed to establish the rapport that will make it possible for the victim to talk comfortably about the experience.

Proof of concealment requires knowing what to look for. The mechanism may be simply continuation of the original misrepresentations, or may require fresh new actions. One technique used is to keep the individual loss small so there will be less checkup and fewer complaints. The perpetrators may also make periodic contacts to explain to the victims why original promises are "temporarily" not being kept. Or such a complex business structure may be established that pursuit is very difficult. Early victims may in fact be paid off for a time as a means of getting more victims involved. Sometimes detailed bookkeeping audits of the records are required for the wrongdoing to be detected. Making the illicit enterprise large enough can also sometimes make the size alone seem to vouch for honesty.

One special investigative technique that is useful in unraveling the complex interrelationships among parties to a scheme to defraud is *link network analysis*, in which special charts are constructed to show the connections among events, persons, organizations, and other scheme components. The charts do not focus on time sequences. Link network analysis is actually useful as a general investigative analysis technique with any complicated crime. Exhibit A and Figure 9-1 demonstrate use of the technique in an actual case.[5]

EXHIBIT A
Case Example Using Link Network Analysis

Recently, in a midwestern state, a classic rip-off of a county's welfare assistance program was uncovered. The scheme was conceptually simple. However, the number of people, addresses, and organizations was large, thus requiring a data structure procedure to keep track of the players.

The originator of the fraud was a welfare caseworker, a woman we will call (fictitiously) Miss Johnson. She was aware that to disperse a check to a needy client, two basic pieces of data were necessary: her approval and the name and address of the client. The latter was computer checked to assure that the welfare agency was not sending more than one check to a recipient.

Miss Johnson persuaded each of fifteen of her actual clients to submit four additional claims, making sure that each claim was to a different name and address. She approved each (of the seventy-five) and the computer, after "verifying" each claim, promptly forwarded the checks. Each of the actual clients (let's call one of them Smith) picked up the fraudulently acquired checks at the addresses given on the claim. After paying a "fee" to the individual at the mail drop, each fictitious person endorsed the checks over to Smith, the actual client. Smith cashed his validly derived check at a bank. He cashed the others at a credit jewelry store (let's call the proprietor Ross) for a fee. Ross covered the "fees" as payments on a set of falsely entered debits in his books. He then deposited the checks to his account. When the checks were cleared and returned to the welfare agency, Miss Johnson was informed that all five checks had been paid. She then went out and got her cut from Smith.

The investigator and prosecutor soon found it difficult to follow all the details of names, addresses, and cash flow; they assumed that for someone hearing the case for the first time, following the details would seem nearly impossible. So, they used a *link diagram* to facilitate their investigation and presentation. As an example, see Figure 9-1, which shows Smith as the client. The investigator and prosecutor had documentary or investigative data to support each line on the diagram. The arrows indicate the flow of the checks. In his court presentation, the prosecutor used a series of fifteen overlays (one for each of the clients involved) to show the magnitude of Miss Johnson's criminal conduct.

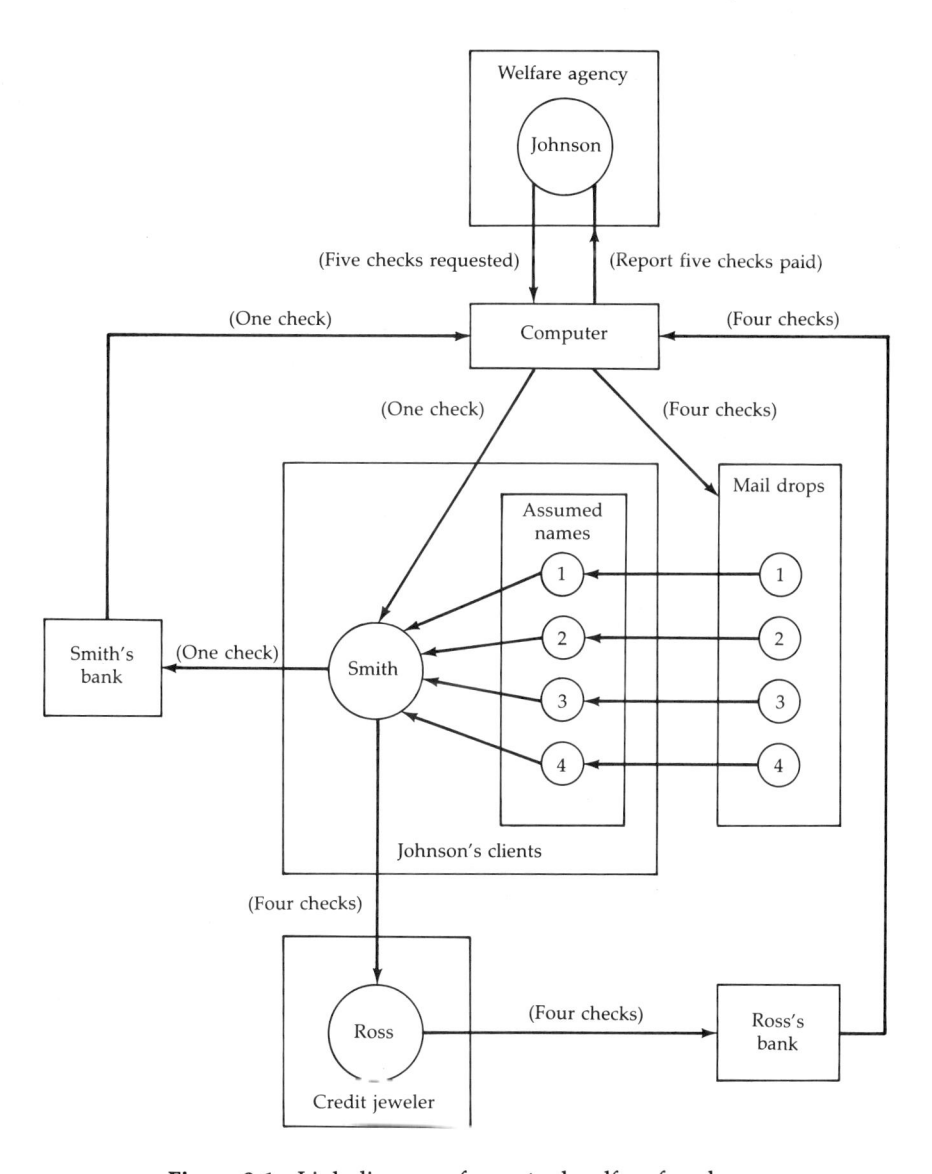

Figure 9-1 Link diagram of an actual welfare fraud case

Another useful analytic technique in fraud and other economic crime cases is construction of *time flow diagrams.* Such diagrams can show the scheme as a series of events connected by related activities. Exhibit B and Figure 9-2 demonstrate use of a time flow diagram. (As in Exhibit A, the names used are fictitious.)

EXHIBIT B
Case Example Using a Time Flow Diagram

On January 15, 1973, the Ace Packing Company, a supplier of meat and poultry to wholesalers and retail markets, found itself short of working capital. John Jones, his father George Jones, and Tom Catlin, the owners of Ace, sought a loan to ease themselves out of difficulties. One of the salesmen employed by Ace, Larry Evans, arranged a loan for them in the amount of $10,000 at an interest rate of 1 percent per week. The loan was advanced by the Carson Trading Corporation, which was owned by Eileen Warren. Ace Packing did not pay off the loan advanced to it by Carson Trading very quickly. As Ace's debt increased, Eileen Warren of Carson Trading insisted upon better financial management of Ace Packing. Her specific demand was that Larry Evans be promoted and made an executive of Ace with broad financial power. The owners of Ace, John and George Jones and Tom Catlin, agreed to this arrangement. On August 3, 1973, Larry Evans was made president of the company with authority to sign all company checks.

Once Larry Evans assumed the presidency and control of Ace Packing, the company began to change its business practices. Whereas Ace had normally made purchases averaging $100,000 per week, several months after Evans assumed his new role in the company, Ace began making large purchases on credit totaling $1.3 million in one six-week period. Many of these purchases were made in response to the demands of new customers brought in by Larry Evans. Among these new customers were the C.W. Meat Company, the Alton Food Corporation, and Walden Poultry Supply, all wholesalers of meat and poultry and all owned directly by Eileen Warren or by one of her relatives. The increases in merchandise purchases by Ace Packing occurred in November and the first two weeks of December of 1973, during the holiday season in which large orders for meat and poultry are not considered unusual.

Combined with new purchasing practices, Ace Packing began to engage in new payment practices. Instead of paying for credit purchases within a seven-day payment period, Ace began delaying payment to those from whom it made purchases. When suppliers began to express concern about nonpayment or delays in payment, Tom Catlin of Ace made personal calls to reassure them that payment would be forthcoming and inducing them to continue forwarding merchandise ordered. In fact, payments were not forthcoming.

Ace's problems in meeting its purchase obligations resulted from two factors: first, in September 1973, a series of meetings involving George and John Jones, Tom Catlin, Eileen Warren, and Larry Evans were held at the behest of Larry Evans. At these meetings, Eileen Warren agreed to greatly increase the C.W. Meat Company's purchases of Ace products. In addition, an informal agreement was made by which Ace would bill C.W. Meat for meat and poultry at only one-half cent per pound over Ace's costs. Thus, because of these agreements, C.W. Meat's purchases for the month of November constituted 60 percent of Ace's sales. The second factor affecting Ace's ability to pay for its orders from suppliers was the fact that the company did not use the payments it received (though rarely covering costs) from C.W. Meat to pay supplier-creditors. This resulted in a large bank balance for Ace. In the last week of November 1973, Larry Evans began making cash withdrawals from the Ace account. By December 6th, these withdrawals totaled $735,000.

During this same period, C.W. Meat Company began modifying the bills it received from Ace so that C.W. Meat was buying meat and poultry for several cents less per pound than Ace was being billed for this merchandise. Both John Jones and Tom Catlin checked these receipts and accepted reductions in payment prices from C.W. Meat.

Ace Packing maintained a corporate bank account at Royal State Bank. When substantially all of Ace's purchases were going to C.W. Meat, C.W. Meat made payment by check to Ace almost upon receipt of delivery. In the beginning, Ace deposited these checks at Royal State Bank and, immediately after each deposit, withdrew the funds. Royal State Bank subsequently refused to permit withdrawals until checks had actually cleared.

On November 22, 1973, at Eileen Warren's suggestion, Evans and John Jones opened another account for Ace Packing at the National Commercial Bank. Both Warren and C.W. Meat maintained accounts at National Commercial. The account at National Commercial was opened with the understanding among Evans, Jones, and bank officials that Ace would be allowed to withdraw funds as soon as the C.W. Meat checks were deposited at National Commercial. As it turned out, the only funds ever deposited in the Ace account at National Commercial were those received from C.W. Meat. Joe Nelson, an agent of C.W. Meat, made all of the deposits to the Ace account.

It was at this same time that Evans began making large cash withdrawals from both Ace accounts. With John Jones, he (Evans) made two large withdrawals from the Royal State Bank. Jones assured bank officials that the money was needed to "pay some trade bills." Jones cosigned the checks. At National Commercial Bank, Joe Nelson introduced Evans to a bank officer as a customer of C.W. Meat. On most occasions Nelson was met at National Commercial by Evans when he (Nelson) made deposits to the Ace account. Immediately after these deposits were made, Evans (with Nelson still present) withdrew from the Ace account almost the precise amount that Nelson had deposited.

By mid-December 1973, the supplier-creditors of Ace Packing were forced to file an involuntary petition in bankruptcy against Ace to seek settlement of their claims for nonpayment. The bankruptcy of Ace appeared to be precipitated by and result from the large withdrawals from Ace accounts made by Evans. The total withdrawals of $735,000 in cash were never found. The state charges that the Ace bankruptcy was a planned and fraudulent one.

The flow of these events is diagrammed in Figure 9-2.

Yet a third investigative procedure of great utility in economic crime cases is a mathematical computation designed to determine the total accumulation of wealth and annual expenditures made by an individual that yields a current net worth estimate. It is based on what is sometimes called the *net worth–expenditures principle*. Although easy to describe, it is sometimes difficult to obtain the data necessary for its application. The investigator finds out what the income from legitimate sources of the target individual has been, calculates what the individual's expenditures have been, and then notes that the excess of expenditures over income were made possible by income from some undetermined source, presumably from the economic crime under investigation. The end result of application of the technique is summarized in Figure 9-3.[6]

Common defenses against the inference that unaccounted-for income came from the illicit enterprise alleged have been that it was gambling income, that the money was not income at all but a gift from some stranger or from a person now dead, and that the money came from previously held capital that had literally been buried rather than kept in a bank. The investigator must be prepared to refute such explanations.

CONTINUING CRIMINAL ENTERPRISE STATUTES

Increasing pressures to do more about economic crime led law enforcement leaders and prosecutors to seek new legal weapons for use in the battle. On the federal level, Congress responded with the Racketeer Influenced and Corrupt Organization (RICO) section[7] of the Organized Crime Control Act of 1970. Its purpose is to provide civil and criminal remedies against the activities of racketeering enterprises engaged in interstate commerce. The interstate commerce requirement is necessary to give federal agencies jurisdiction over what would otherwise be purely a state and local government matter. Some of the states have now enacted similar statutes.[8]

RICO defines racketeering activity in terms of both state and federal law. It includes any act or threat chargeable under state law and punishable by imprisonment for more than one year. The acts or threats may involve murder, kidnapping, gambling, arson, robbery, bribery, extor-

CHAPTER 9 Economic Crime Investigations 141

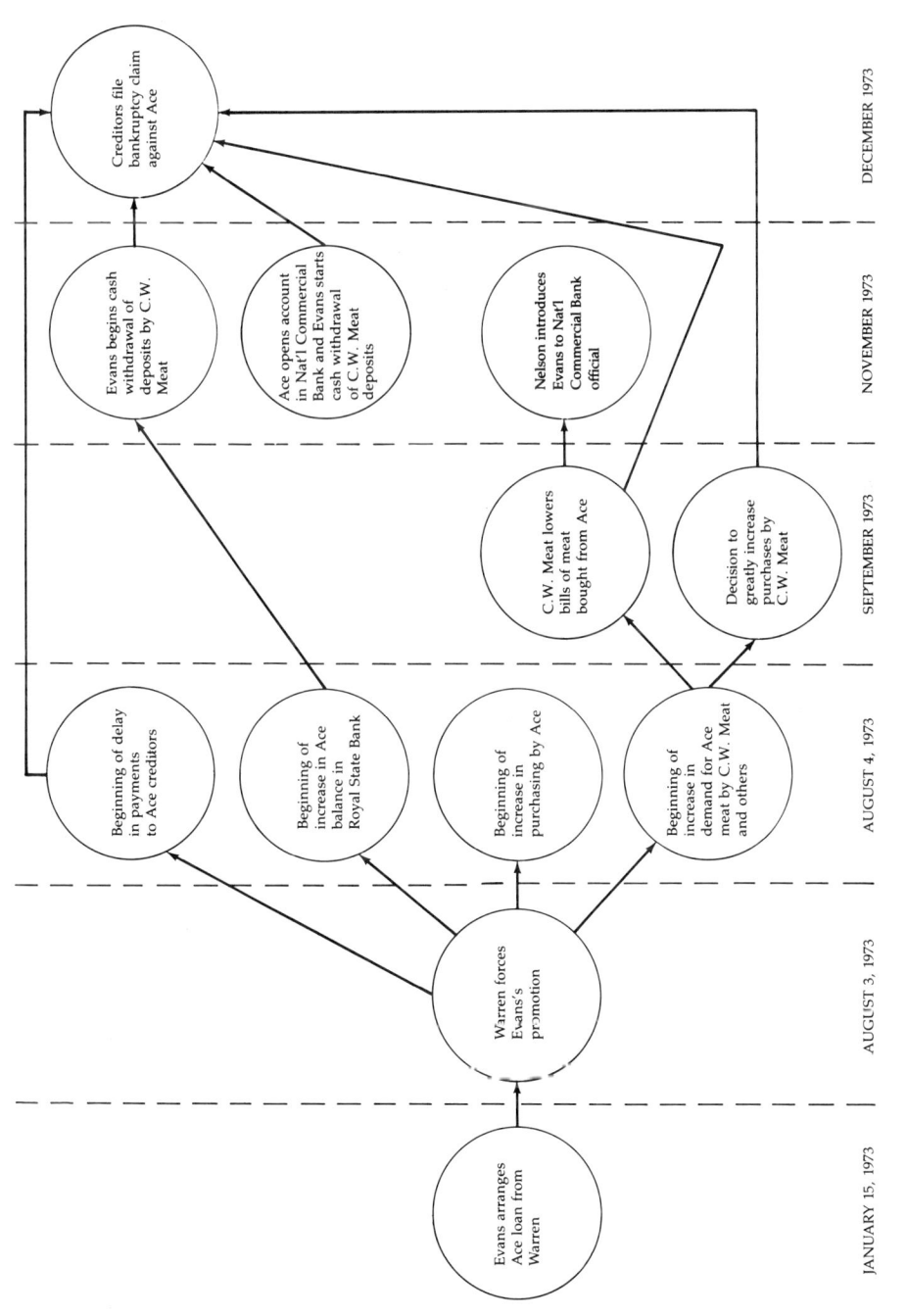

Figure 9-2 Time flow of events in a bankruptcy fraud

	1973	1974	1975	Page No.
FUNDS APPLIED				
Increase in checking account balance	$ 800	$ 2,500	$ 700	13
Increase in savings account balance	1,900	5,300	1,800	23
Down payment on apartment	25,000			25–26
Purchase of securities:				
ABC			20,000	16–19
DEF			5,000	16–19
Purchase of Cadillac (down payment)			5,000	19–23
Purchase of Chevrolet			6,500	19–23
Purchase of diamond ring			5,000	25
Purchase of fur coat			5,000	25
Purchase of travelers cheques		20,000		23–24
Reduction of mortgage on apartment	2,500	10,000	10,000	25–26
Reduction of loan on Cadillac			3,000	20
Total funds applied	$30,200	$37,800	$62,000	
SOURCE OF FUNDS				
Income from furniture store	$16,250	$11,750	$14,375	7
Income from unidentified sources	**$13,950**	**$26,050**	**$47,625**	

Figure 9-3 Source and application of funds

tion, or dealing in narcotics or other dangerous drugs. Racketeering activity also includes any act indictable under a variety of federal laws ranging from bribery, to extortion, to gambling, to actions involving bankruptcy and securities fraud. As is discussed later in this section, this definition has proved broad enough to cover a wide range of economic crime that is incidental to legitimate business operations as well as situations in which the economic crime is the core of a thoroughly illicit business operated by what is popularly called organized crime.

RICO defines a pattern of racketeering activity as two racketeering acts engaged in within any ten-year period. An enterprise is defined as any group of individuals associated in fact, which includes both legal and illegal enterprises. The acts prohibited are use of racketeering income to acquire an interest in an enterprise affecting interstate commerce, use of racketeering income to maintain an interest in an enterprise affecting interstate commerce, or conducting the affairs of any enterprise through a pattern of racketeering activities.

RICO's stiff criminal sanctions of up to twenty years of imprisonment and fine of $25,000 plus criminal forfeitures were upheld as constitutional in 1973.[9] But it also provides for civil remedies that have proved to be very effective. These include orders to persons involved to divest themselves of interests in an enterprise, orders to persons involved restraining them from engaging in any similar enterprise, and orders to reorganize or dissolve an enterprise.

Such orders may be granted as preliminary relief prior to trial. Separate private suits by aggrieved parties for recovery of treble damages are also authorized. These civil remedies have also withstood court challenge.[10] They have been found quite useful because the civil actions from which they result require a lesser standard of proof than do criminal prosecutions, because they take the profit out of the illicit enterprise, and because they close choice channels for distribution of any profit that cannot be reached.

But RICO is not a cure-all.[11] There are weaknesses in and limitations on its use. It is argued that its threat of civil suit is not apt to deter persons who are willing to take the risks of violation of criminal laws. To gain the advantage of the lesser standard of proof, civil rather than criminal contempt proceedings must be used.

The civil action cannot be a criminal prosecution in disguise. There must be a valid and substantial regulatory basis, the proscribed activity must have a genuine adverse effect on the public welfare or commerce, the intent of the legislature must be regulatory rather than punitive, and any punitive effect of the remedy on the defendant must be outweighed by the governmental interest in flexible procedures.

Economic loss to defendants and injury to their reputations, absent forfeitures or imprisonment remedies, are probably not enough to trigger application of the constitutional protections afforded in criminal prosecutions. Because of the Fifth Amendment protection against self-incrimination, the government cannot, in any later criminal prosecution, use testimony obtained from a defendant in an earlier civil action in which the options were to testify or to default. However, the defendant must raise the Fifth Amendment issue in the civil action to earn that protection.

Another restriction on the government is that records obtained in a civil action cannot then be used in a criminal prosecution unless they are of a kind the defendant routinely keeps, unless they involve a noncriminal and regulatory area of inquiry, or unless they are the records of a publicly licensed business.

RICO is being used aggressively against persons alleged to be involved in organized crime.[12] But it is also being used against the abuses of major accounting, banking, insurance, and securities corporations. These organizations seem not to mind traditional civil actions against them but are protesting loudly to Congress their resentment at being classified as "racketeers."[13] One corporation also took its case to the United States Supreme Court. The issue was whether defendants must be convicted of criminal charges before a civil suit for treble damages can be brought. The United States Court of Appeals for the Seventh Circuit, in disagreeing with an earlier decision of the Second Circuit, said:

> RICO may be very broad, but there was nothing careless about its drafting. When Congress deliberately chooses to unleash such a broad statute on the

nation, in the absence of constitutional prohibitions, complaints must be directed to Congress rather than to the courts.[14]

The Supreme Court agreed.[15] As a result, the battle to limit the application of RICO has moved back to Congress. Business interests argue that the statute is being used "to harass and threaten legitimate business."[16] At least one government regulator has agreed with them.[17] Whether Congress will heed their argument remains to be seen. If it does, RICO will serve as an example of a statute that achieved its purpose all too well.

Other federal statutes are also useful to investigators of economic crime. One is popularly known as the Bank Secrecy Act.[18] It has been used in the investigation of illegal laundering of the proceeds from organized and white-collar crime. It is based on the belief that white-collar criminals are using foreign bank accounts to evade capital gains tax on securities transactions, manipulate United States securities markets, violate rules on insider trading, trade in gold, act as depositories for money obtained from illegal activity, and bring money from illegal sources back into the United States as "clean" money loans.[19] The record keeping and reporting requirements of the Act are designed to make it easier for investigators to follow the paper trail that leads to and from economic crime transactions.[20]

There are a number of federal statutes under which assets used in or gained by illegal acts can be seized as forfeited to the United States. Some of the seized assets may be retained by the United States Attorney General for official use by the Department of Justice and may be shared with state and local law enforcement agencies that assisted in the investigation resulting in the seizure.[21] Similar statutes exist at the state level.

SUMMARIZING COMMENTARY

Concentration by law enforcement agencies in the United States on the investigation of economic crime is a relatively new development. It stems from a rather belated realization that white-collar crime not only represents a serious drain on the economy but also results in serious injury to persons. The summer of 1985 saw the first convictions in the history of the United States of business persons for murder when an employee death resulted from unsafe working conditions.[22] The usual investigation, however, involves much less dramatic events.

Investigation of economic crimes presents a special set of legal problems that require close investigator–attorney working relationships. Complex civil and criminal law concepts are involved. Special legal procedures are used to obtain evidence. Civil and criminal sanctions are available. If the investigator is not a law school graduate, an assigned colleague might well be.

Economic crimes generally have five components: a wrongful intent, disguise of purpose, reliance on victim ignorance and carelessness, voluntary victim cooperation, and concealment of the violation. General and specific knowledge, techniques, and skills must be used by investigators in their solution. Among the specialized capacities frequently called upon are those of accountants and auditors. Some investigators have those special capacities; those who do not must seek them out. Among the special techniques used are link network analysis, time flow diagrams, and application of the net worth–expenditures principle.

Special modern statutes at both the federal and state levels are proving to be effective tools in the investigation and prosecution of economic crimes. Among them are the continuing criminal enterprise statutes typified by the federal Racketeer Influenced and Corrupt Organization (RICO) law, which provides civil as well as criminal sanctions. Another is the federal Bank Secrecy Act, which makes it possible to detect and track the laundering of the proceeds from economic crimes. Others are the federal and state laws authorizing the seizure and forfeiture of assets of enterprises engaged in economic crime. Some of those assets can be used to increase the resources of law enforcement efforts against economic crime.

But, for criminal investigators, perhaps the greatest difference between economic and traditional crime cases is the need in the former to live with a single complex case over a long period of time. The case will typically involve not one event with an unknown perpetrator, but a suspect who must be traced through a complicated series of events occurring over a long period of time. These cases require diligence, patience, and persistence. Passage of time is not important as a solvability factor. It is this exclusive involvement with a single case over months and even years that distinguishes economic from traditional crime investigations and from the administrative and legislative agency investigations discussed next in Chapter 10.

STUDY QUESTIONS

1. What are the characteristics of economic crimes that require close cooperation of investigators with lawyers?
2. Why are accountants and auditors very important to such investigations?
3. How can an investigator prove the five usual components of economic crime?
4. How are link network analyses and time flow diagrams used in these investigations?

5. Why is the net worth–expenditures principle sometimes called the seventh basic investigative technique?

RECOMMENDED ADDITIONAL READING

- Blakey, G. Robert, Goldstock, Ronald, and Rogovin, Charles H. *Racket Bureaus: Investigation and Prosecution of Organized Crime*. Washington, D.C.: U.S. Department of Justice, U.S. Government Printing Office, 1978.
- Edelhertz, Herbert, Stotland, Ezra, Walsh, Marilyn, and Weinberg, Milton. *The Investigation of White-Collar Crime*. Washington, D.C.: U.S. Department of Justice, U.S. Government Printing Office, 1977.
- Somers, Leigh Edward. *Economic Crimes: Investigative Principles and Techniques*. New York: Clark Boardman Company, 1984.
- U.S. Department of Justice, Criminal Division. *Investigation and Prosecution of Illegal Money Laundering: A Guide to the Bank Secrecy Act*. Washington, D.C.: U.S. Government Printing Office, 1983.

NOTES

1. See Leigh Edward Somers, *Economic Crimes: Investigative Principles and Techniques* (New York: Clark Boardman Company, 1984), passim.
2. See Peter H. Stone, "Law Firms No Longer Scorn White-Collar Criminal Cases," *The Washington Post* (3 November 1985): F7, c.1.
3. See, for example, Fla. Stat. §§ 812.005–812.14 (1985).
4. This discussion relies on Herbert Edelhertz, Ezra Stotland, Marilyn Walsh, and Milton Weinberg, *The Investigation of White-Collar Crime* (Washington, D.C.: U.S. Department of Justice, U.S. Government Printing Office, 1977), passim.
5. Exhibits A and B and Figures 9-1 and 9-2 are drawn from Edelhertz, Stotland, Walsh, and Weinberg, op. cit., pp. 83–88.
6. The technique is fully illustrated in Richard A. Nossen, *The Seventh Basic Investigative Technique*, originally a separate publication but now most readily available as an appendix to Edelhertz, Stotland, Walsh, and Weinberg, op. cit., pp. 35 et seq.
7. 18 U.S.C.A. §§ 1961–1968 (1970).
8. See G. Robert Blakey, Ronald Goldstock, and Charles H. Rogovin, *Racket Bureaus: Investigation and Prosecution of Organized Crime* (Washington, D.C.: U.S. Department of Justice, U.S. Government Printing Office, 1978), p. 142, n. 65.
9. United States v. Amato, 367 F. Supp. 547 (S.D.N.Y. 1973).

10. United States v. Cappetto, 502 F.2d 1351 (7th Cir. 1974), *cert. den.*, 420 U.S. 925 (1975).
11. This discussion relies on Blakey, Goldstock, and Rogovin, op. cit., passim.
12. See as examples, Mary Thornton, "Nine Charged With Mafia Activities," *The Washington Post* (27 February 1985): A1, c.1; and Margaret Hornblower, "Three Mafia Trials Titillating New York," *The Washington Post* (18 November 1985): A1, c.1.
13. "Businesses Fight RICO Antifraud Law," *The Washington Post* (16 October 1985): A21, c.4.
14. Sedima, S.P.R.L. v. Imrex Co., _____ F.2d _____ (1985); Al Kamen, "Justices to Review Use of Anti-Racketeer Act," *The Washington Post* (15 January 1985): A4, c.1.
15. Sedima, S.P.R.L. v. Imrex Co., _____ U.S. _____ (1985); Stephen Labaton, "High Court Upholds Use of Organized Crime Law in Fraud Suits," *The Washington Post* (2 July 1985): A4, c.1.
16. Michael Abramowitz, "Racketeering Law's Scope Is Debated: Harassment Claimed," *The Washington Post* (25 July 1985): E3, c.1.
17. "Inside the SEC: Reforming RICO," *The Washington Post* (29 May 1985): A19, c.1.
18. The Bank Records and Foreign Transaction Act, Titles I and II, Public Law No. 91-508, 26 October 1970.
19. Criminal Division, U.S. Department of Justice, *Investigation and Prosecution of Illegal Money Laundering: A Guide to the Bank Secrecy Act* (Washington, D.C.: U.S. Government Printing Office, 1983), p. 4.
20. See James L. Rowe, Jr., "Bank Regulators Track Paper Trails in Search of Laundered Transactions," *The Washington Post* (3 March 1985): F5, c.1.
21. See "The Attorney General's Guidelines on Seized and Forfeited Property," 50 Fed. Reg. 24052 (7 June 1985).
22. See "Murder in the Front Office," *Newsweek* (8 July 1985): 58.

LEGISLATIVE AND ADMINISTRATIVE INVESTIGATIONS 10

Investigators play a wide variety of roles in legislative and administrative proceedings. In some situations, their work in these settings is quite similar to what it is in civil cases and criminal prosecutions: it is aimed at producing information about the involvement of legal persons (individuals and organizations) in particular dramatic events. But in many legislative and administrative matters, information must be generated about issues or problems arising from a series of events. What is important is not reconstruction of the past for the purpose of assessing responsibility or culpability, but as a basis for the establishment of guidelines for future conduct in similar situations. Those guidelines may be either new legislation or new administrative rules and regulations.

In addition to their rule-making function, legislatures and administrative agencies do, however, on occasion conduct investigations aimed at fixing responsibility for specific past events. This happens less frequently in legislative than administrative agency settings. Perhaps the most dramatic legislative investigations of this type are those culminating in impeachment trials of state governors or the president of the United States. Somewhat less dramatic but more frequent are hearings aimed at disciplining or expelling a member of the legislative body or a federal or state official.

Administrative agency proceedings that look to fixing responsibility for specific past events concern violations of statutes and regulations. They usually end with modification or revocation of licenses or other rights or privileges conferred in the past, in orders to cease and desist from undesirable conduct, in assessment of monetary penalties, in referral of the matter for criminal prosecution, or in warnings that continuation of the conduct will result in one or more of these punitive actions.

These two kinds of legislative and administrative proceedings are not completely separate, however. Frequently the fixing of responsibility for a dramatic past event will trigger a broader consideration of the general issues raised by that event; this will in turn result in new legislation or new administrative rules and regulations.

In the performance of these functions, legislatures and administrative agencies employ large numbers of persons to produce, organize, analyze, and present the information required for decision making. Sometimes these employees are called investigators, sometimes researchers, and sometimes they have more general titles, such as committee staff members. Their function, however, is investigative. To perform that function well, they must possess the same kinds of knowledge, techniques, and skills as investigators in other settings. For that reason, their basic education and training should be the same.

Past event investigations in these settings are basically the same as in cases where the investigative work product will be used in criminal prosecutions and civil law suits. But there are special considerations that are pertinent to investigative work in these settings. The following sections discuss those considerations in each of these unique environments.

INVESTIGATION FOR LEGISLATIVE ACTION

Legislatures do their work primarily through committees, which may be either standing or ad hoc.[1] A standing committee handles a segment of the legislative business on a permanent basis. An ad hoc committee is appointed on a temporary basis to work on a particular current problem. Both kinds of committee can handle either of the two types of investigations mentioned: a specific dramatic event or the issues raised by a series of events. Investigators assigned to investigation of a dramatic event face a task very similar to work on criminal cases and on cases expected to culminate in civil law suits. Investigators developing information on issues about which legislation is pending find themselves in a less familiar environment. In most cases, the information gathered will be presented at legislative hearings that are a part of the political process.

Legislative hearings have as their purpose the acquisition of information that can be used in the legislative process. However, such hearings can differ markedly in their nature. It is sometimes difficult to tell by whom they are arranged. Ostensibly they will be organized by the staff of the committee holding the hearing; frequently, this will in fact be the case. Sometimes, however, they will be orchestrated by the personal staff of a committee member who has a special interest in the topic concerned. Or it may be a senator or house member who has introduced a bill on the topic concerned. In any of these cases, the actual moving spirit behind the hearing may be a consultant or some interested citizen who has easy access to a key legislator or committee staff person. In some cases, the hearing may actually be arranged by some special interest group that has the necessary access. The ultimate impact that the hearing may have on eventual legislation may well vary depending on who its designers are. These varying political situations may well complicate the work of a participating investigator, but the basic task of accumulating and presenting relevant evidence remains the same.

Just as the moving force behind a legislative hearing may be difficult to identify, so it may not be obvious what the purposes are of those who appear and testify at the hearing. That purpose may be the straightforward one of educating the committee members, and through them the other legislators, by stating on the record reasons for support for or opposition to a pending bill. But the basic purpose of a presentation on behalf of an organization also may be to enhance the credibility of that organization with its members or to obtain favorable attention from the press. The ultimate purpose might be to strengthen the position of the executive director and staff of the organization.

But investigative work product may also be used to influence the legislative process in other ways. Presentation at a hearing may not actually be as effective as direct private presentation of the information to legislators or their key staff people. Where access exists, the information can be used as the basis for drafting specific legislative language for submission as an original bill or as suggested amendments to already pending legislation. Or the information can be provided to a legislator to support a desired position on the issues either in a hearing or on the floor. Where direct access to legislators and their staffs is not available, the information can be supplied to the organization's members who can then use their influence directly with their representatives. An organization might also use the information developed by its investigators to interest other organizations in forming a coalition—with greater influence on a legislature than a single organization. Just how effective presentation of the evidence was by whatever channel may have been chosen will be revealed at committee markup (revision) of the bill and during debate on the floor.

It is these political considerations that set off the work of investigators whose product is presented to legislators from the work of investigators in other settings. The essential task remains the same; only the environment is different.

INVESTIGATION FOR ADMINISTRATIVE ACTION

Administrative agencies have a rule-making function that is very similar to the basic legislative function. It is, in fact, a delegation of power by the legislature that created the agency. In furtherance of that function, there has developed an administrative power to investigate that parallels that of legislatures. The authors of one of the most widely used administrative law textbooks begin their chapter on the topic with this statement:

> We have already developed the theme that the lifeblood of the administrative process is the flow of fact, the gathering, the organization, and the analysis of evidence. Nothing in the law, perhaps, better illustrates the enormously increased reach of government in the last fifty years than does the broadening of the power of administrative investigation.[2]

That power has not gone without challenge. According to another scholar, the traditional administrative law course as taught in the law schools covers three broad areas: "the extent of legislative authority to delegate power to administrative agencies,...the nature of judicial review of agency action...[, and] analysis of the formal aspects of agency procedure."[3] Much of the early controversy has been settled by enactment of the Federal Administrative Procedure Act and by similar state acts.[4] It is within the context of requirements established by such acts that investigators for administrative agencies do their work.

Because it is typical of such laws, the provisions of the federal Administrative Procedure Act (APA) will be summarized in this section. That act governs the exercise of two primary powers of administrative agencies: their power to make, alter, and repeal rules and regulations; and their power to hold adjudicatory hearings on alleged violations of rules and regulations. In furtherance of its purpose to improve and strengthen the process, the APA requires that a general notice of any proposed rule making be published in the *Federal Register*. The agency must then give interested parties an opportunity to participate as a matter of right by submitting written data. Whether oral argument is allowed at an open hearing is left to the discretion of the agency. When a proposed rule has been drafted, it must be published in the *Federal Register* at least thirty days before its effective date.

In the adjudication of alleged violations, the APA requires that the agency grant defendants a fair and open hearing before an impartial and competent tribunal. Notice must be given to the defendant that includes the time, place, and nature of the hearing; the legal authority and grant of jurisdiction under which the hearing will be held; and a summary of the facts alleged and of the law to be applied. Any party to be affected must be given the opportunity to confront any adverse witnesses and to present oral and written evidence on that party's behalf. After conducting the hearing, an administrative law judge will make findings of fact and recommend a decision to the responsible agency leadership. In making its formal decision, the agency may adopt, alter, or reverse the recommendation.

Investigations in the administrative setting present the same basic challenges to investigators as work elsewhere. But again, the environment does make a difference, as does the subject matter. Because administrative agencies focus primarily on regulation of business and industry, investigators may find themselves working closely with lawyers, accountants, and auditors just as they do in economic crime cases.

RELEVANT FEDERAL REGULATIONS AND STATUTES

In addition to having a thorough knowledge of the Administrative Procedure Act, investigators working for those in the private sector whose interests may be affected by federal legislation or administrative action should be aware of other federal statutes and regulations governing such activity. Among these provisions are:

- Federal Regulation of Lobbying Act
- Foreign Agents Registration Act
- Ethics in Government Act
- Department of Justice Standards of Conduct
- Federal Criminal Code sections such as those on Bribery and Graft[5]

These statutes and rules generally cover relationships of government officials with those who seek to influence their actions.

Another kind of federal statute of importance to investigators seeking information is the Freedom of Information Act (FOIA).[6] The Act was passed originally in 1966 and amended extensively in 1974 after the Watergate scandal. It covers all federal executive agencies and most private corporations that are wholly or substantially federally funded. In addition, some states now have similar acts. Anyone can use the Act, but reporters and historians probably resort to it most frequently. The fees attached to production of the information can be stiff. The request process is formal, with provision for appeal in cases of denial.

Although all documents are covered, there are nine exceptions under which an agency may—but is not required to—refuse to furnish the information.

1. The first exception is based on national security. It provides that a request for information may be refused if release would cause some identifiable "damage" to the national security. Usually the information refused will have been classified. Under the classification system established in 1982, the category of *Top Secret* is reserved for information, the unauthorized disclosure of which reasonably could be expected to cause "exceptionally grave damage" to the national security; *Secret* is information that would cause "serious damage"; and *Confidential* information is that which would cause "damage."[7] If a challenge to the decision not to

release the information results in a court case, the judge will read the documents requested in private before coming to a decision.

2. The second exception is for internal agency rules, which Congress decided are simply not of any public interest. Employee parking rules or cafeteria regulations would be typical exceptions of this type. It is uncertain whether general staff manuals would be covered by this exception. The test seems to be whether release would aid in circumvention of regulations or laws.

3. A catchall provision covers information required to be kept secret by other laws where secrecy is clearly required (such as under the Census Act) and that establish criteria for what may be withheld or specify what is to be withheld (such as names, titles, salaries, and number of persons employed by the National Security Agency; certain tax information; and certain patent application information).

4. Trade secrets supplied to the government by a business (such as customer lists, secret formulas, and financial information) are excepted when it can be said that, if revealed, they would hurt the company's competitive position or would impair the government's ability to obtain similar necessary information in the future. This exception does not apply if the government obtained the information from outside sources rather than from the business itself.

5. Executive department privilege exempts working papers, policy drafts, studies and reports used to determine agency policy, and any similar "pre-decisional" documents from required release. This exception does cover documents arising from the attorney–client relationship: any attorney work products, and particularly documents that would reveal the underlying theory and planned trial strategy for pending court cases. It does not cover purely factual portions of any such documents.

6. The sixth exception protects personal privacy. It covers appropriate pertinent documents in personnel, medical, and job evaluation files but not any unrelated documents that might be in such files. Applicants for government contracts are deemed to have waived this right to privacy. The provision allows a balancing test between public need for disclosure and the privacy interest.

7. Some of the files of law enforcement agencies are also excepted. Situations covered are those in which disclosure of the requested information would jeopardize an ongoing investigation where there are concrete prospects of an enforcement proceeding resulting. In claiming the exception, the law enforcement agency must prove that the requested information came from investigative records. The exception will be granted if the law enforcement agency can show that disclosure would interfere with planned enforcement proceedings; deprive a defendant of a right to a fair trial in an impartial adjudication; constitute an unwarranted invasion of personal privacy; disclose the identity of a confidential

source or information furnished entirely by a confidential source; endanger the physical safety or lives of law enforcement personnel; or disclose investigative techniques or procedures that are not generally known. The law enforcement exception, although broad, is certainly not complete. Federal investigators should be aware of the fact that their reports may, in many instances, be available to the public under the FOIA.

8. Some bank reports made to government agencies are covered in the exceptions. Records relating to the examination, operation, or condition of banks where disclosure would undermine confidence in a given bank or in the federal banking system are covered. This exception is used primarily by Federal Reserve Banks and by the Federal Home Loan Bank Board.

9. The last of the nine exceptions is for some oil and gas well data. It allows rejection of requests for information about the location of oil and gas wells of private companies to keep that information out of the hands of speculators. This exception is used only on rare occasions, primarily by the Interior Department, the Federal Energy Regulatory Commission, and the Federal Power Commission.

Despite the nine statutory exceptions, the Freedom of Information Act can serve investigators as a useful source of information. It is, however, a two-edged sword: it can also be used by opposition investigators, as can the Federal Privacy Act.[8] The purpose of the Privacy Act is to make it possible for private individuals to discover what the federal government knows about them and to correct any errors in that information. But in order to get the information, the requesting individual must first furnish information. An investigator's client may wish to use the Privacy Act in connection with a pending action against the government or in defending an action by the government.

The letter of request must provide your full name, date of birth, place of birth, history of foreign travel, home address, and information on any government employment and participation in political groups. It must also be accompanied by a copy of your birth certificate or driver's license to prove your identity. The information provided assists the agency in determining which of its files must be searched and protects against receipt of private records by impostors. The request should specify that both central and field office files be searched. The Federal Bureau of Investigation, which receives a very large number of requests under the Privacy Act, requires that the request be sent directly to the appropriate field office. There is no charge under the Act for search time. All requests must be acknowledged within ten days and filled as soon as possible.

The Privacy Act also contains an important substantive law provision. It prohibits federal agencies from maintaining any records "describing how any individual exercises rights guaranteed by the First Amendment" unless the agency is specifically authorized by law to do so.[9] This makes it illegal for federal agencies to keep files on political dissenters.

SUMMARIZING COMMENTARY

Investigators work in many varied settings in both the public and private sector. This chapter concerns primarily two of the less well known public settings: legislatures and administrative agencies. It also discusses some federal statutes of specific interest to investigators, whether they work for public or private agencies.

Some of the work of legislative and administrative agencies is much like that in other settings, focusing on specific past events and the roles of individuals in them. But much of their work is directed at the exposition and clarification of problems or issues arising out of a series of past events and looks toward laws and regulations that will govern such events in the future.

Generally speaking, investigators working for legislative bodies and administrative agencies must possess the same intellectual bent, draw on the same kind of general body of knowledge, use many of the same techniques and procedures, and show the same kind of dedication required of investigators working in other environments. They, however, must also be concerned about political issues and processes that may be important to their work. They must be thoroughly knowledgeable about the procedures of their employing agency, whether legislative or administrative, which may well be considerably different from court procedures. Their work requires knowledge of economics and of the business and industrial world. And they work on a broader variety of cases in many legislative and administrative investigative positions.

Doing investigative work for a legislature or administrative agency may require more team work with colleagues of different backgrounds and expertise than some other investigative positions require. In that respect, this kind of investigation is more similar to investigation of economic crime than of more traditional crime. And, like investigation of economic crime, it requires at least some knowledge of areas of the law that are not of concern to other investigators. For example, to an investigator employed by an administrative agency, the rules of the Administrative Procedure Act may well be more important than those of civil or criminal procedure.

In addition, a wide variety of special federal statutes may be of importance to investigators, in both the public and private sectors, whose work product will be presented to legislative and administrative agencies. Among these are the Federal Regulation of Lobbying Act, the Foreign Agents Registration Act, the Ethics in Government Act, and the Department of Justice Standards of Conduct along with similar standards of other agencies. The Freedom of Information Act and the Privacy Act may also have special significance in specific situations.

Although perhaps not as extensively developed, the environments of the state legislative and administrative agencies are similar to that of federal agencies. At this level, highly industrialized states present more complex challenges than the more rural agricultural states.

Investigators can find varied and challenging careers in legislative and administrative settings. Their preparation must be essentially the same as that of other investigators, but each of these special environments makes its own demands. In all settings, however, the investigative work product must be organized and analyzed before it can be utilized. Part Three of this book (Chapters 11 and 12) discusses those processes.

STUDY QUESTIONS

1. Is there a significant difference between investigating a single past event and investigating the issues or problems raised by a series of past events? If so, explain that difference.
2. How can political considerations legitimately affect utilization of investigative work product in a legislative setting?
3. Given investigatory documentation of past wrongdoing, what kinds of considerations might lead an administrative agency to seek civil rather than criminal remedies?
4. What effect might there be on investigative procedures if the investigative work product will be used not to punish past wrongdoing but to prevent wrongdoing in the future?
5. What are the nine exceptions to the Federal Freedom of Information Act? For each, state whether or not you believe it is justified and why.

RECOMMENDED ADDITIONAL READING

- Heard, Alexander. *State Legislatures in American Politics.* Englewood Cliffs, N.J.: Prentice-Hall, 1968.
- McNeil, Mary L. *How Congress Works.* Washington, D.C.: Congressional Quarterly, Inc., 1983.
- Rabin, Robert L. *Perspectives on the Administrative Process.* Boston: Little, Brown, 1979.

NOTES

1. Malcolm E. Jewel, *The Legislative Process in the United States* (New York: Random House, 1977), passim; on state legislatures, see Wilder Crane,

Jr., and Meridith W. Watts, Jr., *State Legislative Systems* (Englewood Cliffs, N.J.: Prentice-Hall, 1968), and Alexander Heard, *State Legislatures in American Politics* (Englewood Cliffs, N.J.: Prentice-Hall, 1968); on Congress, see Mary L. McNeil, *How Congress Works* (Washington, D.C.: Congressional Quarterly Inc., 1983), and Michael D. Wormser, ed., *Congressional Quarterly's Guide to Congress*, 3rd ed. (Washington, D.C.: Congressional Quarterly Inc., 1982).
2. Louise L. Jaffe and Nathaniel L. Nathanson, *Administrative Law: Cases and Materials*, 3rd ed. (Boston: Little, Brown, 1968), p. 722.
3. Robert L. Rabin, *Perspectives on the Administrative Process* (Boston: Little, Brown, 1979), p. 2.
4. See the Administrative Procedure Act, 60 Stat. 237 (1946), as amended, 5 U.S.C. § 552a et seq.; for other acts, see, for example, the Uniform Law Commissioners' Revised Model State Administrative Procedure Act, approved at the Annual Conference, July 31–August 5, 1961, in Jaffe and Nathanson, op. cit., p. 1102.
5. See Law and Business, Inc., *Effective Washington Representation: Strategies and Techniques before Agencies, Departments and Congress*, 2nd ed. (New York: Harcourt Brace Jovanovich, 1981), passim.
6. 5 U.S.C. § 552a (1974), as amended. For a sample request letter under FOIA, see Louis J. Rose, *How to Investigate Your Friends and Enemies* (St. Louis, Mo.: Albion Press, 1981), pp. 128–129.
7. 3 C.F.R. § 167 (1982).
8. 5 U.S.C. § 551 et seq. (1966).
9. Ibid., § 552a.

PART THREE

ORGANIZATION AND ANALYSIS OF THE INVESTIGATIVE WORK PRODUCT

> A patient pursuit of facts, and cautious combination and comparison of them, is the drudgery to which man is subjected by his Maker, if he wishes to attain sure knowledge.
>
> Thomas Jefferson
> *Notes on the State of Virginia*

ORGANIZATION OF INVESTIGATIVE INFORMATION

11

Organization of the investigative work product has two principal purposes: preparation of the material for analysis and determination of the direction that the investigation should take from then on. Preparation for analysis includes evaluation of whether each item of information gathered will be admissible in the intended subsequent legal proceeding. The organizational effort begins with the investigation and continues until the case is closed. Without a predetermined but flexible system for organization of the collected data, investigators would soon be swamped with masses of disordered and undigested information.

ORGANIZATIONAL COMPONENTS

Central to the organization of any investigation is the data collection scheme. That scheme must specify who is responsible for obtaining what information, when, and how. One investigator working alone may bear the entire load. If a team is involved, the supervising investigator will make specific assignments. In some cases, the "how" will be a specified routine for a category of investigations. In others, it will be a carefully worked out method for that particular case. In still others, it will be left to the discretion of the responsible investigator. The collection scheme must also specify when and how the information is to be transmitted from the field investigators to the case coordinator. The formality of the scheme will depend on the seriousness of the investigation, whether it is for private or public purposes, and whether the information is being gathered for use in a particular kind of legal proceeding.

One of the primary tools in the assembling of investigative information is the system of running case notes, often called field notes, used by the individual investigator. Three objectives are of overriding importance in making field notes: they must be complete; they must be accurate; and they must be understandable, not only to the maker, but also to third persons who may have occasion to consult them at some later date. Experts frequently recommend that a small loose-leaf notebook be used for the initial recording of information.[1] The notebook should be filled, page by page, and then filed in a safe but accessible place. As soon after the field notes are made as is possible, the information should be recorded in more formal, differently organized reports. Many investigators are provided standard forms for that purpose by their employing agencies. Where such forms are not available, the investigator should use any consistent and logically organized format.

All of the information as obtained must be channeled to the individual responsible for the coordination and direction of the investigation. In a complicated case, the supervisor may well direct that a variety of other files be constructed from the file of individual investigative reports. These new files would be organized to aid analysis. Among them might be files containing information about all persons who figure in the case. Under each name, there would be recorded aliases; a description, with photograph if available; any identifying characteristics; home and business addresses; and a narrative statement of how the person figures in the investigation. A similar file might be built around events, recording for each when and where it occurred, who was involved, and how the event is of importance to the case. An index should be maintained for each separate file to facilitate its use.

Visual aids, such as photographs, sketches, charts, and diagrams, may also be created. Items of physical evidence must be received, receipts given for them, and the items put in a secure place where they are safe from tampering. Most investigative agencies maintain a guarded facility, sometimes known as the property room, for the custody of such items.

In short, the responsibility of the principal investigator on any case is to keep the information that flows to that central position organized in a way that makes it accessible for analysis and for direction of the future course of the investigation. In many situations, particularly in criminal investigations, a field investigator working alone will also bear responsibility for continuing organization and analysis of the evidence being collected.

The responsible investigator or supervisor must evaluate each item of information as it comes in, keeping in mind the rules of evidence that will govern admissibility of the information in later legal proceedings. If a necessary item of evidence would not be admissible because of one of those rules, it must be obtained from some source that does make it admissible.

PERTINENT RULES OF EVIDENCE

All evidence to be relied on at trial must be relevant, competent, and material.[2] It is *relevant* if it tends to prove or disprove an assertion important to the case; *competent* if it was lawfully obtained; and *material* if significant enough to be given weight in the determination by the trier of fact. As the investigative reports come in, items of information in them must be tested by these rules.

Much of the evidence in the eventual legal proceeding in which the investigative work product will be used will be presented through the oral testimony of parties and witnesses. Although the law varies somewhat among jurisdictions, there are a number of disabilities that may make a witness incompetent to testify. In a few states, individuals previously convicted of perjury are still incompetent to testify, although the trend is to allow them to do so.[3] Young children may be held incompetent if examination indicates that they do not have the maturity to understand what is involved in testimony. The same is generally true today for prospective witnesses who have been diagnosed as insane or whose functioning has been impaired by the use of alcohol or other drugs. But even witnesses who may be incompetent to testify in a legal proceeding may be useful during an investigation as sources of leads.

The mere fact that witnesses are allowed to testify does not mean that they must be believed. If at all possible, attorneys will attempt to impeach the testimony of any adverse witness by attacking the credibility of that witness. The chief investigator or case supervisor should therefore insist that field investigators submit information about the competency and credibility of prospective key witnesses, and about the possibility of their testimony being precluded by exercise of a *privilege*. In this context, privilege is the right and duty to withhold or have another withhold information because of some special status or relationship of confidentiality.

When investigative reports contain a reputed admission or a confession in a criminal case, the reports must also show that such statements were not obtained in violation of the defendant's Fifth and Fourteenth Amendment rights against self-incrimination. The report should indicate when the defendant became a suspect, which is when the right arises. If the statement was made thereafter, the *Miranda* warning must have been given if the defendant was in custody,[4] unless one of the exceptions (which are discussed in this section) applies. In addition, because defendants frequently assert that their statements were coerced rather than voluntary, the report should contain a detailed recitation of the circumstances under which the statements were made. The privilege against self-incrimination may in fact not apply (as, for instance, where statements were made spontaneously rather than in response to questioning); this merely underlines the importance of detail in the investigative report of the event.

There may be other privileges regarding communications that are of statutory rather than constitutional origin; these too require special attention in field investigation reports. Among them are communications between spouses, between attorney and client, between priest and penitent, between physician and patient, and between accountant and client. In addition, some states have enacted so-called shield laws that confer a privilege upon news reporters not to reveal their sources.

There is a set of well-established general conditions that must be met before a privilege will be enacted into law.

- The communications must originate in a confidence that they will not be disclosed.
- This element of confidentiality must be essential to the full and satisfactory maintenance of the relationship between the parties.
- The relation must be one which in the opinion of the community ought to be sedulously fostered.
- The injury that would inure to the relation by the disclosure of the communications must be greater than the benefit thereby gained for the correct disposal of litigation.[5]

Field investigators may be faced with these conditions whenever the indicated relationships are involved. Evaluation of the resulting reports must consider whether the situations were properly handled.

In the case of the wife–husband relationship, the privilege of the spouse to suppress any confidential communication is designed to protect the institution of marriage, which even forced testimony might destroy. It is a common law privilege now confirmed by statute and frequently invoked.

Also of common law origin and also frequently used is the now generally codified attorney–client privilege. It is intended to make the services of an attorney to the client more effective. Not only is protection given at trial against disclosure of confidential communications made during the relationship, but that relationship must be allowed to flourish in private. Any breach of that privacy during an investigation, whether accidental or intended, must be reported to the chief investigator. When legal advice of any kind is sought from a professional advisor, the communications relating to that purpose, made in confidence by the client, are permanently protected from disclosure by the client or advisor, except if the client waives that protection. This privilege is a fundamental aspect of the right to counsel.

All but six states now recognize a priest–penitent privilege by statute and the federal courts by judicial decision.[6] Preservation of religious faith as a part of religious freedom is the purpose of this privilege. It is not claimed with nearly the frequency of the two common law privileges just discussed.

Another relatively new statutory privilege is that for confidential communications between physician and patient. Its scope and application vary considerably from jurisdiction to jurisdiction. In some states, the privilege applies only in civil cases, not in criminal prosecutions. Over a third of the states have extended the coverage of the privilege to include psychotherapists, psychiatrists, psychologists, and social workers or some mix of these groups in their relationships with patients.[7] The purpose in each case is to facilitate the flow of information from patient to healer as an aid to diagnosis and treatment.

One of the newest privileges is that for accountant and client. Although not recognized in federal law, many states have established it by statute.[8] As prosecution of fraud and other economic crimes increases, this privilege can be expected to become more important.

State shield laws that allow journalists the privilege of keeping confidential the sources of their information are regarded as extending by statute the First Amendment rights of free speech and the public's right to know. Such laws are still relatively uncommon. If anything, recent trends have been in the opposite direction, particularly in terms of attempts to stop leaks of information from government sources.

When investigative field reports contain information from settings covered by these privileges, the supervising investigator must anticipate that the information will be challenged at trial. If that information is crucial to the case and evaluation of the field report indicates that the challenge will probably be successful, efforts must be made to get the evidence from alternative sources not subject to challenge.

Yet another kind of information that might be found in field reports that may be inadmissible at trial is *hearsay*. Hearsay may be either oral or written; it is information that a prospective witness does not have personal knowledge about—that the witness only heard some other person say or read in a written message from some third person. It is not troublesome if it is the mere utterance of the statement or writing of the document that is important rather than the truth of what is uttered or written. For example, an oral statement or a passage from a written document may be used to prove that the initiator is insane. In that situation the hearsay rule is not involved.

Witnesses are not allowed to testify to what others said or wrote when the testimony is offered to establish the truth of that oral or written statement. The reason is that in such a situation the person who actually made the statement is not present. Defendants have the right to face and cross-examine their accusers, which is not possible when the person is not present. For that reason, the general rule of evidence is that hearsay statements are not admissible.

However, there are many exceptions to the hearsay rule. Among them are the following:

- Spontaneous declarations and excited utterances
- Dying declarations
- Declarations against interest

- Family history
- Regularly kept records
- Official written statements and public records
- Records of past recollection
- Silent or tacit admissions[9]

The other exceptions are of lesser importance to most investigators. Although there are some differences among jurisdictions, the following exceptions discussed here hold true in most.

Under the spontaneous declaration and excited utterance exception to the hearsay rule, declarations and utterances made as part of an event as it unfolds, which are "jarred out of" the speaker by the event, may be testified to by those who heard them. Such statements are actually a part of the event rather than the result of later reflection about that event. The adjectives—spontaneous and excited—used to describe these excepted utterances emphasize their unplanned nature. They are admissible on the assumption that they are true because the speaker did not have time to make a considered statement, did not have time to make up a lie. Although generally referred to as an exception to the hearsay rule, the spontaneous utterance situation is better understood as one in which the hearsay rule simply doesn't apply.

The second exception listed, that for dying declarations, is based on similar reasoning. Such statements are considered to be true because the speaker is assumed not to want to go to meet the Maker having just told a lie. For that reason, the speaker must have believed that death was both near and certain. In most states, the speaker must also have died. In some states, the exception is allowed if the person is simply unavailable. This exception is most useful in cases of homicide in which the victim gives information about the fatal injury just prior to death.

Declarations against interest are admitted as exceptions on very similar grounds. The court asks, "Why would a person make a serious admission against personal interest unless it were true?" The exception does not apply, of course, to admissions and confessions of defendants and other parties, which are admitted on other grounds, but only to statements by nonparties. The interest involved is usually a financial one, but it may be self-incrimination.

As a fourth exception, statements about family history or pedigree are based partially on lack of motive to falsify at the time the statements are made, partly on a belief that the declarant would have accurate information about the matter, and partly on necessity. For hearsay or third-party testimony about the statement to be admitted, it must be shown that the original declarant is not available because of death or for some other good reason; the declarant was related by blood or marriage to the family or was considered as family; and the statement was made before the matter became the subject of a legal proceeding. Among the items of family history that can be included under this exception are dates of marriages, deaths, and births and relationships among family members.

A fifth exception to the hearsay rule is made for records that are kept as a matter of routine over a period of time. Business records are typical, but don't exhaust the category. What makes this exception reasonable is the routine nature of the record, which eliminates any motive to falsify. Any such record made at about the time of the event that it is sought to prove or disprove is admissible.

For the same reason, a sixth exception is granted for official government records required by law. Birth, marriage, and death records are among those most frequently admitted under this exception. Other examples include records kept by courts, motor vehicle departments, prisons, and government weather bureaus.

A seventh hearsay rule exception, that for past recollection recorded, is a bit different in that it concerns a past observation, not of some third person, but of the witness on the stand. In order to be admissible, five conditions must be met.

1. The witness must be shown to lack a present recollection of the event despite efforts at refreshment.
2. The witness must be shown to have had firsthand knowledge of the event.
3. The written statement must have been made at or near the time of the event.
4. The written statement must have been made or dictated by the witness at a time when the witness's recollection was clear and accurate.
5. The witness must testify that the written statement was true and accurate when made.[10]

This exception is frequently used by investigators themselves. They handle large numbers of similar cases, some of which do not reach trial until months or even years have passed. For that reason, the investigator may simply not remember the details of one specific case when called to testify. If the investigator does remember, the testimony must be from that memory, perhaps refreshed by field notes or more formal submitted reports. Only if there is no such present memory do the field notes and reports become evidence of past knowledge recorded. When the notes become evidence and even if only used to refresh memory, they must be made available for inspection by the opposition. For that reason, there must be nothing frivolous in the notes, such as a joke that the investigator wanted to remember. Any such extraneous material can be used to discredit the investigator as nonprofessional.

Last among the particularly common exceptions to the hearsay rule is that available in civil cases for silent or tacit admissions. These are not really statements but conduct when faced with statements or accusations in circumstances that would normally call for refutation. For example, if a person who was flatly accused (in the presence of witnesses) of having committed a wrongful act did not deny the charge but simply looked at the ground in silence, the witnesses could testify to the accusation and the lack of response. The trier of fact could then infer that the lack of denial was an admission of the truth of the accusation made. Because of the Fifth Amendment privilege against self-incrimination, this exception does not apply in criminal prosecutions.

These are not the only exceptions to the hearsay rule, only those most frequently of importance in organizing investigative field reports. Remember that the law is moving toward admissibility of hearsay evidence in ever more situations. For example, after listing a number of specific exceptions, the federal Rule of Evidence grants further exceptions for any

> statement not specifically covered by any of the foregoing exceptions but having equivalent circumstantial guarantees of trustworthiness, if the court determines that (a) the statement is offered as evidence of a material fact; (b) the statement is more probative on the point for which it is offered than any other evidence which the proponent can procure through reasonable efforts; and (c) the general purpose of these rules and the interests of justice will best be served by admission of the statement into evidence.[11]

This movement toward more exceptions has occurred as the law of evidence, which originally developed as judge-made common law, has been codified in recent years into rules of court and statutory provisions. The law of evidence also contains extensive information on the scope of each of the exceptions, by whom, and under what circumstances they can be asserted. In general, this is an area of the law that requires a detailed knowledge of the rules of evidence of the jurisdiction in which the exception is being asserted. It is also an area of the law that all investigators must know well.

Another provision of the law of evidence that the chief investigator who is organizing information from a number of field reports must keep in mind is the *exclusionary rule*. Under this judge-made rule, any illegally obtained item of evidence will be suppressed except in very restricted situations. This applies most frequently to admissions, confessions, documents, and other items of physical evidence that have been obtained as a result of violation of laws regarding arrest, search, and questioning of suspects. Supervisors must be able to judge from the reports of field investigators when illegal procedures were used. The resulting evidence cannot be relied on for courtroom use, nor can any evidence obtained later as a direct result of the illegal action. If the evidence is crucial, it must be obtained a second time by lawful methods untainted by the original illegality.

When documents and other items of physical evidence are legally obtained, they must be processed properly. Complete information must be available in the files about when, where, and under what circumstances they were obtained. The conditions of their custody after discovery and acquisition must be fully documented so that no claim that the items might have been tampered with can be made successfully. Their custody must have been secure enough to preclude any possibility of tampering. The so-called chain of custody must be intact. That requirement having been met, there must also be evidence in the files proving two other facts: that the document or other item is what it purports to be (that it is authentic) and that its message or significance is as alleged. The first factor is the item's external integrity; the second, its internal veracity.

When the item is a document, the *best evidence rule* comes into play. That rule says that the best evidence of what a document contains is the document itself. It requires production of the original document rather than a copy or testimony about the document when the general content of the document is a central issue in the case. Copies or duplicates will be admitted only if the absence of the original is satisfactorily explained, if there is no substantial question about the authenticity of the original, and if use of the duplicate is not unfair to the opposition.[12] Some documents are self-authenticating, such as public records, certified copies of public records, official publications, newspapers, and periodicals. With other documents, authentication is achieved through the testimony of witnesses who can identify the document, frequently by a mark placed on it earlier, and explain its nature and source. Sometimes scientific examination with expert opinion as to its result will be required. In any event, the chief investigator who is organizing the investigative work product must arrange for the identification of the document and explain that arrangement in writing in the case file. The same is true if the contents of the document require interpretation—if the document does not speak for itself.

Similar concerns surround the use of all other physical evidence, which is sometimes called real or demonstrative evidence. Its discovery, acquisition, and preservation (the chain of custody) must be documented. Scientific tests may have to be made, and expert interpretation of the results arranged. All of this is usually a part of the responsibility of the chief investigator who is organizing the work product of the field investigators. It is, however, sometimes delegated to one of the team of lawyers who will present the evidence in some later legal proceeding.

This brief summary of some of the rules of evidence that are important to those organizing investigative information for analysis cannot be more than introductory. Further study in depth will be required before one will be qualified to serve as chief investigator on a complex case that is expected to result in a court trial. In addition, the investigator should not hesitate to consult the prosecutor or other legal advisor, who will present the case in court, concerning the more difficult legal issues about the evidence being assembled.

USES OF INVESTIGATIVE REPORTS

As indicated earlier, organization and analysis of the investigative work product go hand in hand, must begin almost as soon as does the investigation, and will not end until the case is closed. Organization and analysis are separated here for discussion purposes; keep in mind that the separation is artificial. The process of organization and analysis must be continuous because the information produced by the investigation will be used over and over again before its final presentation at trial or in some other legal proceeding. Reviewing the nature of those uses will emphasize the importance of keeping the investigative files up to date.

One of the very early uses of the investigative files will be at status discussions for evaluation of the progress of the investigation. These discussions will be attended by the chief officials involved in the investigation or by their representatives. They involve a review of the information in the files to determine whether the investigation should be continued, redirected, or dropped. Gaps in the information will be identified and steps taken to fill those gaps. The credibility of the evidence will be assessed. Such discussions will be continued throughout the evolution of the case. They will assist the chief investigator in organizing the case files.

Another early use of information in the investigative files will be in affidavits supporting requests for pretrial discovery (depositions, for example), for issuance of subpoenas (including subpoenas duces tecum), and for issuance of arrest and search warrants. In each of these situations, a basis must be established for authorization of the legal process requested.

As the investigation produces more definite results, the information generated will be used in drafting the complaint and subsequent pleadings in a civil court case or administrative proceeding or the formal accusatory document in a criminal case. At this point, strategy decisions will be made as to which of several kinds of legal action will be initiated. In a criminal case, a decision may be made to divert rather than prosecute. If the decision is to prosecute, probable cause to go to trial must be shown at a preliminary hearing or, if required, before a grand jury. Information from the investigative reports will be relied on for these showings. The formal charge is made at arraignment, at which the prosecutor must make a recommendation as to bail, which will again be based on the investigative files. Negotiation that may lead to a settlement in civil actions or a plea bargain in criminal cases also relies on the information in the case files.

Depending on the kind of action to be taken after the investigation, the nature of the investigative records kept and their organization will vary from quite informal to very formal. If the decision concerns a personal or family matter, informality will usually prevail unless a very large economic investment is contemplated. If business, industrial, or public agencies are involved, the record-keeping and organizing processes will be more formal.

SUMMARIZING COMMENTARY

Building an investigative case file begins with the taking of field notes by investigators. As soon as possible, these notes are revised and expanded into investigative reports, sometimes using forms required by the employing agency. Organization of those reports requires not only their ordering but the systematization of the information contained in them into person, event, place, and similarly organized files. The extent of the files to be created will be determined by the seriousness of the case. Their nature will be set by the predetermined investigation plan. Their purpose is to make all of the information generated accessible for analysis, for future direction of the investigation, and for eventual presentation to a decision maker. Organization of the investigative case file also involves evaluation of each item of evidence as to its admissibility in later legal proceedings.

Before any item of information is made a part of the case file, its relevance and competency must be determined and its materiality weighed under the rules of evidence of the jurisdiction. Those rules concern the competence and credibility of witnesses, privileged suppression of confidential communications, admissibility of admissions and confessions by persons accused of crime, and the vagaries of the hearsay rule and its exceptions. The law of evidence is complicated and the chief investigator responsible for organizing investigative field reports into a useful case file must have a working knowledge of that law as it has developed in the jurisdiction.

One provision of the law of evidence of particular importance during organization of the case file is the judge-made exclusionary rule. Under that rule, any illegally obtained evidence is subject to exclusion from trial. This means that admissions, confessions, documents, and other items of physical evidence obtained as a result of arrest, search, and questioning of suspects are subject to challenge. The chief investigator must be sure that the case file demonstrates the legality of such procedures; this legality must be established to meet the suppression challenge.

In addition, the chief investigator must be sure that documents and other items of physical evidence that have been legally obtained are properly processed. The case file must establish the chain of custody that vouches for their integrity: the possibility of their having been tampered with must be eliminated. When a document is to be relied on, the original must be produced unless need for using a duplicate is reasonably established. If scientific tests of physical evidence are required, the chief investigator must arrange for those tests and for their interpretation.

The investigative case file will be used for both internal and external purposes. It must be organized for use in a number of different settings both by investigators and by lawyers. Some of the challenges that the information organized into the case file will be used to meet were described in this chapter. Others are discussed in the next three chapters.

STUDY QUESTIONS

1. What are the primary objectives of an investigator in taking field notes?
2. Why is a simple collection of field investigator's reports not an adequate investigative case file?
3. Why is it helpful to construct person, place, and event files from investigative reports?
4. How can personal computers be used in building investigative case files?
5. What is the basic reason why the person responsible for organization of an investigative case file must have a working knowledge of the law of evidence?
6. What are the different settings in which information from an investigative case file will be used?

RECOMMENDED ADDITIONAL READING

- Gardner, Thomas J. *Criminal Evidence: Principles, Cases and Readings.* St. Paul, Minn.: West Publishing, 1978.
- Kaplan, Eugene J. *Evidence: A Law Enforcement Officer's Guide.* Springfield, Ill.: Charles C Thomas, 1979.
- Swanson, Jr., Charles R., Chamelin, Neil C., and Territo, Leonard. *Criminal Investigation*, 3rd ed. New York: Random House, 1984.

NOTES

1. See, for example, Charles R. Swanson, Jr., Neil C. Chamelin, and Leonard Territo, *Criminal Investigation*, 3rd ed. (New York: Random House, 1984), p. 140.

2. For more extended discussion of the rules of evidence summarized here, see Thomas J. Gardner, *Criminal Evidence: Principles, Cases and Readings* (St. Paul, Minn.: West Publishing, 1978) and Eugene J. Kaplan, *Evidence: A Law Enforcement Officer's Guide* (Springfield, Ill.: Charles C Thomas, 1979).
3. Kaplan, op. cit., p. 30.
4. Miranda v. Arizona, 384 U.S. 436 (1966).
5. Wigmore, John H., *Evidence*, sec. 2285 (Boston: Little, Brown, 1961).
6. Kaplan, op. cit., p. 140; Mullen v. United States, 263 F.2d 275 (1958).
7. Kaplan, op. cit., p. 138.
8. Ibid., p. 1334.
9. Gardner, op. cit., p. 280; this section relies on the discussion in Gardner.
10. Ibid., pp. 211–212.
11. Ibid., pp. 217–218, citing Federal Rule of Evidence, § 803(24).
12. Kaplan, op. cit., p. 280; this section follows generally the discussion in Kaplan.

ANALYSIS OF INVESTIGATIVE INFORMATION

12

Analysis of the incoming investigative work product, like its organization, must begin almost as soon as resources have been committed to the investigation and implementation of the information collection plan has begun. The analysis starts with a new look at the initial information that led to recognition of the problem and to the decision to do something about it. This review will take into consideration what steps have been decided upon to seek a solution to the problem, the kind of decision-making process that will eventually be involved, and the requirements of the setting in which the decision will occur. This initial analysis will pinpoint what must be proved—and to what standard of proof—in order to achieve the objectives of the action being taken. It will then be possible to determine what additional information must be obtained in the collection process. This initial stance of the case is presented schematically in Figure 12-1. The horizontal axis (A–E) of the diagram indicates elements of the case that must be proved. The vertical axis (1–5) indicates items of evidence tending to prove each of the case elements. The letter *I* indicates items already available. Blank cells indicate information yet to be produced by the investigation. When enough cells are filled, the investigation is complete, and the case is ready for presentation in the proceeding. Actually, there is never "enough" information pertaining to any problem situation. There must be some evidence regarding each required element for the case to go forward, but additional corroborating information is always welcome. When the case will go forward after the minimal information is in hand depends upon the importance of that case, which also dictates the resources to be devoted to it.

Ongoing analysis of new information resulting from the investigation may result in one or more of the following:

- Reinterpretation of the previously available information
- Confirmation of the earlier information
- Reaffirmation of the collection plan

	A	B	C	D	E
1	I				
2		I			
3			I		
4				I	
5					I

Figure 12-1 Initial stance of case

- Modification of the collection plan
- Discard of the collection plan
- Realization that the objectives of the investigation cannot be achieved with the currently available resources, within the required time frame, or at all

In making the analysis, each item of evidence must be evaluated as to its probative value and as to its admissibility later in the prospective legal proceeding. This analysis may result in a decision to continue the investigation as planned, to modify the investigative plan, or to abandon the investigation.

CASE COMPONENTS

There can be no investigation plan without clearly defined goals. If the problem is a personal one of some seriousness, say purchase of a new family automobile, there must be an initial determination of the needs. Obviously a sports car with only two seats cannot serve as the only vehicle for a family of five, although it might do for a wife and husband alone. Desirable as well as necessary features in the new car should be listed. In some climates, air conditioning is quite desirable. In other climates, front-wheel drive for better performance in snow might be more important. It must also be determined how much the family can afford to pay, whether financing will be necessary, and, if so, how it can be arranged. When these and similar factors have been thought through, search can begin for the best performing, most aesthetically pleasing vehicle available that meets the family's needs and is within their price range.

Similarly, in a case that is expected to lead to a civil law suit, the components of the case must be determined. If the suit is to be for wrongful injury to the person or damage to property, the precise nature of the injury or damage must be documented. It must also be shown that it was caused intentionally or by negligent conduct toward one to whom the defendant owed a duty of care. It must be proved that the intentional or negligent conduct was that of the person to be sued or by an agent of that person or entity. If negligence is alleged, it must be shown that the plaintiff suffered damage in a specified amount and that the conduct was the proximate cause of the damage. It is not necessary to show actual damage if the tort was intentional. If the suit is to be in contract, it must be shown that there was a contract, a breach by this named defendant, and specified damage to the plaintiff.

In a criminal case, it must be shown that a crime was committed (the famous *corpus delicti*—the body of a crime), and that the defendant committed it. In most cases, there will be an action component *(actus reus)* and a component directed toward the state of mind *(mens rea:* a guilty mind, a criminal intent) in proving that a crime has been committed. Every criminal offense charged has a specific set of elements that must be alleged to exist by the formal accusation. For example, to sustain a charge of common law burglary, the state must allege and prove that there was

1. A breaking and
2. Entering
3. Of the dwelling house
4. Of another
5. In the nighttime,
6. With an intent to commit a felony therein,
7. By the defendant.

This means that the investigation must produce evidence tending to prove each of the seven elements of the alleged crime in order to sustain the charge.

Under modern statutes, burglary has been redefined with varying sets of elements in different jurisdictions. For example, the current Florida statute on burglary reads:

810.02. Burglary
1. "Burglary" means entering or remaining in a structure or a conveyance with the intent to commit an offense therein, unless the premises are at the time open to the public or the defendant is licensed or invited to enter or remain.
2. Burglary is a felony of the first degree, punishable by imprisonment for a term of years not exceeding life imprisonment or as provided in § 775.082, § 774.83, or § 774.084, if, in the course of committing the offense, the offender:
   a. Makes an assault or battery upon any person.
   b. Is armed or arms [himself or herself] within such structure or conveyance, with explosives or a dangerous weapon.
3. If the offender does not make an assault or battery or is not armed, or does

not arm [himself or herself] with a dangerous weapon or explosive as aforesaid during the course of committing the offense and the structure or conveyance entered is a dwelling or there is a human being in the structure or conveyance at the time the offender entered or remained in the structure or conveyance, the burglary is a felony in the second degree, punishable as provided in § 775.082, § 775.083, or § 775.084. Otherwise, burglary is a felony in the third degree, punishable as provided in § 775.082, § 775.083, or § 775.084.[1]

This statute creates a number of related offenses that cover many more situations than did common law burglary.

In addition to proving the substantive elements as set out here for any court action, the investigation should determine which court has the inherent power to decide the case (jurisdiction) and in which county or city that court may hear and determine the case (venue). It may also be necessary as a practical matter for the investigation to produce facts that tend to prove some point that is not legally required but that experience shows is most helpful in obtaining the desired result. For example, motive—as opposed to intent—for commission of a crime is never legally required for conviction. But as a practical matter, the judge or jury may refuse to believe that this defendant committed the offense unless motive is shown. On the other hand, it is not uncommon for there to be no apparent motive for some specific offense.

It is not always easy to determine what the components of a case are. Not even all crimes have as simple a definition as that set out for common law burglary. For example, a single substantive criminal law statute may create over one hundred related but unique criminal offenses, each with a distinct set of elements that differs in some way from each of the other offenses created by the statute. Consider the Model Penal Code provision regarding bribery of public officials as an illustration of this problem of statutory analysis. The recommended statute reads:

Section 240.1 Bribery in Official and Political Matters
A person is guilty of bribery, a felony of the third degree, if [that person] offers, confers, or agrees to confer upon another, or solicits, accepts or agrees to accept from another:
1. any pecuniary benefit as consideration for the recipient's decision, opinion, recommendation, vote or other exercise of discretion as a public servant, party official or voter; or
2. any benefit as consideration for the recipient's decision, vote, recommendation or other exercise of official discretion in a judicial or administrative proceeding; or
3. any benefit as consideration for a violation of a known legal duty as public servant or party official.

It is no defense to prosecution under this section that a person whom the action sought to influence was not qualified to act in the desired way whether because [he or she] had not yet assumed office, or lacked jurisdiction, or for any other reason.[2]

An investigator concerned with this statute would first notice that it creates two clusters of offenses: the first is concerned with those offering bribes, the second with those soliciting or accepting bribes. The investigator would also note that it discusses bribery in three different kinds of situations: general discretionary official and political activity; proceedings that are judicial or administrative in nature; and situations involving known legal duties of public servants and party officials. This makes six basic categories of offenses: giving bribes in three different situations, and taking bribes in the same three situations. In analysis of the statute, it is wise to treat each of these six categories separately to avoid confusion. Diagramming each category also helps.

Turning first to the cluster of offenses by offerors of bribes to influence general discretionary official and political activity, the concerned investigator might come up with an analysis of the elements of those offenses that looks like this:

1. Offering, or
    a. Conferring, or
    b. Agreeing to confer,
2. Upon another
3. A pecuniary benefit
4. As consideration for that other's
    a. Decision as a public servant, or
    b. Decision as a party official, or
    c. Decision as a voter, or
    d. Opinion as a public servant, or
    e. Opinion as a party official, or
    f. Opinion as a voter, or
    g. Recommendation as a public servant, or
    h. Recommendation as a party official, or
    i. Recommendation as a voter, or
    j. Vote as a public servant, or
    k. Vote as a party official, or
    l. Vote as a voter, or
    m. Exercise of discretion as a public servant, or
    n. Exercise of discretion as a party official, or
    o. Exercise of discretion as a voter
5. By the defendant.

The analysis reveals a group of five-element offenses. Two of the elements, numbers one and four, are stated in the alternative, with three alternatives for number one and fifteen alternatives for number four. This means that the *small portion* of the statute thus far considered contains forty-five separate and distinct although closely related offenses (3×1×1×15×1=45). To illustrate, one offense has elements 1, 2, 3, 4, and 5; a second, elements 1a, 2, 3, 4, and 5; a third, elements 1b, 2, 3, 4, and 5; a fourth, elements 1, 2, 3, 4a, and 5; a fifth, elements 1a, 2, 3, 4a, and 5; a sixth, elements 1b, 2, 3, 4a, and 5; and so on.

A second set of forty-five offenses is revealed if we consider the phrase "solicits, accepts or agrees to accept from another" instead of the phrase "offers, confers, or agrees to confer upon another." This means that the statute read through subsection (1) creates ninety separate and distinct substantive criminal offenses. Actually, those twelve offenses with elements 4c, 4f, 4i, and 4o may not have been intended by the drafters of the statute, but they are there. If not intended, the statute is badly drafted.

Moving on to subsection (2) of the statute, a similar analysis reveals another forty-eight separate and distinct offenses. Subsection (3), in turn, shows an additional twelve such offenses for a grand total of one-hundred and fifty.

Yet another complication is the fact that statutes contain a good bit of non-element language. The last paragraph of the Model Penal Code bribery statute negates a potential affirmative defense. Others contain affirmative defenses, labeling language, punishment provisions, special rules of procedure and evidence, examples, definitions, incorporation by reference language, and much more. That non-element language complicates recognition of the elements for the uninitiated.

Even offenses that are more common than bribery require analysis. Typical might be public drunkenness, which is proscribed by the Model Penal Code in this language:

> A person is guilty of an offense if [that person] appears in any public place manifestly under the influence of alcohol, narcotics or other drug, not therapeutically administered, to the degree that [that person] may endanger [himself or herself] or other persons or property, or annoy persons in [the] vicinity.[3]

Using the diagrammatic technique again, the following analysis of offense elements emerges:

1. Appearing in any public place,
2. Manifestly under the influence of
    a. Alcohol, or
    b. A narcotic, or
    c. A non-narcotic drug,
3. Not therapeutically administered,
4. To the degree that the person might
    a. Endanger himself or herself, or
    b. Endanger others, or

c. Endanger property, or
   d. Annoy persons in the vicinity,
5. By the defendant.

Here one finds a group of five-element offenses. Two of the elements, this time numbers two and four, are stated in the alternative, with three alternatives for number two and four alternatives for number four. This simple statute then creates twelve separate and distinct although closely related offenses ($1 \times 3 \times 1 \times 4 \times 1 = 12$). This is more like the usual run-of-the-mill criminal offense. But the law enforcement and prosecuting officials must charge and be prepared to prove the correct—and only the correct—offense in a given case. These examples demonstrate the difficulty in some criminal cases of clearly defining the goals of the investigation.

After the investigative objectives have been spelled out, it is clear what the information from the field reports must tend to prove, but the degree of certainty of that proof must still be specified. Most persons know that criminal cases must be proved beyond a reasonable doubt. Fewer know that the usual standard of proof in civil cases is a preponderance of the evidence but that, for some civil actions (those involving fraud, for example), the standard is clear and convincing evidence. Each of these standards has its own reason in the law.

The least rigorous of the standards is the usual civil test of a preponderance of the evidence. Where preponderance is the rule, the judge or jury need only be convinced that the evidence is slightly in favor of one party to justify a judgment for that party. The customary reason given by the courts for that rule is that, in the common civil suit, both parties are exposed to the same risk. Either the plaintiff loses on the claim for a given amount of money or the defendant is assessed and must pay the same amount. Because the risk is about the same, the preponderance rule seems to be justified.[4]

The most rigorous standard is the criminal test of proof beyond a reasonable doubt. An excellent statement of what that standard means is found in the *United States Manual for Courts-Martial*.

> By reasonable doubt is intended not a fanciful or ingenious doubt or conjecture but substantial, honest, conscientious doubt suggested by the material evidence, or lack of it, in the case. It is an honest, substantial misgiving, generated by insufficiency of proof of guilt. It is not a captious doubt, nor a doubt suggested by the ingenuity of counsel or court and unwarranted by the testimony, nor a doubt born of a merciful inclination to permit the accused to escape conviction, nor a doubt prompted by sympathy for [the accused] or those connected with [the accused]. The meaning of the rule is that the proof must be such as to exclude not every hypothesis or possibility of innocence but any fair and rational hypothesis except that of guilt; what is required is not an absolute or mathematical certainty but a moral certainty.[5]

The reason frequently given by courts for this much more severe standard is that the risk to the defendant on erroneous conviction is much greater than the risk to the state on erroneous acquittal. Erroneous conviction may involve loss of freedom and even of life; erroneous acquittal involves only a slight increase in the number of crimes that already go unpunished.

Between these two standards in severity is that of clear and convincing evidence. This standard is sometimes used in civil cases, such as those involving fraud or involuntary civil commitment to a mental institution—cases resulting, rightly or wrongly, in tarnishing of the defendant's reputation. Frequently these are cases that, although civil, involve moral turpitude. Although the conduct is not sufficiently antisocial to be classed as criminal, it does result in loss to the defendant of something more than just money. Which standard of proof must be met in a given case obviously affects the amount of evidence that must be produced by the investigation.

When an investigation has turned up some evidence tending to show the existence of every element of the action that must be proved *(prima facie evidence)*, a *prima facie case* has been made. This assures that the case will be considered on its merits by the trier of fact, whether judge or jury. The case still may not be won, however, because the opposition may successfully refute the prima facie evidence on one or more necessary elements.

In judging when an investigation has produced "enough" evidence on a necessary element of the case, the chief investigator responsible for analysis of the field reports must consider not only the information in the reports but what rebuttal evidence the opposition will probably offer on that element. The analysis must anticipate what the opposition's case might be. That judgment requires experience.

INVESTIGATIONS FOR PLANNING PURPOSES

Thus far in this chapter, the discussion has focused primarily on only one kind of investigation: that which seeks to reconstruct events in the recent past so that responsibility for those events can be established. But there is another kind of investigation as well: that which seeks to establish a basis for future action. In that situation there must also be collection of the information followed by its organization and analysis. In both kinds of cases, one of the first fruits of the analysis will be discovery of gaps in the information—information that is needed but not yet collected. The gaps may exist for a variety of reasons. It may be that the need for the data was not recognized in the original investigative plan. In that situation, the plan must be amended and the information sought. Or it may be that the information simply doesn't exist, that the persons involved in the activity simply didn't record it and hence could not themselves produce it. Then the analyst must make an educated guess as to what the information would be if it could be found. That estimate might not stand up in court but it will serve for future planning purposes and for design of attempts to obtain information from which the point may reasonably be inferred. When evidence on necessary elements of prospective civil or criminal court cases cannot be found, the investigation must be closed, either temporarily or permanently.

Making educated guesses about missing data in an investigation-for-planning-purposes requires special qualifications. First of all, it takes a sound and broad background knowledge about the general environment in which the problem under investigation exists. That can be obtained either through general education or specialized training. Second, it requires an intimate knowledge of all of the information that is available from the investigation of the problem: the guesser must have a comprehensive knowledge of the case file. And third, knowledge of history and of human nature are also important. Given these qualifications, the analyst can make the best estimate of what the missing information would be if it were available.

When all of the information that can be acquired is at hand, a number of possible solutions or possible next steps will emerge from the data. Chances are that no one of these will be ideal: each will have both advantages and disadvantages; each will be a compromise. In that situation, the alternative solutions should be presented to the decision maker with a complete discussion of their respective advantages and disadvantages.

ANALYSIS OF REPORTS FOR INVESTIGATOR EVALUATION

A secondary purpose for analysis of investigative field reports is evaluation of the performance of individual field investigators. As indicated in Chapter 7, increasingly greater resources are being devoted to investigations in many settings in both the public and private sectors. Management of those resources has become a very important function.

In performing that function, the chief investigator looks for both quality and quantity of the investigative work product. Quality means producing the needed information through ethical and legal procedures, being certain about the weight to be accorded to the information from each source, and reporting that information completely, accurately, and with clarity. Quantity means being able to obtain the necessary information with a minimum expenditure of time and other resources.

In assessing individual investigator performance, the supervisor will look for strengths and weaknesses. Special strengths should be noted and commended. They should also be exploited. An investigator who demonstrates special interests and talents should be given as many cases as possible in which that special interest and talent will make a difference. Consideration should also be given to whether the talent is teachable. If so, one of that investigator's assignments should be to develop the necessary teaching materials and to teach the knowledge or skill to fellow investigators in periodic in-service training sessions.

When performance weaknesses are discovered, the supervisor must determine whether they result from personal lack of capacity for investigative work; from poor preparation; or from some systemic weakness in the selection, training, assignment, and supervision of investigators. Of greatest concern are weaknesses that seem to be inherent in the investigative unit, that are demonstrated by most or even all of the field investigators. Such weaknesses require consultation with agency leaders about possible changes in unit structure, personnel selection and training methods, or assignment and operational procedures. But it may also be determined that the weakness is inherent in the individual investigator. In that case, the supervisor may decide that additional training is the answer. Or the individual's performance may be due to stress from some personal or family problem. In such a situation, referral for individual or family counseling may be indicated. However, in some cases, the supervisor may decide that the individual simply does not have the interest or capacity for investigative work. In that event, transfer into some other position in the agency or company should be attempted. If transfer is not possible, the person should be counseled to seek other employment. If that suggestion is ignored or unproductive, the person should be discharged, although, particularly in public employment under civil service laws, that action may be difficult to achieve. Pending transfer or discharge, the individual usually can be assigned to some simple task within the unit that can be performed well on a temporary basis.

SUMMARIZING COMMENTARY

Analysis of the information in accumulating reports from field investigators is necessary as a check on progress in implementing the investigative work plan, in assessing the continued effectiveness of that plan, and in assessing the performance of individual investigators under the plan. The substantive aspect of the analysis will be directed at how well the investigation is producing the evidence necessary to prove the elements of the prospective civil proceeding or criminal prosecution. To make the judgment, the analyst must know what those elements are.

For personal decisions, the processes of setting the objectives, devising the usually informal data collection plan, performing the field investigation necessary to implement that plan, and analyzing the collected information for its bearing on the objectives will usually all be carried out by one person, with minimal assistance from others.

When some kind of civil court action or other similar legal proceeding is anticipated, the elements necessary for success in the action must be known to the supervisor or other analyst of the investigative reports. In the civil realm, those elements usually include some wrong done to the plaintiff by the defendant that resulted in damage to the plaintiff that can be measured in monetary terms. Each of these components of the case must be supported by information obtained in the investigation.

In criminal cases, the analyst must know the elements of the crime to be charged. This means analysis of substantive criminal law statutes and of the information in the investigative reports to determine what kind of fit exists between the two. Analysis of substantive criminal law statutes is a skill that investigators and analysts must develop. Because of the complexity of the statutes, it can be mastered only through guided practice.

When the necessary elements of the case that must be proved are known, the analyst must then determine what and how much evidence there is in the case file tending to prove the existence of each of those elements. When the evidence on a particular element would, if believed, establish existence of that element, there is prima facie evidence on the element. When there is prima facie evidence on every necessary element, a prima facie case has been established. Having a prima facie case means that a decision on the merits must be made by the trier of fact, be that judge or jury. It does not mean that the case will automatically be won. A prima facie case can be refuted by countervailing evidence presented by the opposition.

How much evidence will be required to win a case depends on a number of factors.

- The standard of proof for that kind of case
- The weight given to the evidence presented
- The amount of contradictory evidence presented by the opposition and the weight given to that evidence
- The substantive impression that the case as a whole makes on the decision maker(s)

In most civil cases, the standard of proof is a simple preponderance of the evidence. In civil cases in which some stigma attaches to the defendant, the standard is usually clear and convincing evidence. In criminal cases, the most rigorous standard is required: proof beyond a reasonable doubt. The analyst must judge whether the information in the case file meets the appropriate standard of proof in deciding whether the investigation can be considered complete or must continue. That judgment will be based in part on an estimate of the weight that will be given to each item of evidence.

It is also necessary for the analyst to make some estimate of the probable strength of the evidence that will be offered by the opposition. That estimate will be based on information from pretrial discovery, on information presented at preliminary hearings, on information acquired during pretrial conferences, as well as on information from the investigative case file. Usually the attorney who will be responsible for presenting the case at trial or other contemplated legal proceeding will have participated in the information-generating preliminary procedures and hence will be primarily responsible for the pretrial estimate of the strength of the opposition's case.

When the investigation is made for planning purposes, the issue is not whether there is enough evidence to prove a case, but whether all of the relevant information available has been collected, given the resources at hand. When it is decided that it has, the analyst must make educated guesses to fill in any remaining blanks. Once that is done, the file is studied for possible solutions to the problem. Several usually present themselves, each with advantages and disadvantages. Each of the several must be described by the analyst in detail and presented to the decision maker for choice. No choice will be an ideal solution; any choice will be a compromise.

In addition to substantive analysis of the investigative field reports, attention must be paid to what they can tell about the performance of the individual investigators filing those reports. Strengths and weaknesses must be identified and faced. In extreme cases, that something might include discharge of an incapable investigator. In other situations, the task will be the more pleasant one of commendation and planning for more effective use of demonstrated superior knowledge and skill. In still other cases, unit training needs will be identified.

At some point, the case analyst will decide that the investigation is complete and can be scheduled for presentation to the eventual decision maker. Chapters 13 and 14, Part Four of this book, cover that presentation phase of the process of determination of fact.

STUDY QUESTIONS

1. Why must the first step in the analysis of investigative work product be a reevaluation of the initial information that triggered the investigation?
2. Organization and analysis of the information in a case file usually

reveal gaps in what is required. What steps can be taken to fill those gaps?
3. How does an analyst know what the evidence in a case file must prove?
4. What are the general objectives of proof in civil cases? In criminal cases?
5. Why are different standards of proof used in different legal proceedings?
6. Describe briefly one effective procedure for analyzing a substantive criminal law statute.

RECOMMENDED ADDITIONAL READING

- Bailey, F. Lee. *To Be a Trial Lawyer.* Marshfield, Mass.: Telshare Publishing, 1982.
- Wilson, James Q. *The Investigators: Managing FBI and Narcotics Agents.* New York: Basic Books, 1978.

NOTES

1. Fla. Stat. § 810.02, as amended.
2. American Law Institute, *Model Penal Code and Commentaries* (Philadelphia: American Law Institute, 1980), Part 2, Vol. 2, pp. 4–48. The American Law Institute is an elite self-perpetuating group of American lawyers interested in law reform. Its Model Penal Code has not been adopted in toto by any jurisdiction, but many sections have been adopted and it has otherwise been quite influential in every jurisdiction that has revised its substantive criminal law since the Code provisions became available in 1962.
3. American Law Institute, *Model Penal Code* (Reprint of proposed official draft) (Philadelphia: American Law Institute, 1962), p. 225; the statute further discusses classification of and punishment for the defined offenses.
4. See the discussion in the concurring opinion of Justice Harlan in In re Winship, 397 U.S. 358 (1970).
5. President of the United States, *United States Manual for Courts-Martial,* Rev. Ed. (Washington, D.C.: U.S. Government Printing Office, 1969), pp. 13–14.

PART FOUR
PRESENTATION OF THE FACTS

Pretrial preparation has often been compared to a part of the iceberg that sank the *Titanic,* namely the part that was under water (about 87 percent of the whole). You may not be able to see it from a distance, but you know damned well it's there. The trial itself is like the portion that sticks up out of the water for all to see.

F. Lee Bailey
To Be a Trial Lawyer

If you want to win a case, paint the judge a *picture* and keep it simple.

John W. Davis (personal communication to G. J. Miller)
Annual meeting of Scribes, 21 August 1955

PREPARATION FOR PRESENTATION 13

As the time approaches for final presentation of the information to a decision maker, the role of the investigator in serious, complicated cases shifts from an accumulator of evidence to an assistant to whomever will present it. The presenter will usually be a lawyer. In legal proceedings it will always be one of a special breed of lawyers: a litigator or trial attorney.

Information does not speak for itself. It must be presented effectively. That presentation will vary considerably with the kind of fact-finding procedure involved. With personal and minor official decisions, it may well be informal. In serious official matters, it will be quite formal. The more serious the case, the more extensive the preparation, and the more extensive the investigator's role in that preparation. Criminal trials are probably the most formal settings that an investigator will encounter, and among them a complex trial for economic crime may require the most intensive preparation. For those reasons, this chapter will stress preparation for the trial of a complicated white-collar crime.

CASE PREPARATION

A number of considerations govern case preparation. The information must be organized to show that it includes proof of each of the necessary elements of the offense charged. As a practical matter, it should also show motive. Beyond those basic requirements, it must show the broad economic impact—hence the importance—of the case. That factor will ensure vigorous prosecution and, later, will influence the sentencing of those convicted.

As a preliminary matter, the case files will be used to draft the formal charge and to establish a theory on which trial of the case will be based. They will then be used as the basis for obtaining a finding of probable cause at a preliminary hearing before a magistrate to proceed to trial, or for obtaining a finding of true bill on an indictment submitted by the prosecutor to a grand jury. The information in the file will be used to prepare the prospective witnesses, to obtain stipulations from the defense to simplify the issues to be addressed at trial, to plan requests for disclosure of the defense case, to prepare answers to defense disclosure requests, and to seek pretrial conferences. The case files should allow anticipation of the theory upon which the defense will be based and of specific elements of that defense. The case is then poised for trial, but effective plea bargaining, which may obviate trial, may occur.

The extent to which the investigator will participate in this pretrial preparation will vary with prosecutors and investigators. This is a very interesting facet of the case to which an investigator can make a major contribution and from which he or she can learn a great deal. For these reasons, the investigator should attempt to attend and participate in as many of the various pretrial conferences and proceedings as possible. Preparation for trial is obviously not a single act; as has been emphasized repeatedly, it is a continuing process that should begin early in the investigation. It should probably involve several status conferences with the prosecution staff. When the chief investigator decides that the investigation is complete, a final formal submission report should be made to the prosecutor.

SUBMISSION OF THE CASE TO THE PROSECUTOR

There is no one best format for the final investigative report submitting a case to the prosecutor. Any logical, well-organized structure will do. This section contains a digest of the conventional wisdom about format.[1]

It is recommended that the case submission report begin with an introductory paragraph containing the basic facts. First might be a list of the names, ages, addresses, and occupations of the proposed defendants. Next could come citation of the statute or statutes violated, followed by a brief statement of the complaint or other circumstances that launched the investigation. A second paragraph might give greater detail on the nature and scope of the violations, indicating their geographic spread, their monetary impact, and the categories and number of victims. A third paragraph could present the evidence tending to prove the existence of each of the necessary elements of the offense, after which there might be a narrative statement of how the investigation developed. Then the personal and criminal histories of the proposed defendants can be outlined. This initial section of the submission report might end with a list of prospective witnesses accompanied by a summary of what each can contribute to the case.

The second section of the report might be devoted to statements taken from the witnesses. There should be a written report of each interview with a prospective witness, including persons victimized by the crimes. Each report should be complete, with both incriminating and exculpatory information, if any, included. The first reported interview with any given person should contain an appraisal of the witness's probable effectiveness on the stand, including any information, such as a criminal record, that might be used by the opposition to attack the credibility of the witness.

A third section of the submission report might describe any documents or other physical or real evidence that the investigation has produced. The authenticity, chain of custody, and inherent significance of each item should be discussed, with a list of witnesses who can testify to each of those attributes of the item. Tape recordings and videotapes should be treated like other items of real evidence, with special emphasis given to demonstrating their authenticity.

Wherever useful to achieve greater clarity in the submission report, visual aids should be included. The progression of events can be illustrated with time flow diagrams. Relationships among those involved can be shown with link network analysis charts, and profits to the participants can be demonstrated using net worth–expenditure charts. Maps showing the geographic spread of the case might also be useful. These graphics might later be enlarged for use during presentation of the case to the decision maker.

Standard agency procedure may include a prescribed format for the final investigative report submitting the case to the prosecutor. If there is no standard procedure, a format such as that outlined here might be used. As with any report, accuracy, completeness, and conciseness are required.

USES OF THE CASE SUBMISSION REPORT

Attorneys responsible for presentation of the case to the decision maker will use the final investigative report in a number of ways, among which will be pretrial discovery, pretrial conferences, the drafting of stipulations, the preparation of witnesses (including expert witnesses), plea bargaining, the drafting of trial briefs, and the preparation of the trial case file.

As noted earlier, the pretrial discovery process available in both civil and criminal cases is a two-way process. Each side is subject to discovery by the other. Revealing the apparent strength of the case of the state to the defense encourages guilty pleas that save court time. Frank disclosure by the state also meets the requirements of the *Brady* doctrine requiring that any possible exculpatory evidence obtained by the prosecution be passed on to the defense.[2] It also makes requests for a *bill of particulars* (a more detailed statement of the facts on which the case is based) unnecessary, and tends to lead to stipulations that restrict and sharpen the issues to be contested at trial. Full disclosure can avoid criticism by the court at trial for attempts to achieve surprise. The prosecution should not, however, release the detailed statements of witnesses unless required to do so. Minor inaccuracies and generalities that they contain, although not exculpatory in the *Brady* doctrine sense, might be used to impeach the witness at trial. Most of the information used by the prosecutor in the discovery process will be obtained from the case submission report.

Pretrial conferences also require reliance by the prosecution on the case submission report. Such conferences are encouraged by judges as an aid toward settlements and plea bargains that will help clear court dockets.[3] In addition to leading to agreement on complicated legal issues, the pretrial conference can also lead to stipulations on factual and procedural matters on which agreement was not reached in earlier discovery. Stipulations are frequently made as to the authenticity and integrity of the chain of custody of documents, tape recordings, and other items of physical evidence. They are also commonly used to facilitate admission of previously prepared and marked bank and business records to be offered as exhibits. As a matter of strategy, prosecutors in economic crime cases are loathe to stipulate as to the impact of the fraud because live testimony from the distressed victims has a profound effect on a jury. Judges do their best to encourage stipulations. When agreed upon, they should be reduced to writing and signed by the prosecutor or plaintiff's attorney, the defense attorney, and the defendant.

At the pretrial conference there may also be judge-inspired settlement of remaining evidentiary issues about such matters as the disclosure of the statements of witnesses, about the use of visual aids, and about the need for demonstrating that proffered evidence is relevant to the case. Although they do save court time, there is some skepticism about whether they save judge time. Some judges are moving toward tighter scheduling of cases as an alternative that may lead to less expenditure of their time.

Investigative case submission reports are also useful to presenting attorneys in the preparation of witnesses for testimony at trial. In fact, attorneys often delegate preparation of at least some witnesses to a trusted investigator who is assisting in preparation for trial. Witness preparation is both lawful and ethical as long as it does not seek to falsify the testimony of the witness. Among its legitimate purposes is orientation of the witness to the physical layout of the courtroom (where to sit, the mechanics of being called and sworn) so that the witness will be more relaxed in that environment, which facilitates accuracy in testifying. It is also proper to make witnesses aware of how their testimony fits into the overall structure of the case—that it is important. Witnesses should be told that their answers to questions should be complete yet as brief as possible, that they should give only the information requested. They should be told about the legitimate purposes of cross-examination, that the mere act of cross-examination is not an attack on their truthfulness, but the exercise of a constitutional right of the defendant. This knowledge will help them to keep their composure on cross-examination. At this point, any possible grounds for attack on their credibility by the opposition should also be discussed with witnesses. Finally, because witness preparation of this kind is both lawful and ethical, witnesses should be instructed to admit that they have discussed with their attorney or the investigator how best to convey the information desired of them accurately, completely, and concisely.

Presenting attorneys will usually want to prepare (or be prepared by) expert witnesses personally. If the expert is inexperienced as a witness, all of the preparation just discussed will be necessary. The experience (both as a witness and as a practicing professional) and qualifications of any prospective expert witness must be verified. Then the attorney and the expert should discuss just how the expert opinion and the facts on which it relies can best be presented. Carefully prepared hypothetical questions are sometimes used. When an older, well-experienced expert witness works with a young, relatively inexperienced attorney, the process that develops is actually preparation of the attorney by the witness, rather than vice versa.

While preparing for trial, prosecutors will usually engage in plea bargaining. The purpose is to conserve scarce resources. The goals are to obtain a fair plea and a sentence that will further protection of society and be proportionate to the seriousness of the criminal conduct. Plea bargains are made with the defense attorney, not with the defendant, although they must be approved by the defendant. The bargain can be to drop all charges, to reduce the number or seriousness of the charges, to drop other pending cases and charges, to separate cases of codefendants, or to waive various formal requirements. Because sentencing is the province of the judge or jury, the prosecutor cannot promise a particular sentence, only agree to recommend that sentence to the sentencing authority. Plea bargains can be made at any time prior to the verdict at trial. Usually the prosecutor will accept pleas to more greatly reduced charges very early in the proceedings. Closer to or at trial, such pleas will not be acceptable simply because the state has then invested an increased amount of time and money in the case. When bargaining with the defendant's attorney, the prosecutor is almost completely dependent on the investigative case submission report for information.

Among the factors that the report and the bargaining process must address are the seriousness of the offense, the strength of the government's case, and any aggravating or mitigating circumstances. With respect to seriousness, the prosecutor will be concerned with whether the offense was against property or the person, whether a weapon was used, and whether damage to property or injury to the person resulted. Regarding the strength of the government's case, the prosecutor must know the probable impact and credibility of prospective witnesses; whether the victim or any prospective witnesses are reluctant to testify; the probable weight of the state's evidence generally; whether any of the evidence is subject to suppression; relevant policies of the prosecution; and whether there are strong defenses available, such as alibi or insanity. Mitigating or aggravating circumstances may include the background of the defendant, whether the victim or any other persons were injured, and the extent of any property damage caused. When a bargain is made, to ensure credibility, the investigator must see that it is kept.

Investigative case submission reports are also used as the basis for preparation of trial briefs. Trial briefs are written by attorneys when specific complex legal issues are expected to arise at trial. Although they concern questions of law, those questions arise out of the facts and how those facts are to be proved, information whose primary source is the investigative case submission report. It is usually that report which alerts the presenting attorney to the probable need for the trial brief.

One last purpose served by the investigative case submission report is to furnish the information needed by the presenting attorney for assembling the master case file to be used in the trial or other legal proceeding. Before addressing that process, however, more attention to anticipating the case of the opposition is merited.

ANTICIPATING THE OPPOSITION

One of the important aspects of preparation for legal proceedings is anticipation of the opposition's case. Surprise in any such proceeding, dramatic as it may be, does not lead to good results. The party surprised may not be able to marshal available countervailing evidence effectively, which may lead to unwarranted loss of the case—a miscarriage of justice. The party achieving surprise, if the unanticipated evidence is overwhelming, could have used it earlier to win the case at much less cost, both in money and time.

Recognition that surprise is an evil has led to legal procedures designed to prevent it. Although the law varies from one jurisdiction to the next, the anti-surprise procedures usually include authorization to take *depositions* (formal statements made under oath in the presence of attorneys for all parties who wish to be represented) from all prospective witnesses. The anti-surprise procedures include formal pretrial discovery orders that are used extensively to obtain documents relevant to the case from the opposition. Pretrial conferences may be held in which each side explores the strengths and weaknesses of the opposition case. These conferences are held in the presence of a judge who urges both sides to find a basis for settlement. For a party actually injured, settlement saves time and money, gets the compensation for damages earlier, and avoids the risk of an incorrect adverse verdict at trial. For the culpable party, time and money that further proceedings would require are saved, the payment of damages may be reduced somewhat in amount, and the risk of assessment of very high damages by a jury is avoided. Negotiation for settlement is one of the finest lawyer's arts. In criminal cases, the counterpart is plea bargaining.

In all of this activity, being able to anticipate accurately the opposition's case is crucial.[4] To demonstrate what is involved, consider the anticipation of possible defenses in a criminal fraud case. One such defense might be that no misrepresentation was made. The defense might argue that the advertising and other materials were simply badly worded, subject to interpretations other than those intended, but that no intent to defraud was present. The defense may even assert that the materials were screened in advance by a lawyer who approved their use. The argument may assert that no reasonable person would have interpreted the material as did those now claiming to be victims, that their greed made them read something into the material that was not only not intended but that in fact was not there.

In another kind of fraud case, the defense might allege that only a simple business failure, not a scheme to defraud, was involved. And in fact, being faced with business failure is sometimes the motivation for launching a scheme to defraud. Whether such a scheme was actually implemented or whether the losses were due simply to business failure is a question for the jury. They should be persuaded that there is evidence of actual positive misrepresentation before they can bring in a guilty verdict.

Similarly the defense might argue that the product or service furnished was worth what was paid, so that there was no fraud. But in the eyes of the law, there was fraud if the product or service was not as described, even if it was worth something. Part of this defense might be a claim that refunds were made whenever requested. Again, whether there was in fact fraud is a question for the jury.

Taking another tack, the defense might argue that what are alleged to be fraudulent misrepresentations were merely sales "puffing," the kind of zealous exaggeration that has always been a part of sales. They may also be justified as permissible expressions of opinion. But claiming that an article or service has specific qualities that it really does not is more than puffing; it is fraud. Again, the question is one for the jury.

Other defendants may argue that they are not responsible for unauthorized deceptive acts and misrepresentations of over-zealous sales representatives and other agents. As a general rule, the law provides that the statements of an agent are binding on the principal if they were made within the scope of employment and with the actual or apparent authority of the principal. If it can be shown that the same statements were made by different agents at different times in different places, a strong case has been made that the statements were authorized by the principal.

Or it may be asserted that the defendants are not responsible for oral agreements not included in the written contract. This is reliance on the *parol evidence rule,* a rule that excludes oral or other extrinsic evidence by which a party seeks to contradict, vary, add to, or subtract from the terms of a valid written agreement or instrument. But the rule makes exception for cases of fraud, mistake, or accident. If fraud can be shown, the parol evidence rule will simply not apply.

The initial anticipation of possible defenses will have been supplemented by the several pretrial processes that produce additional evidence about the prospective defense. It will also be furthered by the investigators' and lawyers' previous experience with the kind of case involved.

MASTER CASE PRESENTATION FILE

When a case is finally scheduled for trial, the responsible attorney needs a set of files that are different from those assembled during the investigation for use during the various pretrial processes.[5] The master case file for trial should have at least three sections.

1. A case summary
2. An outline of the order in which evidence will be presented
3. Memoranda of law on legal points that are expected to arise during the trial

The case summary section contains a brief overview of what the case is all about. The attorney probably has a number of cases pending for trial, and this one may be scheduled on short notice quite some time after completion of all pretrial activity. In addition to refreshing the attorney's memory concerning the general outlines of the case, the summary section will contain information about the current status of any settlement or plea bargaining negotiations that have been in progress.

The second feature of the attorney's file might well be an evidence checklist detailing the order in which the witnesses and other evidence will be offered at trial. It should include complete information on how each witness can be reached at any time, and what preparations have been made for the production of documents and other items of physical evidence. This section will serve as a guide to actual presentation of the case in the courtroom.

Section three of the master case file contains a list of any legal points yet to be decided on pretrial motion and of any evidentiary problems that are expected to arise as the trial progresses. It also contains the legal memoranda that have been prepared discussing those legal points. This ensures that pretrial orders will be obtained on all remaining points that need not be disputed, and serves as a guide for quick, effective, and interesting presentation of the evidence in the case. With the master case file assembled, the attorney is now ready for the trial or other legal proceeding to begin.

SUMMARIZING COMMENTARY

When a case reaches the point at which the completed investigative work product is about to be put to use, the role of the investigator shifts from being the principal to being an assistant to the attorney litigating or managing the case. In that new role, the investigator will be a source for backup information and possibly a prospective witness. Or the investigator may become simply an interested observer of the resulting legal procedure.

In the preparation of important cases, the investigator's potential role is of crucial importance up to the time the case is ready to go to trial. The trial attorney assigned to the case may well know nothing about it; the attorney may be totally dependent on the investigator and investigative reports for information necessary to pursue the case. In a few very big, important, and complicated cases, a trial attorney may have been assigned when the investigation was initiated, but such situations are relatively rare. In most cases, investigative agencies develop cases and then submit them to an office of attorneys for presentation in a variety of legal forums. In some situations, the investigators may seek legal advice during the investigation, but even those cases are not very frequent.

When the newly assigned trial attorney begins preparation for presentation of the case, the primary source of information on which all subsequent actions will be based is the investigative agency's case submission report. From it will come the information needed to draft a civil complaint or a formal accusation of violation of criminal law, to develop a theory on which the case will be advanced, to show probable cause to proceed to trial, or to obtain an indictment. It will also be used in discovery procedures, in pretrial conferences, in preparation of witnesses, and in settlement or plea bargaining negotiations. For all of these reasons, the case submission report of the investigative agency must be complete, accurate, concise, and well organized.

No matter how good the case submission report, having an investigator who assisted in its compilation as an assistant in its interpretation and use is of great value to the trial attorney. In many cases, such an investigator-assistant can take the major or even entire responsibility for preparation of the witnesses. That assistant can also make the necessary custodial arrangements for presenting documents and other items of physical evidence, and can make sure that witnesses are present when and where needed.

Investigator-assistants to trial attorneys can be helpful in anticipating defenses that may be used by the opposition. In this regard, the investigator's experience will be different than that of even a senior attorney. The investigator's experience will have produced an insight into possible defenses that the attorney alone would not possess. Working together, the attorney and the investigator can probably ensure that there will be no surprise in the defense.

And finally, the investigator can assist the trial attorney in converting the investigative case submission report into a master case file, which can aid the attorney at the trial. All of these are interesting activities that represent the culmination of an entire investigative effort. They are activities to which the investigator can make a major contribution and from which he or she can learn a great deal. For these reasons, both the investigator and the investigative agency should try to maximize the investigator's participation in the pretrial activities that constitute preparation for trial. The next stage, the role of the investigator in the final presentation of the investigative work product at trial, is discussed in Chapter 14.

STUDY QUESTIONS

1. Why is it more productive for an investigator to remain as an assistant to the attorney in pretrial activity and trial of a case than to move on immediately to another investigative assignment?
2. When proof of motive is so important as a practical matter, why isn't it given more legal significance?
3. What is the purpose of having so many pretrial activities in which the investigator can play such a crucial role?
4. Why is there so much emphasis on witnesses and their prospective testimony in the processing of cases toward decision making?
5. Why is there movement toward elimination of surprise in actions at law?

RECOMMENDED ADDITIONAL READING

- Bailey, F. Lee. *To Be a Trial Lawyer.* Marshfield, Mass.: Telshare Publishing, 1982.

- Cound, John J., ed. *Civil Procedure: Cases and Materials*, 3rd ed. St. Paul, Minn.: West Publishing, 1980.
- Kamisar, Yale, ed. *Modern Criminal Procedure: Cases, Comments, Questions*, 5th ed. St. Paul, Minn.: West Publishing, 1983.
- Kerstetter, Wayne A., and Heienz, Anne M. *Pretrial Settlement: An Evaluation*. Washington, D.C.: Law Enforcement Assistance Administration, 1979.

NOTES

1. See, for example, the suggestions in Herbert Edelhertz, Ezra Stotland, Marilyn Walsh, and Milton Weinberg, *The Investigation of White-Collar Crime: A Manual for Law Enforcement Agencies* (Washington, D.C.: U.S. Department of Justice, U.S. Government Printing Office, 1977), pp. 195–198, and in National District Attorneys Association, *The Prosecutor's Manual on Economic Crime* (Washington, D.C.: National District Attorneys Association, 1977), pp. 121–122.
2. Brady v. Maryland, 373 U.S. 83 (1963); see Chapter 4 for a detailed discussion of this case.
3. See generally, Wayne A. Kerstetter and Anne M. Heienz, *Pretrial Settlement: An Evaluation* (Washington, D.C.: Law Enforcement Assistance Administration, 1979); John J. Cound, ed., *Civil Procedure: Cases and Materials*, 3rd ed. (St. Paul, Minn.: West Publishing, 1980); and Yale Kamisar, ed., *Modern Criminal Procedure: Cases, Comments, Questions*, 5th ed. (St. Paul, Minn.: West Publishing, 1983).
4. National District Attorneys Association, op. cit., p. 129; Edelhertz, Stotland, Walsh, and Weinberg, op. cit., pp. 123–143.
5. This discussion follows that in F. Lee Bailey, *To Be a Trial Lawyer* (Marshfield, Mass.: Telshare Publishing, 1982), pp. 97–101.

CASE PRESENTATION 14

An investigation culminates in use of the information that it produces in a final presentation to a decision maker. That final use may be preceded by a number of intermediate uses, may itself be only the last of a series of potentially final presentations, and will vary in format and style with the setting in which it occurs.

Among the intermediate uses of information resulting from an investigation, perhaps the earliest will be in briefings of the investigative team members. These may be purely informational, bringing all of the field investigators up-to-date on progress thus far to aid them in meeting ongoing demands for additional specific information. Or they may be in the nature of brainstorming sessions designed to reinvigorate an investigation through reinterpretation of the existing information, through development of new ideas on how to obtain needed additional information, through reassessment of the strengths and weaknesses of the case as it stands and of the probable case of the opposition, and through suggestions as to new sources of support for the investigation.

Another kind of intermediate presentation will be in progress reports to supervisors designed to revalidate the project, to continue the flow of resources, and to obtain new or different resources. Or presentation may be designed to document the basis and need for legal process to obtain information from reluctant sources, to prevent opposition actions that might unfairly prejudice the case being built, or to preserve assets or other aspects of the current situation pending a final decision on the issues. Among the process and procedures sought might be discovery (depositions, subpoenas duces tecum), search warrants, injunctions, writs of mandamus, arrest warrants, and determinations of probable cause to proceed.

Yet another kind of intermediate presentation of the investigative work product might come in negotiation or bargaining that could achieve the project objectives without going the full route to final decision making:

achievement of a settlement (either out of court or through approval of a consent decree) in a civil action or of a plea bargain in a criminal case.

A potentially final presentation differs from the intermediate primarily in that it might terminate the project. It may also differ in scope, detail, and formality. Most will only be potentially final because review of what otherwise might be the final decision is frequently possible, although it may not be sought. There is, however, an end of the line after which further review is not possible. In civil actions, it is frequently necessary to exhaust possible administrative remedies before resorting to court action. When a trial court decision has been reached, there may be possible review by at least one higher appellate court as a matter of right, or such a court may have discretion to allow review. That intermediate appellate court decision, in turn, may be subject to review by a court of last resort. Each such presentation must, however, anticipate the possibility that it may be the last chance to obtain a favorable ruling.

Any presentation of information from an investigation must be based on a clear definition of the issues, careful collection of the relevant information, sound analysis of the collected information, and logical organization of the analyzed work product for the kind of presentation required.

IMPACT OF THE SETTING

Setting does have a definite impact on the presentation of the case. It will dictate who makes the presentation, the kind of assistance that the presenter can have, the procedures to be followed during the determination, the burden and quantum of proof, the rules of evidence to be used, and the remedy that can be obtained.

In most personal and informal organizational settings, the investigator will also be the person making the presentation. Application of custom will usually govern the result, although in some cases legal rules will be involved. A friend or relative may be present simply as a supporter or to speak, either formally or informally, in support of the position sought. In a work setting, the petitioning individual may be represented by a union official, frequently called a shop steward. In a growing number of such cases, an attorney may be involved, particularly if there is no immediate settlement of the issues involved at the first level of consideration.

In nearly all formal governmental settings, the individual may today be represented by a lawyer, although that has not always been true. In most criminal proceedings, the state is now required to furnish an attorney if the defendant cannot afford to hire one. What began as a requirement only at trial has now been pushed further and further back into pretrial proceedings.

Procedures also vary with setting. Custom again governs in most personal and informal situations, with private organizations frequently using Robert's *Rules of Order* as their guide. Formal personal or union contracts of employment may also be involved. In formal governmental settings, whether administrative or judicial, procedures are usually established by law. Common law precedent, rules of court, administrative regulation, or a statutory code of procedure may govern. Common law provisions have now largely given way to consciously promulgated written rules.

Usually the burden of proof is on the party initiating the action: on the plaintiff in a civil case and on the state in a criminal prosecution. In most personal and informal organizational settings, there is no formal burden or quantum of proof involved. For formal governmental and judicial proceedings, the burden and quantum of proof are determined by law.

Sometimes on a particular issue, the burden of going forward with the evidence shifts from the party bearing the general burden of proof. In that case, the opposition must raise the issue and present some evidence to support their position. The ultimate burden of persuasion then rests on the party generally bearing the burden of proof. The standard of proof specifies how heavy that burden is. As was discussed in detail earlier (in Chapters 2 and 12), the standard in most civil cases is proof by a preponderance of the evidence, but it may be clear and convincing proof. In criminal cases, the burden is proof beyond a reasonable doubt.

In some situations, the burden of proof may be affected by a presumption. For example, if a will cannot be found, it is presumed to have been revoked by the testator. If a letter is regularly addressed and mailed, it is presumed to have been received by the addressee. If a person is absent for seven or some other stated number of years without explanation or communication, that person is presumed to be dead. Some presumptions are rebuttable and others are conclusive. A conclusive presumption cannot be attacked by introducing evidence to the contrary. The so-called presumption of innocence in criminal cases is not really a presumption at all, but merely a popular way of stating that the burden of proof in criminal cases always rests on the state.

The setting in which the determination is to be made also dictates the rules of evidence, if any, to be used. In personal and informal determinations of fact, formal rules of evidence are seldom used. Instead, the decision makers use common sense in deciding what to believe and how much weight to give the evidence. In more formal settings, rules of evidence generally do apply, rules that have the force of law. Rules of evidence were traditionally judge-made common law rules. Today the rules are usually established with legislative approval as rules of court, promulgated as administrative regulations, or created by statute. They govern offers of proof. As such, they are procedural rules applied during determination of fact that protect a decision maker from hearing assertions that cannot be evaluated properly by that decision maker.

Setting also determines the remedy that may be obtained. In criminal cases, the classic punishments on conviction are monetary fine, probation, incarceration in a local jail or regional prison, or death. Today judges may also require restitution to the injured party, payment of medical expenses, service to the community, or some other innovative remedy. In most jurisdictions, sentencing is the province of the judge. A few states, Virginia among them, require juries to sentence as well as convict.

Although provisions vary with the jurisdiction, the sentencing authority usually has a number of sources of information available in addition to that developed during the trial. One important source is the presentence report, prepared by a probation officer, that furnishes information on the background and current life situation of the defendant. Because the report may well be influential, it is customarily made available to the defendant, after information regarding confidential sources has been eliminated, so that the defense can check it for accuracy. The sentencing authority may allow rebuttal of factual assertions made in the report.

In addition, there may be available at sentencing a report of observation of the defendant by mental health experts. There may also be recommendations from police investigators, from the prosecutor, and, in all except capital cases,[1] from victims as well as from the defendant, family, and friends. For sentencing purposes, unsworn testimony, rumor, hearsay, and other evidence not admissible at trial may be considered for what it is worth. The formal rules of evidence do not apply. It is proper for the sentencing authority to consider such factors as the defendant's age, health, character, associates, conduct at trial, lack of repentance, and previous activities while on pretrial release, probation, and parole. The nature of the crime, possible deterrence of others who might commit the same crime, other pending charges or indictments, perjury on the witness stand, prior convictions, and the details of those crimes may also be considered. The sentencing process is much more free and open than the trial. This may change, however, for a move to establish guidelines to govern sentencing decisions is underway.[2]

In civil cases, the usual remedy is money damages, technically a legal remedy. Equitable remedies, such as restitution, specific performance, transfer of specific property, and injunctions are also available. Administrative proceedings may result in any of these remedies, in a cease and desist order, in loss of a license, in a change in permissible charge rates, or in similar administrative action.

Personal decisions will result in choice of the personal action to be taken. In less formal organizational settings, one's role or status in the organization may be affected. These variations in result of determinations of fact obviously depend on the setting, as do the other factors just outlined. They must be considered in presentation of the case, as must a number of other preliminary concerns.

SPECIFIC PRELIMINARY CONCERNS

There are a number of difficult preliminary decisions to be made in some case presentations. One involves choice of the forum. For example, it might be possible to bring a civil action in any one of several counties within a state, in any one of several states, or in either a state or federal court. The same may be true in a criminal case where a series of related criminal acts took place in several jurisdictions within a short period of time prior to apprehension of the suspect or suspects.

Many factors will be involved in the choice of forum in such cases. Take, for example, the manufacture, possession, and sale of liquor upon which taxes are not paid. Frequently this violates both federal and state law. In such a situation, choice of which jurisdiction will prosecute may well depend on the respective laws of the two jurisdictions regarding confiscation of equipment and other property used in the criminal activity. One jurisdiction may authorize seizure and sale of the property (such as airplanes, automobiles, trucks, or boats) without payment to lien holders; the other may require payment of such liens. If the law enforcement officials believe that the lien holder is actually bankrolling the operation, they will prosecute in the jurisdiction that does not require payment to lien holders in order for the action to be a more effective financial deterrent to future operations. The reputations of the prosecutors of the two jurisdictions for effectiveness, the reputations of the judges for severity or lenience, or the availability of investigative or prosecutive resources may also be crucial. Although investigators may not be making the final decision on choice of forum, they will contribute to that decision.

Another difficult decision will be whether to request trial by judge alone or trial by jury.[3] Among the issues recognized by attorneys in deciding whether to waive trial by jury is whether the judge can successfully merge the two functions of deciding legal and factual questions. A second concern is that, in deciding the admissibility of evidence, the judge must hear all of the testimony usually kept from a jury. If the judge's decision is against admission, can the judge, when deciding the factual issues, ignore what was heard about evidence that was denied admission? It is also true that a judge cannot possess the variety of community views represented in a jury. Then there is belief that trial of both fact and law by a judge results in fewer reversals on review and very seldom in mistrials. Judge trials are more economical and are usually considered by attorneys to be more consistent and predictable than trials by jury. But if the decision is to request trial by jury, the attorney must face the issue of how the jurors are to be chosen. Investigators can be quite helpful in that process.

F. Lee Bailey, a very successful trial lawyer, states that he tries to select jurors who have a "healthy self-confidence balanced by a modicum of humility," jurors "who respect the rights and needs of others," and "who have an air of being able to look out for themselves, and at the same time an inclination toward generosity to others."[4] But in most cases, lawyers must make judgments as to whether prospective jurors possess such characteristics without a great deal of information about them.

How much information an attorney has about prospective jurors when making choices depends on the resources available for investigation of those on jury panels. This depends, in turn, on the nature and importance of the case. Generally speaking, the greater the stakes involved in the trial, the greater the resources available for investigation and other efforts to support jury selection.

In most cases, a list—of names, addresses, and occupations—of the persons on the jury panel from which trial jurors will be chosen will be available to the lawyers several weeks in advance. In some cases where experience indicates that attempts may be made to intimidate or endanger jurors (such as some narcotics cases), so-called no-name jury panels will be used; these lists are not available until the day of trial. When the list is available in advance, investigators may be asked to annotate it with specific kinds of information about each prospective juror. In some jurisdictions, a jury book may be available containing information about jurors based on their prior jury service.

If resources are available, a number of other techniques may be used to get additional information useful in jury selection. Among them are community public opinion surveys, use of mock juries, and observation of prospective jurors by social scientists sitting at the elbow of the attorney in the courtroom during selection procedures.

Public opinion surveys are designed to determine how different segments of the community (such as occupation groups) react to issues that would be raised at the trial. If at all possible, persons identified from old jury lists are used because they are considered to be more representative of prospective jurors than a random sample of residents from the community at large. The issues stressed might be as varied as abortion, authoritarianism, control of corporations, police misconduct, or sterilization of certain categories of people.

Mock juries are presented with facts similar to those expected to be raised at the trial. The mock deliberations of the jury are then observed for clues as to how certain categories of prospective jurors might react to the case. This technique is expensive, costing anywhere from about twenty thousand to two-hundred and fifty thousand dollars. Obviously, very high stakes would have to be involved to merit such expenditures, but verdicts in some cases today do run to hundreds of millions and even billions of dollars.

When courtroom observation of prospective jurors is used, the experts hired are usually psychologists or sociologists. The technique is based on an assumption that the observed actions of a person are a clue to that person's attitudes.

Regardless of the source of the information, its use comes in the *voir dire*—the oral examination of prospective jurors by the opposing attorneys or by the judge and attorneys. The goal of the process is to eliminate jurors who might be biased against one side of the case. That might be accomplished by *challenge to the entire panel* (because, for example, the selection process discriminated systematically against some group); this is often called *challenge to the array*. It might be achieved by *challenge for cause* (for example, a showing that a prospective juror is closely related to a party to the suit, or does not believe in capital punishment in a case where that is a possible result). There is no limit to the number of challenges for cause. Or a jury panel member might be eliminated by *peremptory challenge*, for which no cause need be shown. Peremptory challenges are limited in number, with varying allowances in different kinds of cases in different jurisdictions. For example, ten peremptory challenges might be allowed each defendant in felony cases and only three per defendant in misdemeanor cases.

Among the areas of inquiry typically involved in the voir dire are

- Bias or prejudice based on race, national origin, political belief, religion, lifestyle, or sexual preference
- Whether the person would give more weight to a police officer's testimony simply because of that status than to the testimony of other witnesses
- Whether the person has previously been a juror in a similar case and, if so, the impression that experience left
- Whether the person is acquainted with any of the parties, anticipated witnesses, or lawyers involved
- Whether the person, any relative, or close friend has ever been involved in similar events and, if so, how they were treated and what impact the experience had
- Whether the person has been exposed to media coverage of the case
- What the person's attitude is toward a trial theory of a party (such as a defense of self-defense or of insanity)
- Whether the person has any educational, political, or religious beliefs that might influence attitude toward the issues involved (for example, concerning child abuse, spouse abuse, rape, abortion, or fraud)

Voir dire is the first chance of the lawyer and the investigator to make an impression on those who will be jurors. This impression must be a good one. Courtesy and respect must be shown along with firmness. Peremptory challenges must be exercised in a way that does not raise antipathy but in a fashion that will aid the case. And some anticipated problems with the evidence in the case should be raised and dealt with, such as the innocence of a darting child, the unavoidability of knocking down a pedestrian, or the previous criminal record of the plaintiff. These actions of the presenting attorney rely heavily on the information in the final investigative case submission report. With these preliminary matters out of the way, presentation of the principal investigative work product to the decision maker can begin.

PRESENTATION CONCERNS

When the time finally comes for the presentation, the attitude of the one making it is all-important.[5] It must be one of respect for the decision maker based on understanding of the task of decision. The role of the advocate is to give all possible aid to that task. Above all, a reputation for absolute trustworthiness in presentation of the amassed information must be earned. With that kind of reputation for honesty and forthrightness established, the presenter can turn to consideration of the most effective way in which the necessary information can be presented. The process begins with an opening statement.

Opening statements are brief summaries of the cases that the advocates intend to present. They begin with an explanation of what the party represented is asking for, and of the facts on which that request is based. The evidence to be submitted to prove those asserted facts is reviewed. Reference is made only to evidence that is sure to be admitted. Overstatement can result in a mistrial. The opening of the opposition, which comes second, describes the defense evidence to be submitted in contradiction to that of the plaintiff. If a jury is involved, it is at this point that the establishment of rapport with the jurors begun during voir dire must be made firm. The advocate addresses the decision makers simply and directly, both in words and in actions. Promise to prove facts during the proceeding must be limited to what the investigative work product will support.

Next comes presentation of the evidence through direct examination of witnesses and through identification and submission of real evidence marked as exhibits. The goals are to establish—in the most effective way—those facts that tend to prove the case and to minimize the effectiveness of the anticipated case of the opposition. Among the lessons of experience are to be respectful of all involved, to be fair but firm, and to maintain an even mien—never to show surprise. Because most evidence is presented through witnesses, the advocate must know well what the investigative report contains about the witnesses.

Knowledge of one's witnesses—of their probable effectiveness, of their ability to handle the complexity of their evidence, of their respect for and appreciation of the oath, and of their ability to handle cross-examination—comes from pretrial interviews with and preparation of those witnesses. Write ups of the interviews will be included in the investigative case submission report, and the preparation may well have been carried out by an investigator. That preparation, which is both legal and ethical, will make the presentation a smooth one. The witness will know why the case is being tried, how this bit of evidence fits in and why it is important, and that the evidence should be presented in a straightforward manner, without prompting through the asking of leading questions by the presenter.

Knowledge of one's witnesses also makes possible the ordering of their testimony in a logical manner, usually building the case chronologically. It makes it possible to begin and to end with strong witnesses, with the last witness, particularly in a complex case, being able to clean up any loose ends. Familiarity with the witnesses makes it possible to use short, concise, and direct questions designed to elicit yes or no answers. There should be only limited use of questions that elicit narrative answers.

One of the principal problems with investigators when they appear as witnesses stems from the fact that trials may come months or even years after the investigation was completed. In the interim, a number of similar cases may have been investigated. The investigator may have forgotten the crucial details of the instant case. As indicated earlier, there are two remedies for that situation: refreshment of the investigator's recollection from case notes or use of the investigator's original notes as the evidence (*past recollection recorded*). To use these remedial processes, the case presenter must be thoroughly familiar with the case file.

When presenting cumulative evidence, the attorney must know when to quit. Some corroboration of important testimony by an independent witness increases the weight of that testimony, but too much repetition slows down the proceedings, becomes boring for the trier of fact, and immerses salient points in a sea of testimony. An evaluation of whether what the witness has to say is worth the trouble of appearance must be made. Only witnesses who pass that test should be called. For maximum impact, be as brief as possible while still presenting the case completely and well.

Within general limits, each advocate has a right to present the case as desired; the opposition also has the right, and in most cases the obligation, to cross-examine witnesses as they appear. The purpose of cross-examination is to explore the perception, memory, articulation, and candor of the witness.[6] Every witness should be prepared for cross-examination as well as for direct examination. The purpose of cross-examination must be made clear. The right of the other attorney to ask leading questions must be explained. The witness should be instructed to be cooperative, to answer the questions briefly but truthfully, and not try to do battle with the cross-examiner. Any anticipated testimony that might be used to contradict the witness should be reviewed. Whether the witness has made any prior statements that might be used for impeachment (discrediting) of the witness should be explored.

Regarding cross-examination, trial lawyers agree on three basic rules.

1. Don't cross-examine unless you must, unless the witness has hurt your case or can provide crucial evidence not otherwise available.
2. Don't ask a question unless you know and are prepared to accept the truthful answer.
3. Don't ask questions beginning with *what, when, where, why,* or *how* unless with very good reason. Stick to questions requiring yes or no answers.

There are three phases to cross-examination: extraction, closing, and impeachment. In extraction, the attorney seeks to elicit anything helpful to his or her case that the witness might know. Closing is the cutting off of any escape route when the cross-examiner has decided to attempt to impeach the witness. When this is done, there must be no possible explanation for the admitted situation available to the witness other than the discrediting one. Closing is accomplished by getting every detail of the witness's story on the record. Pointing out the discrepancy or contradiction is impeachment or discrediting of the witness.

Impeachment through cross-examination requires careful planning. Exactly how did the witness hurt the case? Is there contradicting evidence? Is the witness firm enough in making the assertions to prevent escape? Is the weakness of the testimony in the witness's perception, memory, or candor? Inability to articulate will seldom be the cause. With all of this information in mind, the impeachment process begins. Its scope is limited to the subject matter of the direct testimony and the credibility of the witness.

In short, good cross-examination requires painstaking preparation. Whether to cross-examine at all must be carefully considered. If undertaken, the points to be made should be outlined. The cross-examiner's concentration must be on the answers of the witness. An associate should write down the answers. For successful impeachment, the improbability or impossibility of the events as alleged by the witness must be shown through the use of simple language in directive and leading questions. It builds points slowly to a strong ending. Cross-examination should not lead simply to a repetition of the direct testimony. The questioner should not assume anything not in evidence, should not ask a question to which the truthful answer is not known, and should remain calm. Cross-examination is an art mastered by all successful trial lawyers.

After cross-examination, the attorney who presented the witness for direct testimony has an opportunity to repair any damage done. This redirect examination is usually very short and is limited to matters raised on cross-examination, but can be quite telling if the cross-examination is not well done.

As discussed in Chapter 4, both direct and cross-examination of expert witnesses require special care. For success, the requirement is thorough preparation. Expert testimony does not bind the jury. It is to be considered along with all other evidence presented and given such weight as it is deemed to deserve. Issues to be considered include whether the opinion is based on sufficient education and experience, whether the reasons given to support it are sound, and whether the opinion outweighs other evidence presented in the case. As with all other evidence, final evaluation of expert testimony is the task of the trier of fact.

A matter that frequently arises in criminal cases is whether and when evidence of previous crimes can be admitted. The general rule is that such evidence is not admissible if offered to show simply that the defendant is a person of bad character or has a propensity to commit crimes.[7] In most jurisdictions it can be admitted in at least five specific situations: to show motive, intent, absence of mistake, the identity of the defendant, and a common scheme or plan. Although motive is not an element of any criminal offense, its showing is frequently persuasive to the trier of fact that the defendant actually committed the offense charged.

Previous offenses may have included threats to the victim of this offense or a special relationship between the alleged perpetrator and the victim that may be relevant in proof of motive. Intent may be proved if the defendant can be shown to have committed a pattern of similar crimes. If the defendant claims accident or self-defense, commission of previous similar crimes can be shown to discredit those defenses. Commission of similar crimes previously in the same manner as this one can be shown to identify the defendant as perpetrator in the instant case. Such offenses are sometimes called signature crimes. And it may be shown that the instant offense was part of a larger criminal scheme. Testimony about the commission of the underlying felony in a felony murder case is one example; theft of an automobile later used in a bank robbery is another. In order to use testimony of the commission of previous crimes for these purposes, a basis must be established. The judge must be convinced that the other crime will be probative evidence for the purpose for which it is offered, that it is necessary for the purpose offered, and that its probative value is not outweighed by its possible prejudicial effect.

When the party initiating the action has presented all of the desired evidence to prove its case, the opposition then presents its defense in much the same manner. Witnesses are presented for direct examination, cross-examination, and redirect examination. Physical evidence is identified, marked, and submitted. When those processes are complete, both sides present their closing arguments.

In making their closing or final arguments, the opposing attorneys emphasize the importance of the case, go over the duty of the jury, comment on the burden of proof, argue the weight to be accorded to specific items of evidence, discuss reasonable inferences that can be made from the evidence, and comment on the credibility of specific witnesses. The lawyers in closing may not state their personal beliefs about the matters at issue; appeal to the passions or prejudices of the jury; or, in a criminal case, comment on the defendant's failure to testify.

More might be said specifically about closing arguments in criminal cases. The prosecutor will usually discuss the elements of the offense charged and the state's evidence tending to prove the existence of each of those elements. Admitted documents and other physical evidence will be used in that summary. The testimony of particularly strong witnesses will be highlighted and attempts made to bolster that of weaker witnesses by showing corroboration by other witnesses and by arguing that the witness has no motive to lie. The case of the defendant can be attacked by asking whether it is reasonable or whether it is only a desperate theory, claim, or contention that does not raise a reasonable doubt.

The defense, on the other hand, will usually stress the duty of the jury to acquit if there is any reasonable doubt on any element of the offense, will attack the credibility of the witnesses for the state, and will frequently mention the state's failure to produce more positive witnesses. The defense attorney may show sympathy for the victim, if deserved, but argue that there is not sufficient evidence to show that the wrong was committed by this defendant. In most jurisdictions, this is the last chance for the defense to speak; the prosecution has the final word. Where this is the case, the defense will probably mention it. The defense may not argue any matter not in the record, that the defendant should not be subjected to the severe possible penalty, or that the defendant is in need of the sympathy of the jurors.

The prosecution has the last word in rebuttal of the case of the defense in most jurisdictions. In that rebuttal the prosecutor will seek to reinforce the state's case and will repeat the theory of the prosecution. In most jurisdictions, the judge will then charge the jury, explaining its task once again and summarizing the applicable rules of law. In some jurisdictions, this charge by the judge may come before the final arguments of the attorneys. The jury will then be sent to the jury room to begin its deliberations.

In many criminal cases, the defense will move for a directed verdict of acquittal after the state and defense cases have been closed. That motion must be granted if the judge is convinced that the evidence and all permissible inferences from the evidence, when viewed in the light most favorable to the government, is such that a reasonable juror must have reasonable doubt as to the existence of one or more of the essential elements of the offense. If granted, the jury must enter a verdict of acquittal as directed by the judge. The jurors do not actually deliberate about the case.

Investigators must be familiar with these presentation processes to carry out their investigations effectively and to participate intelligently in the final proceedings. Being able to participate in the use of their work product also motivates the investigator to dedicated service. It converts the work from being simply a job into an interesting career.

SUMMARIZING COMMENTARY

Investigators see their work product used both in intermediate and in potentially final presentations. Those that are intermediate serve in a variety of ways to push the case forward. Of those that are potentially final, one will in fact end the case.

Just how and by whom presentations of the information developed in the investigation will be made depends on the nature of the case (whether administrative, civil, or criminal) and on its setting. The setting will dictate who makes the presentation, the procedures to be followed, the burden and quantum of proof, the rules of evidence to be used, and the remedy that can be obtained.

When a case goes all the way to final formal determination in a legal proceeding, a number of preliminary concerns must be faced. One of them is choice of the forum. Another is whether, when a court trial is scheduled, the right to a jury trial should be waived and the judge allowed to try both the factual and legal issues. If a jury is to be used, there must be preparation for choice of jurors, which requires further investigation of the background of potential jurors. In the shaping of the jury, there may be challenge to the entire panel, challenge of individuals for cause, or peremptory challenge. This shaping involves a decision by the presenter as to the characteristics of jurors to be sought. The courtroom process of jury selection is called voir dire.

After the opening statements, the moving party presents its case, largely through the testimony of witnesses, each of whom is then subject to cross-examination by the opposition. When the moving party finishes, the defense submits its case in a similar manner. In criminal cases, the defense frequently moves for a directed verdict of acquittal when the prosecution has completed its case and again when the evidence for the defense has been presented. The equivalent in a civil action is a motion to dismiss the case. When that is not granted, closing arguments are made, the judge instructs the jury on the law, and the jury begins its deliberations.

It is a fortunate presenter who has the assistance of the chief investigator on the case during preparation for and at the final presentation. It is also a fortunate investigator who is allowed to play that role, which makes it possible to see the final culmination of the investigative efforts.

STUDY QUESTIONS

1. Intermediate presentations of investigative information are frequently made. Of what significance is that fact to investigators?
2. Why are most full presentations of the case built by investigation only potentially final?
3. What impact does the setting have on potentially final presentations?
4. Why is knowledge of one's witnesses important in potentially final presentations?
5. When should an advocate cross-examine an adverse witness?

RECOMMENDED ADDITIONAL READING

- Bailey, F. Lee. *To Be a Trial Lawyer.* Marshfield, Mass.: Telshare Publishing, 1982.
- Dershowitz, Alan. *The Best Defense.* New York: Random House, 1985.
- Weston, Paul B., and Wells, Kenneth M. *Criminal Evidence for Police,* 2nd ed. Englewood Cliffs, N.J.: Prentice-Hall, 1976.

NOTES

1. Booth v. Maryland, _____ U.S. _____, 107 S.Ct. 2529, 96 L.Ed. 440 (1987).
2. For background on the federal guidelines, which have been adopted, see "Special Report: Guidelines Go to Congress; August '88 Implementation Prepared," in "News from the Sentencing Commission," *The Third Branch* 19, no. 5 (May 1987).
3. See F. Lee Bailey, *To Be a Trial Lawyer* (Marshfield, Mass.: Telshare Publishing, 1982), pp. 108–111; Robert E. Oliphant, ed., *Trial Techniques with Irving Younger* (Minneapolis, Minn.: National Practice Institute, 1978), pp. 5–16; John R. Wing, ed., *The Jury: Techniques for the Trial Lawyer* (New York: Practicing Law Institute, 1983), passim.
4. Bailey, op. cit., p. 119.
5. See Oliphant, op. cit., passim; Wing, op. cit., passim; and Leonard

Packel and Delores B. Spina, *Trial Advocacy: A Systematic Approach* (Philadelphia: American Law Institute—American Bar Association Committee on Professional Education, 1984), passim.
6. In general, see the works cited in Note 5 and Robert L. Habush, *Art of Advocacy* (New York: Matthew Bender, 1986), passim.
7. See, for example, Section 404(b) of the Federal Rules of Evidence.

GLOSSARY

Associative evidence Evidence used to show a connection between two objects; for example to connect or associate an individual with a scene. *See also* Individuation.

Bill of particulars In common law practice, a written statement or specification of the particulars of the demand for which an action at law is brought, or of a defendant's set-off against such demand (including dates, sums, and items in detail), furnished by one of the parties or the other, either voluntarily or in compliance with a judge's order.

Brute facts Facts standing by themselves, without reference to their relationship to other facts and without interpretation as evidence of the truthfulness or falsity of some assertion. *See also* Indifferent facts.

Challenge To object or take exception to. Three challenges are available in jury selection. Challenge to the entire panel, often called challenge to the array, can be made if some partiality or default can be shown in the process by which the jury was drawn. Challenge for cause is a challenge to a juror for which some cause or reason is alleged. Under peremptory challenge, available in criminal practice, each side is allowed to challenge a certain number of jurors, without assigning any cause. *See also* Voir dire.

Clear and convincing evidence The evidence necessary to meet the more stringent of the two civil action standards of proof. *See also* Preponderance of the evidence.

Control The investigator who is directing an informant.

Criminalist Forensic scientist whose work product is routinely used in legal proceedings, primarily in criminal cases. *See also* Forensic scientist.

Deposition Sworn testimony of a witness taken upon interrogatories, not in open court, and intended to be used in trial.

Determination of the issues The decision that one line of evidence meets the required standard of proof such that matters at issue can be settled with one outcome rather than another.

Discovery The disclosure of facts, titles, documents, or other things that are necessary to the party seeking the discovery as a part of a civil or criminal cause or action pending or to be brought or as evidence of the party's rights or title in such proceeding. *See also* Pretrial discovery.

Experimental research Behavioral and social science research in which one variable is changed while others are held constant in order to assess the consequences of the change.

Falsification Process by which science disproves its tentative hypotheses and theories. This can be done by observation showing that facts implied by the theory do not exist.

Findings of fact Facts accepted by the trier of fact as having been proved to exist, to be relevant, and to be worthy of weight in making the required determination of issues involved in the matter.

Forensic scientist Scientist whose work product is routinely used in legal proceedings. *See also* Criminalist.

Hearsay Evidence not proceeding from the personal knowledge of the witness, but from the mere repetition of what the witness has heard others say. Hearsay evidence is admitted only in specified cases, when necessary.

Historical research A behavioral and social science research approach consisting of the patient reconstruction of the past. Research by one kind of behavioral and social scientist, a professional historian.

Hypothesis A tentative assumption made for the sake of argument or to draw out and test its logical or empirical consequences. *See also* Theory.

Identification Proof of identity; proof that a person, subject, or article is the very same as alleged, charged, or reputed to be; proof that an item of physical evidence falls into a certain category. *See also* Individuation.

Indifferent facts Items subject to observation that need no interpretation. *See also* Brute facts.

Individuation A refinement of identification in determination of fact whereby a person, subject, or article is identified and shown to be different from all others. *See also* Identification.

Interrogation The questioning of a suspect, perpetrator, or individual who is reluctant, or who refuses to cooperate with the interviewer. Control of the interviewee and of the direction of the discussion have traditionally been aspects of interrogation. *See also* Interview.

Interview A meeting—either in person or not—in which information is obtained from a person. As a result of *Miranda v. Arizona,* most of the differences between an interview and an interrogation have been eliminated. *See also* Interrogation.

Link diagram Analytic technique used in fraud and other economic crime cases to illustrate complicated linkages between persons involved. Each connection should be supported by documentary or investigative data. Arrows are used to indicate the flow. *See also* Time flow diagram.

Link network analysis Investigative technique in which special charts are constructed to show the connections among events, persons, organizations, and other scheme components. These charts, which do not focus on time sequence, are used to unravel the complex interrelationships among parties to a scheme to defraud.

Management of criminal investigation (MCI) A concept for improving the organization and management of the investigative function of police agencies. Under MCI, patrol officers have increased investigative responsibility in a wide range of cases. They are assisted by investigative specialists and by a centralized departmental investigative unit. MCI's five components are initial investigation, case screening, management of the continuing investigation, police-prosecutor relations, and continual monitoring of investigative performance.

MCI *See* Management of criminal investigation.

Net worth–expenditures principle Mathematical computation designed to determine the total accumulation of wealth and annual expenditures made by an individual. The net worth–expenditures principle is used to determine whether expenditures exceed known accumulation, indicating an unaccounted for source of income.

Observation research Behavioral and social science research consisting of developing and recording additional knowledge about the present.

Parol evidence Oral or verbal evidence; that which is given by word of mouth, the ordinary kind of evidence, given by witnesses in court.

Parol evidence rule Under this rule, when parties put their agreement in writing, all previous oral agreements merge in the writing and a contract as written cannot be modified or changed by parol evidence, in the absence of a plea of mistake or fraud in the preparation of the writing. *See also* Parol evidence.

Preponderance of the evidence The lesser of two common standards of proof, one of which must be met in civil legal proceedings. The evidence must produce the stronger impression, be given the greater weight, and be more convincing as to its truth when weighed against the opposing evidence. *See also* Clear and convincing evidence *and* Proof beyond a reasonable doubt.

Pretrial discovery Enforced production of documentary evidence. This encompasses motions to produce, subpoenas duces tecum, interrogatories, depositions, and search warrants. *See also* Discovery.

Prima facie case A case in which the evidence in the litigant's favor is sufficiently strong for the opponent to be called on to answer it; prima facie evidence is provided for every element of the case. A case established by sufficient evidence and that can be overthrown only by rebutting evidence adduced on the other side. *See also* Prima facie evidence.

Prima facie evidence Evidence good and sufficient on its face, evidence that is sufficient to establish a given fact or the chain of facts claimed, but that can be overthrown only by rebutting evidence adduced on the other side.

Privilege A right or immunity granted as a peculiar benefit, advantage, or favor. Many different privileges exist under the law, ranging from privilege under civil law to that under maritime law.

Problem definition A process including three prerequisites: a thorough knowledge of the context, intellectual capacity to form intuitive insights, and careful consideration of problem symptoms.

Proof beyond a reasonable doubt A standard of proof that must be met in certain criminal prosecutions. This proof precludes every reasonable hypothesis—not all possible hypotheses—except that which it tends to support. *See also* Clear and convincing evidence *and* Preponderance of the evidence.

Standing A personal interest in the outcome of an issue sufficiently direct and substantial to authorize one to seek legal or other official resolution of the issue.

Survey research Behavioral and social science research in which information is gathered about some population by interviewing a representative sample of that population.

Theory A plausible or acceptable general idea of the root of the problem based on facts, suppositions, and conclusions that are continually subjected to reexamination to determine whether they can continue to be relied on. *See also* Hypothesis.

Time flow diagram Analytic technique used in fraud and other economic crime cases to show the scheme as a series of events connected by related activities. *See also* Link diagram.

Tort (From the Latin *torquere,* to twist; *tortus,* twisted, wrested aside.) A private or civil wrong or injury. A wrong independent of contract. Three elements of every tort action are existence of legal duty from defendant to plaintiff, breach of duty, and damage as proximate result.

Tortious Wrongful; of the nature of a tort. *See also* Tort.

True bill A term used in criminal practice to signify the endorsement made by a grand jury upon a bill of indictment. A bill of indictment is declared a true bill when the grand jury find it sustained by the evidence given them and when they are satisfied of the truth of the accusation.

Truth A substantial conclusion based on valid reasoning from premises believed to be correct in the light of current knowledge. *See also* Validity.

Validity A formal concept in scientific reasoning in which a stated implication is valid if it is logically correct, if the implied conclusion must follow from the previous assertion. Valid reasoning from a false premise leads to a false conclusion. *See also* Truth.

Value set A set of predispositions, derived from one's cultural background, education, training, occupational and life experiences, that determines the way one sees the world and interprets observed facts, including the evidence presented in legal proceedings.

Voir dire Preliminary examination of one presented as a juror or witness, where the person's competency, interest, and other relevant factors can be reviewed and objected to if necessary. *See also* Challenge.

READINGS FOR INVESTIGATORS — APPENDIX A

Investigators, like other professionals, can never stop reading. They also can never find the time to read everything that they should and would like to read. The purposes of this appendix are to help investigators become aware of relevant publications as an aid to them in setting priorities for their available professional reading time and to list some of the publications that may be consulted during research on particular problems that may be encountered during an investigation.

GENERAL READING

As indicated in the text, investigators must know at least a little bit about a lot of things. For that reason, they should have as a base a broad liberal arts education rather than a narrow and technical training. When their formal education is completed, they must keep their general knowledge base up-to-date through a personal reading program. A good place to start and from which to get leads for more comprehensive treatments of subjects of interest is with a good daily newspaper such as the *New York Times*, *Washington Post*, *St. Louis Times Dispatch*, or *Los Angeles Times*. The paper chosen should be read carefully every day.

Not all of the investigator's reading can be career oriented. Investigators must also remain well-rounded, whole persons, which means that their general reading should also be dictated by their general noncareer interests. Local, national, and world issues should be followed; hobbies pursued; interests in literature and the arts developed; and even reading for pure entertainment undertaken to enhance the investigator's qualifications and performance.

CAREER ORIENTED READING

When an investigator has settled on a career direction, that choice will suggest both general reading in fields surrounding the area in which the substance of the investigations will lie and specific reading in that area. An investigator who reads extensively in cognate fields will be surprised at how often that reading will be useful in an investigation. For example, one who becomes a specialist in the investigation of criminal homicides should read legal articles on the law of homicide, medical articles on diagnosis of cause of death, sociological articles dealing with conditions in our society that lead to homicide, as well as materials on homicide investigation.

Persons who choose investigation as a career will find a wide variety of journals available whose specific focus is investigative matters. Because so many investigations are in support of some kind of anticipated legal proceeding, the reviews and journals published under the auspices of the nation's law schools are very important. The law reviews discuss both substantive law in the areas where investigations are common and the procedural rules, such as the rules of evidence, that govern the procedures. The best access to this resource is the *Index to Legal Periodicals*, which is similar to the more general *Readers' Guide to Periodical Literature* with which most of us are quite familiar. Similar indexes to the criminal justice literature are now available.

Titles of magazines and journals of specific interest to investigators follow. (Addresses or other publication information is included for some of the materials.) This list is not complete, but does include references found useful by many investigators.

Addictions (Alcohol and Drug Addiction Foundation, 344 Bloor Street, Toronto, 179, Canada)
American Journal of Clinical Pathology
American Journal of Forensic Medicine and Pathology
Association of Firearms and Tool Mark Examiners Journal
Australian Journal of Forensic Science

Bulletin on Narcotics (United Nations, Division of Narcotics, Geneva, Switzerland)

Canadian Society of Forensic Science Journal
Corrections Today
Corrective and Social Psychology Journal
Crime and Delinquency
Criminal Defense
Criminal Justice and Behavior
Criminal Justice Policy Review
Criminal Law Review
Criminology: An Interdisciplinary Journal

Detonator Magazine
Drug Dependence

Drug Enforcement

F.B.I. Law Enforcement Bulletin
Fingerprint and Identification Magazine
Fire and Arson Investigator Journal
Forensic Photography
Forensic Science Gazette
Forensic Science International
Forensic Science Society Journal

International Association of Arson Investigators Journal
International Criminal Police Review
International Drug Report
International Journal of Forensic Dentistry
International Journal of the Addictions
International Microform Journal of Legal Medicine and Forensic Science
Investigative Reporters and Editors Journal
Investigator

Journal of Criminal Law, Criminology and Police Science
Journal of Criminology and Police Science
Journal of Drug Issues
Journal of Forensic Medicine
Journal of Forensic Sciences
Journal of Legal Evidence
Journal of Police Administration
Journal of Police Science and Administration
Journal of Polygraph Science
Journal of the Canadian Society of Forensic Science
Journal of the Forensic Science Society (British)
Justice Quarterly

Keepers Voice

Law and Order

Medical Science and Law
Medicine, Science and the Law
Medico-Legal Journal
Military Police Journal

National Employment Listing Service (Includes investigative positions)

Police Chief
Police Journal (British)
Police Law Quarterly
Police Times
Polygraph (American Polygraph Association)

Polygraph Law Reporter
Polygraph Review
Privacy Journal

Response to Violence in the Family
Royal Canadian Mounted Police Gazette

Safe Schools Bulletin
Security Register
Security World

Trial Lawyers Guide

World Association of Document Examiners Journal

Zeitschrift für Rechtsmedizin/Journal of Legal Medicine (German)

In addition to these journals, a number of association newsletters and commercially published digests are also available to investigators; some of them are listed here.

American Association of Correctional Psychology
Arson Analysis Newsletter
Arson Resource Exchange Bulletin

Computer Security Digest
Corporate Fraud Digest
The Criminologist (American Society for Criminology)

Detective

Economic Crime Digest (National District Attorneys Association)
Exchange (World Association of Document Examiners Newsletter)

Forensic Serology News

Identification News
Identification Officer
Insurance Crime Prevention and Justice Report
International Association of Automobile Theft Investigators Newsletter

Narcotics Newsletter
News and Views in Forensic Toxicology

On the Line (American Correctional Association)

Security Blanket
Security Digest

Today (Academy of Criminal Justice Sciences)

These sources supplement the books and monographs that appear regularly. The addresses of and subscription information on these publications—and many others—may be found in the *Index to Criminal Justice Periodicals* available in university libraries. They are also found in the more general Ayer's *Directory of Publications* (published annually) or *Ulrich's International Periodicals Directory* (supplemented by *Ulrich's Quarterly*), either or both of which should be available in your public library. Also helpful are two National Institute of Justice publications, *A Network of Knowledge: Directory of Criminal Justice Information Sources* and *Expanding Knowledge in Criminal Justice: Publications of the National Institute of Justice 1978–Date*, latest editions.

An additional source of information that should not be overlooked is the occasional graduate student master thesis or doctoral dissertation that reports research of interest to investigators. These are indexed and available through your local library's interlibrary loan service.

AGENCIES AND ORGANIZATIONS OF INTEREST TO INVESTIGATORS

APPENDIX B

This appendix presents a list of many of the agencies and associations in which investigators may be interested. As an investigator, you may wish to join one or more of these organizations. Or you may wish to consult them to obtain expert advice about problems encountered during investigations. Remember that this list is not complete; you are sure to find other useful organizations during your work. Addresses for some of these organizations change with some frequency. In addition, in seeking aid from psychiatrists and other medical experts, the latest editions of the *Directory of Medical Specialists*, *Who's Who in America*, and *Biographical Directory of the Fellows and Members of the American Psychiatric Association* will be helpful. Other associations can be identified and their addresses obtained from the annual *Encyclopedia of Associations*, available in your local public library.

Academy of Criminal Justice Sciences, University of Nebraska at Omaha, 1313 Farnam on the Mall, Omaha, NE 68182-0115

American Academy of Correctional Officers, 1417 Willow Avenue, Des Plaines, IL 60016

American Academy of Forensic Sciences, 225 South Academy Boulevard, #201, Colorado Springs, CO 80910

American Academy of Neurology, 4005 West Sixty-fifth Street, Minneapolis, MN 55435

American Academy of Psychoanalysis, 125 East Sixty-fifth Street, New York, NY 10021

American Association of Correctional Psychologists, c/o Allen K. Hess, Ph.D., Department of Psychology, Auburn University, Auburn, AL 36830

American Association of Mental Health Professionals in Corrections, c/o Dr. John S. Zil, 2615 E. Clinton Street, Fresno, CA 93703

American Board of Forensic Psychiatry, c/o Medical and Chirurgical Faculty of Maryland, 1211 Cathedral Street, Baltimore, MD 21201

American Board of Odontology, c/o Homer R. Campbell, D.D.S., 6800 C Montgomery NE, Albuquerque, NM 87109

American Board of Pathology, c/o 112 Lincoln Center, 5401 West Kennedy Boulevard, Box 24695, Tampa, FL 33623

American College of Legal Medicine, 1340 North Astor Street, Chicago, IL 60610

American Correctional Association, 4321 Harwick Road, College Park, MD 20740

American Electroencephalographic Society, Marquette University School of Medicine, Milwaukee County Hospital, Milwaukee, WI 53233

American Federation of Police, 1100 Northeast 125th Street, North Miami, FL 33161

American Humane Association, P.O. Box 1266, Denver, CO 80201

American Justice Institute, 725 University Avenue, Sacramento, CA 95825-6793

American Neurological Association, 710 West 168th Street, New York, NY 10032

American Psychiatric Association, 1700 Eighteenth Street NW, Washington, DC 20009

American Psychological Association, 1200 Seventeenth Street NW, Washington, DC 20036

American Society of Clinical Pathologists, 445 North Lake Shore Drive, Chicago, IL

American Society of Crime Laboratory Directors, c/o Jerry Chisum, California Department of Justice, 2213 Blue Gum Avenue, Modesto, CA 95351

American Society of Criminology, Suite 212, 1314 Kinnear Road, Columbus, OH 43212

American Society of Forensic Odontology, c/o Dr. James D. Woodward, School of Dentistry, University of Louisville, 2301 S. Third Street, Louisville, KY 40292

American Society of Questioned-Document Examiners, 1415 Esperson Building, Houston, TX 77002

Armed Forces Institute of Pathology, Washington, DC 20306

Arson Resource Center, 16825 South Seton Avenue, Emmitsburg, MD 21727

Association of Firearm and Tool Mark Examiners, 7857 Esterel Drive, La Jolla, CA 92037

Association of Paroling Authorities, c/o New Jersey State Parole Board, P.O. Box 7387, Whittlesey Road, Trenton, NJ 08625

Center for Human Toxicology, University of Utah, Salt Lake City, UT 84112

Chicago Law Enforcement Study Group, Room 303, 109 North Dearborn Street, Chicago, IL 60602

College of American Pathologists, 230 North Michigan Avenue, Chicago, IL 60601

Computer Protection Systems, Suite 4, 711 West Ann Arbor Trail, Plymouth, MI 48170

Crime and Justice Foundation, 19 Temple Place, Boston, MA 02111

Criminal Justice Statistics Association, Suite 122, 444 North Capitol Street NW, Washington, DC 20001

Drug Enforcement Administration, Forensic Science Section, 1405 I Street NW, Washington, DC 20537

FBI Laboratory Division, Tenth Street and Pennsylvania Avenue NW, Washington, DC 20535

FBI Training Academy, Forensic Science Research Training Center, Quantico, VA 22135

Forensic Sciences Foundation, Suite 201, 225 South Academy Boulevard, Colorado Springs, CO 80910

Forest Products Laboratory of the Forest Service, United States Department of Agriculture, Madison, WI 53707

Independent Association of Questioned-Document Examiners, 518 Guaranty Bank Building, Cedar Rapids, IA 52401

Institute of Applied Science, 1920 W. Sunnyside Avenue, Chicago, IL 60640

Insurance Crime Prevention Institute, 15 Franklin Street, Westport, CT 06880

International Association for Identification, P.O. Box 139, Utica, NY 13503

International Association for Shopping Center Security, P.O. Box 1275, Atlanta, GA 30301

International Association of Arson Investigators, 25 Newton Street, P.O. Box 600, Marlboro, MA 01752

International Association of Auto Theft Investigators, 12416 Feldon Street, Wheaton, MD 20906

International Association of Bomb Technicians and Investigators, P.O. Box 6609, Colorado Springs, CO 80934

International Association of Coroners and Medical Examiners, 2121 Adelbert Road, Cleveland, OH 44106

International Association of Law Enforcement Firearms Instructors, Inc., P.O. Box 598, 2 White Place, Brookline Village, MA 02147-0598

International Criminal Police Organization, 26 rue Armengaud, 92210 Saint-Cloud, France

International Juvenile Officers Association, 8700 North Port Washington Road, Fox Point, WI 53217

International Narcotic Enforcement Officers Association, Suite 310, 112 State Street, Albany, NY 12207

International Reference Organization in Forensic Medicine and Sciences, c/o Dr. William G. Eckert, Laboratory, St. Francis Hospital, Wichita, KS 67214

International Society of Crime Prevention Practitioners, P.O. Box 1284, Rockville, MD 20850

Law Enforcement Standards Library, National Bureau of Standards, United States Department of Commerce, Washington, DC 20234

Milton Helpern International Reference Center for Forensic Sciences, Box 95, Wichita State University, Wichita, KS 67208

National Alliance for Safe Schools, 501 North Interregional Road, Austin, TX 78702

National Association of Medical Examiners, 1402 South Grand Boulevard, St. Louis, MO 63104

National Automobile Theft Bureau, 10330 South Roberts Road, 3A, Palos Hills, IL 60465

National Burglar and Fire Alarm Association, Suite 1120, 1120 Nineteenth Street NW, Washington, DC 20036

National Center for the Prevention and Control of Rape, National Institute of Mental Health, Parklawn Building, Room 6C-12, 5600 Fishers Lane, Rockville Lane, Rockville, MD 20857

National Center on Child Abuse and Neglect Information Center, Children's Bureau, P.O. Box 1182, Washington, DC 20013

National College for Criminal Defense, College of Law, University of Houston, Houston, TX 77004

National Crime Information Center, Federal Bureau of Investigation, Tenth Street and Pennsylvania Avenue NW, Washington, DC 20535

National Employment Listing Service, Criminal Justice Center, Sam Houston State University, Huntsville, TX 77341

National Rural Crime Prevention Center, 2120 Fyffe Road, Columbus, OH 43210

National Training Center for Polygraph Science, Suite 1400, 200 West Fifty-seventh Street, New York, NY 10019

Police and Security Section, Association of American Railroads, 1920 L Street NW, Washington, DC 20036

Police Executive Research Forum, 2300 M Street NW, Washington, DC 20037

Police Services Resource Center, Suite 500, 918 F Street NW, Washington, DC 20004-1482

Resource Center on Family Violence, 2000 P Street NW, Washington, DC 20036

Terrorism Research and Communication Center, Room 501, 110 West Fortieth Street, New York, NY 10018

United States Department of the Treasury, Bureau of Alcohol, Tobacco, and Firearms, Forensic Science Laboratory, 1401 Research Boulevard, Rockville, MD 20850

United States Police Canine Association, 8616 Trumps Hill Road, Upper Marlboro, MD 20772

World Association of Document Examiners, 111 North Canal Street, Chicago, IL 60606

INDEX

Abramowitz, Michael, 147
Accountant–client privilege, 165
Accountants, 72
Active listening, 87
Actus reus, 176
American Law Institute, 186
Administrative Procedure Act, 155
   summary, 151
Administrative proceedings, 148
   adjudicative, 148
   investigative, 148
   penalties, 148
   problem definition, 148
   rule making, 148
Admissions, 69, 90–94, 163
   voluntary, 163
Adversary system, 42
Ahern, James F., 128
Ake v. Oklahoma, 79, 85
Alibis, 59, 69
American Bar Association, 42
American Enterprise Institute, 64
Anticipating the opposition, 194
   possible defenses, 195
Arbitration, 13, 14, 16
Arizona v. Hicks, 46
Assault and homicide, 120
Assertion, 19
   compound, 7
   conditional, 7
   conjunctive, 7
   consequent component, 7
   hypothetical, 7
   implicative, 7
   as proposition, 7
   simple, 7
Attorney–client privilege, 164
Audigators, 134
Audit, 72
   bookkeeping, 73
   normal, 72

Auditors, 72
Autopsy, 76, 121
Axiom, 8

Bailey, F. Lee, 186, 198, 199, 213
Bank Secrecy Act, 144
Barzun, Jacques, 29, 30
Belief systems, 15
Bennett-Sandler, Georgette, 114
Bequai, August, 127, 128
Bernstein, Carl, 26
Beveridge, W. I. B., 17
Bias, 43
Biderman, Albert D., 127
Bill of particulars, 191
Bioengineering, 22
Blakey, G. Robert, 146, 147
Bloch, Peter B., 114
Booking, 38, 44
Bookkeeping, 72
Booth v. Maryland, 213
Brady v. Maryland, 59, 67, 191, 199
Brandeis, Louis D., 32
Brookings Institution, 64
Bruske, Ed, 102
Brute or indifferent facts, 9, 15, 69
Burden of proof, 202
   presumption of innocence, 202
   presumptions, 202
Burglary, *see* Larceny, burglary, and robbery

Caldwell, Robert G., 128
California Bureau of Criminal Identification and Investigation, 119
Cameras, 81, 83
Canon of Parsimony, 6
Canvass of scene, 90
Caretakers, 98
Case files, 174, 185
Case presentation, 200
   bargaining, 200

Case presentation *(continued)*
  charge to the jury, 211
  choice of forum, 204
  closing arguments, 211
  components, 201
  evidence presentation, 207
  impact of the setting, 201
  intermediate use, 200
  judge or jury, 204
  jury selection, 205
  negotiation, 200
  opening statement, 207
  opposition case, 211
  potentially final, 200, 201
  preliminary concerns, 204
  progress reports, 200
  setting impact, 201
  team member briefing, 200
  witnesses, 207
Case screening, 107, 109
Chain of custody, 72
Chambers v. Maroney, 46
Chamblis, Bill, 127, 128
Chamelin, Neil C., 30, 67, 128, 172
Chapman, John W., 45
Chemists, 76, 77
Children, 98
  abuse, 98
  interview procedures, 98, 99
  verbal communication, 99
Chimel v. California, 46
Chronology, 70
Civil sanctions, 73
Classified material, 152
  confidential, 152
  secret, 152
  top secret, 152
Closing arguments, 211
  rebuttal, 211
Cognitive interview, 100
Coles, Gregory L., 102
Collection, 49
  of information, 49
  plan, 20, 49
Collingwood, R. G., 17
Colloquialisms, 96
Colorado v. Sporleder, 46
Common law burglary, 176
  elements, 176
Complainants, 51
Compromise, 182
Computers, 74, 81, 82, 84
Confession, 69, 91–94, 163
  voluntary, 163
Confidential communications, 171
Conspiracy, 131
Contempt power, 39, 44
Contraband seizure, 35

Coroners, 71, 76
Corpus delicti, 176
Corruption, 26
Cound, John J., 199
Crane, Wilder, Jr., 156
Crime analysis units, 106, 119, 126
Crime commission, 119
Crime laboratory, 71
Crime scene search, 60
Criminal enterprise statutes, 140
  RICO, 131, 144
Criminal investigation management, 105
  conditions for success, 109
Criminal law, 116
  enforcement, 103
Criminal law statutes, 176
  analysis, 108, 176
  complexity, 177
  elements, 176
  non-element language, 179
Criminalists, 70
Cross-examination, 71, 96, 208

David, Pedro R., 127, 129
Davis, John W., 187
Deception, 96
  detection, 96
  motive, 97
Decision makers, 9–16, 20, 24, 27, 28, 69, 71, 83, 184, 200, 207
Decision making, 3, 4
  formal, 4
  governmental, 4
  group, 4
  informal, 4
  personal, 4
Deduction, 7, 16
Defense theory, 190
  anticipation, 190
Delaware v. Prouse, 46
Dentists, 56, 78
Department of Justice Standards of Conduct, 152
Depositions, 57
Dershowitz, Alan, 213
Description, 16
Determination, 10
  defined, 10
Determination of fact, 28
  analysis, 3
  organization, 3
  presentation, 3
Determination of the issues, 10
Dexter, L. A., 101
Dinges, David F., 85
Dioxyribonucleic acid, 77
Diplomatics, 70

INDEX

Directed conversation, 86, 100
  skills, 100
Directed verdict, 211
Direct examination, 71, 211
Discovery, 57
  civil, 57
Discretion, 12, 15, 37, 40, 41
Distortion, 96
  accidental, 96
  purposeful, 96
District of Columbia, 35, 61
Documents, 56, 65, 74
  accuracy, 75
  authenticity, 60, 75
  best evidence rule, 60
  credibility, 60
  examination of, 75
  exemplars, 75
  external validity, 60
  internal validity, 60
  motions to produce, 57
  pretrial discovery, 57, 59
  search warrants, 60
Douglas, Jack D., 128
Drug abuse, 125
  investigative procedures, 125
Due process, 59

Eck, John, 45, 112, 114, 115, 129
Economic crime, 130
  accounting problems, 133
  categories, 132
  civil penalties, 130
  components, 131, 134, 145
  cost, 130
  criminal sanctions, 130
  defense bar, 130
  defenses, 140
  investigative approaches, 134
  legal problems, 130, 144
  link network analysis, 135, 145
  net worth–expenditures principle, 140, 145
  penalties, 145
  problems, 130
  prosecution, 132
  team investigation, 134
  time flow diagrams, 137, 145
  useful statutes, 144
Edelhertz, Herbert, 146, 199
Effective listening, 86
Electronic surveillance devices, 36
Empiricism, 8
Empiricists, 8, 16
Epigraphy, 70
Ethical restraints, 40
  criteria, 40
  moral philosophy, 40

Ethical restraints *(continued)*
  personal code, 40
  situations, 41
  use of information, 42
Ethics in Government Act, 152
Evans, Bergen, 19, 30
Evans, Cornelia, 19, 30
Evidence, 9, 171
  acceptance, 1
  associative, 70
  best evidence rule, 169
  chain of custody, 61
  collection techniques, 29
  documentary, 56, 74
  exclusionary rule, 168, 171
  exculpatory, 59
  false, 42
  fingerprints, 73
  firearms, 75
  as fruit of poisonous tree, 40
  hearsay, 165
  illegally obtained, 42
  interpretation, 69
  motion to suppress, 40
  physical, 60, 64, 65, 77
  planting, 41
  of previous crimes, 210
  real or demonstrative, 169
  sample, 72
  scientific, 68–70
  serological, 76
  strength estimate, 184
  technicians, 119
  toxicological, 76
Exclusionary rule, 168, 171
Exhumation, 121
Experts, 68
  availability, 71, 74
  background, 71
  briefing, 72
  character, 71
  chemists, 76
  credibility, 71
  document examiners, 74
  financial, 73
  fingerprint, 73
  firearms, 75
  forensic pathologists, 76
  independent, 74
  need for, 71
  pathologists, 76
  qualifications, 74
  scientific, 69
  serologists, 76
  suitability, 71
  toxicologists, 76
  types, 83

Experts *(continued)*
  uses, 83
  utilization, 70
Explanation:
  as modified deductive process, 16
  in scientific reasoning, 7

Fact, 9
  analysis, 20
  as assertion, 9
  brute or indifferent, 9
  definition, 9
  as event, 9
  as evidence, 9
  finding, 9, 15
  organization, 20
  presentation, 10, 20
  synthesis, 20
Fact presentation, 10
  economic crime, 189
  formal, 189
  informal, 189
  investigator role, 189
  preparation, 187
  preparation components, 189
  to the prosecutor, 190
  submission report, 190
Federal Bureau of Investigation, 119
Federal Energy Regulatory Commission, 154
Federal Home Loan Bank Board, 154
Federal Power Commission, 154
Federal Privacy Act, 154
Federal Regulation of Lobbying Act, 152
Federal Reserve Banks, 154
Fences, 123
Field notes, 171
Field reports, 180
Fifth Amendment, 163
Findings of fact, 9
Fingerprints, 70, 74, 77
  computers, 74
  development, 74
  exemplars, 74
  latent, 74
  search, 73
  single print, 74
Finley, Joseph E., 128
Firearms experts, 75
Fisher, Ronald P., 102
Follow up, 87
Foreign Agents Registration Act, 152
Forensic:
  odontologists, 77, 78
  pathologists, 76, 121
  scientists, 70
Formal implication, 7
Fourteenth Amendment, 163

Frank, Judge Jerome, 11, 17
Fraud, 130
Frazier, Robert L., 114
Freedom of Information Act, 152
  exceptions, 152
Freund, Paul A., 45

Gardner, Thomas J., 66, 67, 172, 173
Gaulman v. *United States*, 46
Geiselman, R. Edward, 102
Gerber, Samuel R., 101
Gert, Bernard, 40, 42, 45, 46, 47
Godkin, E. L., 32
Goff, Colin H., 127
Goldstock, Ronald, 146, 147
Graff, Henry F., 29, 30
Greenberg, Ilene, 114, 115
Greenfield, James, 129
Greenwood, Peter, 115
Griswold v. *Connecticut*, 45

Habush, Robert L., 214
Harding v. *State*, 85
Heard, Alexander, 157
Hearsay, 165
  declarations against interest, 166
  defined, 165
  dying declarations, 166
  exceptions, 165
  government records, 167
  past recollection recorded, 167
  pedigree, 166
  routine records, 167
  spontaneous utterance exception, 166
  tacit admissions, 167
Heienz, Anne M., 199
Heritage Foundation, 64
Hilts, Phillip J., 85
Historians, 14, 15, 18, 19, 25, 26, 70
Homicide, *see* Assault and homicide
Homosexuals, 121
Hornblower, Margaret, 147
Hot pursuits, 35
Hypnosis, 80, 83
Hypotheses, 7
  falsification, 7
Hypothetico-deductive method, 8

Identification, 70
Identification requests, 38
Idioms, 96
Illicit enterprise, 117, 140
Illinois v. *Gates*, 46
Illinois v. *Lafayette*, 46
Imagination, 15, 25
Impeachment, 148
Implicans, 7
Implicate, 7

Inbau, Fred E., 67, 84, 85
Individuation, 70
Induction, 7, 16
Industrial espionage, 23
Inference, 14
Informants, 51, 52, 59, 65, 112, 126
  anonymous, 55
  choice of, 53
  control, 53
  crimes by, 55
  development, 53
  identity disclosure, 54
  immunity, 53
  management, 53
  motives, 52, 53
  payment, 55
  protection, 53
  risks, 54
  termination, 55
  types, 52
  undercover, 52
Information analysis, 174
  for admissibility, 175
  case components, 175
  civil cases, 175
  criminal cases, 176
  initial, 174
  for investigator evaluation, 182, 183
  jurisdiction, 177
  missing data, 181
  motives, 177
  objectives, 183
  for probative value, 175
  purposes, 182
  results, 174
  solutions, 182
  venue, 177
Information organization, 159
  collection scheme, 161
  components, 161
  continuing process, 161
  custody, 162
  evaluation, 162
  event files, 162
  file indexes, 162
  person files, 162
  purposes, 161
  rules of evidence, 162
  running case notes, 161
  transmittal, 161
  visual aids, 162
Information packs, 62
Inheritance, 11
Initial investigation, 107
Injunctions, 131
In re Winship, 186
Insanity, 59
Inspector generals, 73, 117, 134

Insurance, 122
Intelligence, 24, 29, 119, 126
Interior Department, 154
Interpretation, 11
Interrogation, 50, 56, 88, 90, 100
  control, 90
  court decisions, 91
  defined, 90
  goal, 90
  procedures, 90
Interrogatories, 57
Interview, 65, 88
  assessment, 94
  beginning, 94
  closing, 95
  cognitive, 94
  end, 94
  importance, 50
  initial, 49
  mechanics, 100
  middle, 94
  parts, 100
  record, 96
  subject types, 50
Interviewing, 88
  actors, 88
  aged persons, 89
  agency guidelines, 100
  assessment, 96
  children, 89, 98
  complainants, 88
  conditions, 96
  cooperation, 96
  eye witnesses, 88, 89
  firmness, 92
  flexibility, 100
  hostile persons, 89, 91
  inconsistencies, 95
  injured persons, 88
  invalids, 89
  language facility, 96
  locating interviewees, 89
  names, 95
  nervousness, 97
  notes, 94
  observers, 94
  physical abuse, 92
  police protection, 98
  politeness, 91
  postponement, 93
  preparation, 97
  priorities, 88
  privacy, 93
  probing, 92
  procedures, 89, 91, 93, 94, 95
  proscribed procedures, 92
  rapport, 93, 94
  recording, 94

INDEX

Interviewing *(continued)*
resources, 90
setting, 93, 100
special cases, 97, 98, 100
summary, 95
suspects, 91
temper, 92
threats, 92
unethical procedures, 93
weather conditions, 89
Intuition, 15, 25
Investigation, 15, 18, 28
administrative, 25, 148
for administrative action, 150
arrests, 107
arson, 120
assault and homicide, 120
assessment of, 107
assignment, 108
attorneys', 24
burglary, 120
Central Intelligence Agency, 104
centralization, 104
clearances, 107
closed, 107
commonalities, 118, 126
continuing, 107
convictions, 107
covert, 22, 29, 119
criminal, 51, 104
defined, 19
economic crime, 130
ethical restraints, 32
executive, 24
federal, 104
goal, 3
in-house, 23
initial, 105
larceny, 120
legal guidelines, 29, 31, 32, 43
legislative, 24, 148
for legislative action, 149
management, 90, 103
mass media, 23
method, 28
military, 24, 104
offense types, 126
overt, 22
patrol, 105
personnel, 25
plan, 49, 65, 118
plan components, 49
for planning purposes, 181, 185
police, 103
principles, 3, 28
private, 23
proactive, 119, 126
procedures, 118

Investigation *(continued)*
prosecution's, 107
public, 24, 25
purposes, 28
reactive, 119, 126
robbery, 120
sexual assault, 120
shortcomings, 106
social workers, 25
solvability, 107
supervision, 108
traditional crimes, 116
unsuccessful, 31
Investigative information, 27
analysis, 174
organization, 161
Investigative reporters, 18, 27, 70
Investigative reports, 170
accusatory documents, 170
affidavits, 170
analysis, 170
case status determination, 170
complaints, 170
formality, 171
forms, 171
Investigators, 18
administrative, 148, 155
area, 104
arson, 124
case presentation, 108
coordinator, 161
corruption, 104
drug abuse, 125
economic crime, 130
evaluation, 108
failure, 31, 182
field, 161
generalists, 104, 120
intelligence, 25
jobs, 103
legislative, 148, 155
memory refreshment, 208
past recollection recorded, 208
perjury, 41
persistence, 26
political settings, 155
practice, 27
preparation, 25, 29, 126
pressure from superiors, 42
principal, 162
in prosecution, 108
retraining, 109
role shift, 189, 197
specialist, 104, 120
supervisory, 161
theft, 122
training, 26

Investigators *(continued)*
    undercover, 119
  Issue briefs, 62

Jaffe, Louis L., 157
Jefferson, Thomas, 159
Jenck's Act, 59
Jenkins, Iredell, 1
Jennings, Margaret S., 66, 67
Jewel, Malcolm E., 156
Johnson, John M., 128
Judges, 10, 15, 56, 69, 73, 83, 92, 107, 180, 184
    administrative, 13
    administrative law, 151
Jurisdiction, 103
    federal police, 104
Juries, 10, 56, 69, 73, 83, 107, 180, 184
Justice systems, 12
    civil, 4
    criminal, 4

Kamen, Al, 85, 102, 147
Kamisar, Yale, 199
Kaplan, Eugene J., 172, 173
Karchmers, Clifford H., 129
Kelley, Clarence M., 66
Kerstetter, Wayne A., 199
King, Harry, 127, 128
Klockars, Karl B., 127, 128
Kohler, Wolfgang, 17
Kraus, Leonard I., 127
Kuckich, Diane S., 30

Labaton, Stephen, 147
Laboratories, 71
    crime, 103
    mobile, 74
Larceny, burglary, and robbery, 122
    burglars, 123
    definitions, 122
    hostages, 124
    insurance, 122
    investigative procedures, 122
    private investigators, 124
    professionals, 123
    robbers, 123
Larson, J. A., 101
Law, applied to facts, 10
Lawler, Robert, 46
LEGIS, 62
Legislative hearings, 148
    alternatives, 150
Legislative proceedings, 148
    adjudicative, 148
    investigative, 148
Lesko, Matthew, 63, 66, 67

Levi, Edward H., 66
Levine, Samuel F., 129
Library of Congress, 61
Lie detection, 79, 83, 90
Line-up, 39
Linguistics, 70
Link network analysis, 136, 145
Lloyd Morgan's Canon, 6

MacGahan, Aileen, 127
Management of criminal investigation (MCI), 105
    adoption, 112
    advantages, 105
    components, 105, 107, 109
    defined, 105
    expansion, 110
    field testing, 106
    fine tuning, 110
    monitoring, 108
    portability, 112
    revision, 110
    solvability factors, 106
    support, 106
    variations, 105
Marshall, Thurgood, 79
Master case presentation file, 196
    evidence, 196
    memoranda of law, 196
    summary section, 196
McNeil, Mary L., 156
Mediation, 13, 14, 16
Medical examiners, 71, 76
Mens rea, 176
Methods, 20
    investigation, 20
    research, 20
    scientific, 20
Militia, 103
Miranda v. Arizona, 91, 101, 173
    confessions, 90
    custody, 91
    rights, 91
Misprision of felony, 56
Modus operandi, 61
Moenssens, Andre A., 67, 84, 85
Moses, Ray Edward, 67, 85
Moskowitz, Daniel B., 66
Muckrakers, 117
Mullen v. United States, 173
Myren, Richard A., 128

Nader, Ralph, 26
Narcotics, 125
Nardini, William, 128
Nathanson, Nathaniel L., 157
National Crime Information Center, 119
National guard, 103

National Law Enforcement Intelligence Unit, 119
National Library of Medicine, 62
National Referral Center, 62
National Science Foundation, 22, 30
National Security Agency, 153
Negotiable instruments, 122
Net worth–expenditures principle, 140, 145
Neurologists, 78, 79
New York State Identification and Intelligence System, 119
Norton, Loran A., 127, 128
Nossen, Richard A., 146

Occam's razor, 6
O'Hara, Charles E., 89
O'Neill, William Matthew, 17
Oliphant, Robert E., 213
Opinion, 69
Organized crime, 117, 131
Orientation, 49
Orne, Emily Carota, 85
Orne, Martin T., 85
Osterburg, James, 69, 84, 85

Packel, Leonard, 214
Paleography, 70
Paper trail, 57, 134
Pennock, J. Roland, 45
Pen register, 37
Pennsylvania v. Mimms, 46
Perpetrators, 51, 118
Personal computers, 81, 82, 84
Petersilia, Joan, 115
Philcox, Norman W., 128
Photo identification, 39
Physical anthropologists, 56, 77
Physical evidence, 119
  custody of, 172
  processing, 169, 172
Physician–patient privilege, 164
Physicians, 98
Plans, 20
  collection, 20
  investigative, 20, 21, 27
  research, 27
Poisonous tree, 40
Police, 103
  agenda, 116
  contract service, 103
  education, 106
  federal, 104
  federal support, 106
  highway, 103
  Interpol, 104
  radio, 103
  research, 106
  state, 103

Political process, 12, 28
Polygraph, 79
Prediction, 16
Presentation of information, 15
Presentation preparation, 189
  role of the investigator, 189
Pretrial discovery, 57
  civil, 57
Priest–penitent privilege, 164
Prima facie case, 181, 184
Prima facie evidence, 181, 184
Priorities, 88
Private eyes, 23
Privileged communications, 163
  general conditions, 164
  privileges, 163
Probability, 18
Problem definition, 15, 20, 21
  change, 49
  government investigators, 29
  imagination, 5
  intuition, 5
  jurisdiction, 22
  knowledge of context, 6
  skills, 5
  from symptoms, 6
Property room, 162
Propositions, 16
Prosecution, 108
  arraignment, 108
  charge, 108
Protective custody, 99
  children, 99
Psychiatrists, 78, 98
Psychologists, 79
Public corruption, 117, 118
Public order, 116

Rabin, Robert L., 156, 157
Racketeer Influenced and Corrupt Organization Statute (RICO), 140
  court challenge, 143
  criticism, 144
  penalties, 140
  provisions, 140
Rand Corporation, 104
  MCI studies, 106
Rape, 121
Rationalism, 8
Rationalists, 16
Reasons, Charles E., 127
Redirect examinations, 210
Reference sources, 61, 65
  commercial firms, 61, 64
  data banks, 61, 64
  government agencies, 61, 62
  libraries, 61, 62
  private associations, 61

Reference sources *(continued)*
    think tanks, 61, 64
    trade associations, 63
Reiss, Albert J., Jr., 127
Reports, 49
    initial, 49
Research, 18, 28
    applied, 19, 22
    basic, 19, 22
    defense, 23
    defined, 19, 28
    design, 64
    expenditures, 22
    experimental, 21
    government, 22
    historical, 21
    industry, 22
    in-house, 23
    national security, 23
    objectives, 28
    observation, 21
    public policy, 23
    scientific, 20
    survey, 21
    university, 22
Research approaches, 28
Research design, 49
Research personnel, 25
    preparation, 25, 29
Reward and promotion system, 109
Right to privacy, 32
    aspects, 33
    becomes law, 32
    history, 32
    interviewing, 94
    limitations, 32
Ringel, William E., 67
Robbery, *see* Larceny, burglary, and robbery
Robert's *Rules of Order,* 202
Rock v. Arkansas, 85
Rogovin, Charles H., 146, 147
Rose, Louis J., 29, 30, 157
Rose-Ackerman, Susan, 128
Rovario v. United States, 66
Rowe, James L., Jr., 147
Royal, Robert, 101
Rules, 10, 11, 12, 15
    discovery, 57
    of evidence, 14
    general, 7
Rules of court, 202
Rules of evidence, 162
    competence, 163
    materiality, 163
    relevance, 162
Rural crime, 125
    drug cultivation, 126

Rural crime *(continued)*
    rustling, 125
    theft, 125
Russell, Harold F., 127

Schmidt, Anne, 102
Schneckloth v. Bustamante, 46
Schroeder, Oliver, 101
Schultz, Donald G., 127, 128
Schutt, Steven, 101
Science, 68
Scientific method, 20
Scientific reasoning, 7
    contingent, 8
    necessary, 8
Scientists, 14
    historians, 14
    physical, 14, 16
    social, 14, 16
Searches, 33
    anonymous informant, 34
    automobiles, 36
    confidential informants, 34
    consent, 35
    evidence in plain view, 35
    exigent circumstances, 36
    incident to an arrest, 36, 38
    items seizable, 35
    plain view, 35
    probable cause, 33
    surveillance, 34
    totality of the circumstances, 35
    without warrant, 35
    warrant execution, 35
    warrants, 33
Secretor, 77
Sedima, S.P.R.L. v. Imrex Co., 147
Self-incrimination, 60, 163
Self-study, 68
Semen, 77
Serologists, 76, 77
Settings, 3, 12, 13, 15, 18, 50, 155
    administrative, 13
    governmental, 13
    impact, 27
    investigation, 20
    judicial, 13
    legislative, 13
    organizational, 50, 51
    private, 13
    research, 20
    scientific, 14
Settlement, 192
Sexual assault, 121
Shafer, Robert Jones, 30, 67, 84
Shield laws, 26, 164
Sinclair, Upton B., 26, 30
Smith, Dwight C., Jr., 117, 128

INDEX

Smith, Henry D., 19
Smith, Robert Ellis, 45, 46
Smithsonian Institution, 62
Smith v. Maryland, 46
Social agencies, 98
Solvability factors, 107, 112
Somers, Leigh Edward, 66, 84, 146
Sound recorders, 81, 83
Sources of information, 49
Specialists, 22
Specialization, 68
   advantages, 105
   disadvantages, 105
   formal, 105
   informal, 105
Speedy trial, 14
Spina, Delores B., 214
Stakeout, 21
Standard of proof, 10, 184
   administrative, 13
   beyond reasonable doubt, 18, 26, 180
   civil cases, 180
   clear and convincing evidence, 18, 180
   criminal cases, 180
   preponderance of the evidence, 18, 180
Standing, 40
Stanford Research Institute, 106
   MCI studies, 106
Starrs, James E., 84, 85
State ex rel. Collins v. Superior Court, 85
State v. Collins, 85
State v. Valdez, 85
Steffens, Lincoln, 30
Sting operations, 123
Stipulations, 191, 192
Stop and frisk, 38
Stone, Julius, 17
Stone, Peter H., 146
Stotland, Ezra, 146, 199
Submission report, 190
   format, 190
   master case file, 194
   plea bargaining, 193
   preparation of witnesses, 191, 192
   pretrial conferences, 191, 192
   pretrial discovery, 191
   submission, 197
   trial brief preparation, 194
   uses, 191
   visual aids, 191
Subpoenas duces tecum, 57
Suicide, 121
Surprise, 194
   prevention, 194
Surveillance, 21
Suspects, 51, 73, 91
Swanson, Charles R., Jr., 30, 67, 128, 172

Talese, Gay, 128
Target, 22
Technology, 22, 81, 83, 84
   utilization, 81
Tenth Amendment, 103
Teresa, Vincent, 128
Territo, Leonard, 30, 67, 128, 172
Terry v. Ohio, 46
Testimony, 72
   cross-examination, 59
   expert, 83
   impeachment, 59
   oral, 13, 163
Texas v. Brown, 46
Theory, 6
   building, 6
   confirmation, 8
   conflicting, 7
   falsification, 7
   infirmation, 8
   multiple, 7
   precision, 6
   range, 6
   simplicity, 6
   testing, 7
   verification, 8
Thornton, Mary, 147
Time flow diagrams, 145
   example, 138
Time restraints, 26, 27
Toba, Yoshihide, 84
Torres, Donald A., 114
Tort, 69, 77
Toxicologists, 56, 77
Trace material, 69
Tracing persons, 89
Trade secrets, 58
Transmitters, 82, 84
Truth, 7, 9

Undercover agents, 126
United States v. Amato, 146
United States v. Booth, 46
United States v. Cappetto, 147
United States v. Harrison, 46
United States v. Matlock, 46
United States v. McCarthy, 46
United States v. Minnick, 46
United States v. Ross, 46
United States v. Santana, 46
United States v. Wade, 46
Unlawful burning, 120
   definition, 124
   investigative procedures, 124
Use of force, 26

Validity, 7
Value set, 11, 12, 15

Varrin, Robert D., 30
Vicarious experience, 87
Victims, 51, 56, 112, 117, 118, 120, 132, 190
Voir dire, 206

Waldron, Ronald J., 114
Walsh, Marilyn E., 128, 146, 199
Ward, Richard H., 101, 102, 114, 115
Warden v. Hayden, 67
Warrants, 105
Warren, Samuel D., 32
Washington Post, 26
Wasserman, Robert, 115
Watergate, 26, 117
Watts, Meridith W., Jr., 157
Weidman, Donald R., 115
Weinberg, Milton, 146, 199
Weinreb, Lloyd L., 46
Welch v. United States, 46
Wells, Kenneth M., 213
Westin, Alan F., 128
Weston, Paul B., 213
White-collar crime, 116, 144, 189
Wife-husband privilege, 164
Wigmore, John, 173

Wilensky, Harold L., 30
Wilson, George C., 115
Wilson, James Q., 127, 128, 186
Wing, John R., 213
Wire taps, 36
 court authorization, 37
 procedures, 37
Witnesses, 11, 24, 39, 41, 51, 52, 56, 59, 94, 112, 118, 191, 208
 competence, 171
 credibility, 52, 163, 171
 cross-examination, 43, 52
 expert, 56, 71, 73
 incompetence, 163
 lay, 69
 locating, 51
 observation conditions, 51
 personal characteristics, 52
 preparation, 191
 preparation legality, 192
 preparation purposes, 192
 weight, 163
Woodward, Bob, 26
Wormser, Michael D., 157

Ybarra v. Illinois, 46